"In this collection of essays, he focuses on the lives of great writers, social activists, spiritual seekers and psychologists."
— *The Renaissance Universal Journal*

"A man of profound spiritual awareness writing of matters of the heart and the mind."
— *Doris Grumbach, SMITHSONIAN Magazine*

"McCarthy has the intriguing ability to weave the reader into his own web of absorption with the minds and thoughts of his inner companions, gently helping us share his own excitement and delight of discovery of truly beautiful people."
— *National Catholic News Service*

"A reflection of quiet brilliance . . . The book is a joy."
— *America*

"Carefully, lovingly, and with humor McCarthy gives you men and women you can respect. . . ."
— *The Washingtonian*

The Best in Paperbacks from Acropolis

Inner Companions

Personal Encounters with Enduring Thinkers

by Colman McCarthy

AN ORACLE TRADEPAPERBACK
ACROPOLIS BOOKS LTD. • WASHINGTON, D.C. 20009

ORACLE TRADEPAPERBACK 1978
©Copyright 1975 by Colman McCarthy

ACROPOLIS BOOKS LTD.
Colortone Building, 2400 17th St., N.W.
Washington, D.C. 20009

Printed in the United States of America by
COLORTONE PRESS, Creative Graphics Inc.
Washington, D.C. 20009

Library of Congress Cataloging in Publication Data
McCarthy, Colman.
    Inner companions.

    1. Biography. I. Title.
    CT104.M23   920'.02   75-31846
    ISBN 0-87491-054-4
    ISBN 0-87491-270-9 pbk.

Inner
Companions

Inner Companions

Colman McCarthy

A

Acropolis Books Ltd.

2400 17th Street, N.W., Washington, D. C. 20009

ACROPOLIS BOOKS LTD.
Colortone Building, 2400 17th St., N.W.
Washington, D.C. 20009

Printed in the United States of America by
COLORTONE PRESS, Creative Graphics Inc.
Washington, D.C. 20009

Library of Congress Cataloging in Publication Data
McCarthy, Colman.
   Inner companions.

   1. Biography. I. Title.
CT104.M23   920'.02   75-31846
ISBN 0-87941-054-4

First Printing, November 1975
Second Printing, June 1976

Denise Levertov, Reed Whittemore, Michele Murray, J. F. Powers, Sigrid Undset, E. B. White, Claude McKay, Mary Lavin, Edwin Arlington Robinson, Brendan Behan, William Carlos Williams, Willa Cather, Flannery O'Connor, Jean Toomer, Richard McKenna, Heinrich Boll, Sean O'Casey, Dorothy Day, Danilo Dolci, George Seldes, Emma Goldman, A. J. Muste, Aldo Leopold, T. Thomas Fortune, Paulo Freire, Harry Caudill, W. E. B. DuBois, John Muir, George Orwell, St. Benedict, Rabbi Abraham Heschel, William Penn, St. Teresa, Paul Hanly Furfey, Daniel, St. James, Charles de Foucald, Swami Bhaktivedanta Prabhupada, James Pike, The Curé of Ars, St. Francis, Florida Scott-Maxwell, Miguel de Unamuno, Viktor Frankl, Raissa Maritain, Carl Jung, Sir John Eccles, Simone Weil, Alfred Adler, Rudolf Dreikurs, Josephine Johnson, Tu Fu, Henrik Ibsen

All Real Living is Meeting.

Martin Buber

To Mav, Jim, Johnny, and Eddie—my

lively and cheerful outer companions.

Acknowledgments

MY SPECIAL THANKS TO Philip Geyelin, editor of "The Washington Post" editorial page. His roots are French, and the excellence of his long career in journalism epitomizes the ideal expressed by one of France's lasting lights, Henri Bergson: "Act like a man of thought and think like a man of action." Much of the material in this book first appeared, in different form, on the "Post's" editorial page, and did so by Phil Geyelin's kindness and encouragement.

Others to whom I owe debts, both for help in writing this book and for past generosities, include Morton Mintz, Howard Simons and Paul Richard of "The Washington Post," Sargent Shriver, Gilbert Harrison, Gene Patterson, Tom Kelly, Marye Picone, Beatrice Thomas, Bernard Shulman, the community at Spring Hill College, Mobile, Alabama, and my spirited colleagues on the editorial page staff. My mother and three brothers have provided me with ever thrumming amounts of intellectual stimulation, ranging from their views on the state of the Republic to the nature of my golf swing, both in rickety shape. My late father, a country lawyer for forty-three years and a Republican back in the days before the hacks took over that party, believed that nothing better opened the mind of a child than a home library. He provided one, and I am still catching up on books he was talking about twenty-five years ago.

Most of all, I continue to run up debts to Mav McCarthy, the woman with whom I live. I know it is customary for male writers to offer thanks to their wives for the latters' robotic sacrifices while the "opus" was being written. But my own wife has better pursuits than

9

Contents

Preface

WHEN I BEGAN WRITING for *The Washington Post* in 1968, I knew that a newspaper runs on both the tradition and the obligation of trying to tell and explain what is happening. A journalist should clear today's air of yesterday's fogs, hoping that his copy has a little sun to it, at least for the few minutes a reader runs his eyes over the inches of type. But that broad definition of journalism, telling and explaining, is a mansion of many rooms, and regularly I have had the fortune to be given the key to one of the least used of them. It is the room in which what is happening has little to do with an event of yesterday, nor with quoting the almighty words of our political godlets, nor with headlines or deadlines. Instead, in this room, the hot, breaking news may be what Simone Weil discovered when she went among the factory workers of France, or what St. Benedict said to the fathers and brothers of Monte Casino in the sixth century, or what Claude McKay thought of America when he came here in 1914, or John Muir's experiences in Yosemite, or Denise Levertov's ideas about teaching poetry to the young. Such revelations can have the freshness of this morning's newspaper, if you haven't heard them, and perhaps more urgency, because already they possess the quality of having endured.

With this in mind—all news isn't new—I began contributing to the *Post's* editorial page ongoing columns called "Thinkers and Their Thoughts." The pieces have been appearing usually once a month, which is about the rest period I need to recuperate from the columns and editorials the remainder of the time on politics, the mischief of the powerful, the victimization of citizens and other realities that keep this earth from being a vale of joy. It is humbling sometimes

15

when after delivering a piece that puts into the frying pan, say, a deadhead politician and thinking, wait until the reader sees this character flailing and kicking in the heat, to meet a living reader a day later and hear her refer not to my sizzler of yesterday but to a column some years back on Sigrid Undset or Danilo Dolci. Such experiences—humility is good for us, no matter how often the security guard at the *Post's* door is told not to let it in—affirm Santayana's belief: "Tell me to what you pay attention and I will tell you who you are."

Those who have told me they pay attention to the writers, poets, philosophers, artists, saints and observers whose ideas are gathered here are usually people with touches of the renegade in them, citizens who want to go to the heart of the matter, or at least the aorta. These are the fugitive souls fleeing the cheap or crass of our times and refusing to enroll quietly in their local behavior-modification center. In *Leaves of Grass*, Walt Whitman lined up with them:

> *I am for those that have never been master'd,*
> *For men and women whose tempers have never been master'd,*
> *For those whom laws, theories, conventions, can never master.*

> *I am for those who walk abreast with the whole earth,*
> *Who inaugurate one to inaugurate all.*

These are the intellectually alive who hunger for life, though not the kind satisfied with the side dishes that America's institutions often serve up—the empty calories of television, the fast foods of many high schools and colleges where mastering information—burger-bits of knowledge—has replaced exposure to wisdom. Many of the institutions and political parties want it that way: the system needs lazy minds, spirits of low literacy and souls seldom touched by the refinement of reflection or thought. The blockhead is no more a threat to the decreed way than the hothead. In the classrooms, how can even the most tireless teacher not feel frustrated when students keep pouring in year after year, benumbed and dulled, having logged thousands of hours of television since babyhood? In a scrimmage pitting arts and letters against call letters, there is no doubt which is smeared. Many school officials believe that students should be required to take a foreign language—Spanish usually, sometimes French or German. The officials have been too long in the front office; the children down the corridor are already being taught a foreign language: English.

The sadness of this is not that we have so many citizens coming out of our schools who can't read intelligently—which is true enough—but that they are easy to fool, and that the foolers constantly ply their craft. One of the last times I looked at television—several years ago—the advertising industry was working hard to dupe and gull: in one sixty-minute period, polysteel tires from Goodyear, chromacolor television sets from Zenith and quatrecolor from Panasonic, and powerpoint pens from Papermate were touted. What gibberish words are those—polysteel, chromacolor, quatrecolor and powerpoint? They have no meaning outside the context of the ad, so how can meaning exist inside? It doesn't. But since the clever copywriters who concoct these ads persist in the belief that millions of viewers have little or no intelligence that can be insulted, well, keep insulting them with empty language that sounds impressive. Fool them. Lure them to the store. Get their money. Meanwhile, the question on some minds is not whether a company makes a chromacolor or quatrecolor TV set but whether or not the product will catch fire—as ten-thousand did in one recent year, most of them color sets.

It is no coincidence that politicians rely on advertising techniques. They know the advantage: people think in words, but if they are used to empty words then they must have empty heads. Feed them any kind of word salad, a leafy green slogan, that is easily digested. Thus, a Richard Nixon was able to say that he waged war to win peace, a slogan on a level of deceit with his predecessor's Great Society. Some politicians talk in brand name idiom—the WIN button of Gerald Ford, thought up by an ad agency—not because they have evil minds but because they operate on the theory that most people have inactive minds. The system depends on illiterates, and the more of them that can be produced the less likely anyone will demand an accounting from those in power.

Everyone must form his own resistance, to keep himself in a knowing, critical and educated habit of mind, to see that his consciousness is ever forming and his spirit ever a fund open to regular contributions. The pieces I have written here have been my own way of making the effort to stay on fire with a love of learning, and also to fight off those who would choke my imagination and curiosity by stuffing it with guff and cant. With these pieces—a gathering of miniatures—I have been educating myself in public. I believe that the discovery of tastes is the essence of education more than filling the mind with information. I think of a high school student who came by recently and talked about his school. "In just the past month," he

17

said, "I've been assigned papers on Wordsworth, Homer and Shakespeare. I haven't written a one. I hate it. What do I care about those ancient creeps." The question was asked rhetorically, but the student looked at me knowingly, expecting the routine adult answer: "But you must learn about great minds like Wordsworth, Homer, Shakespeare and all the other shapers of Western Civilization." Actually, my sympathies were with the student, and I said so. His mind was a throat, and his school was cramming down nothing but indigestibles. More, it was destroying his taste for any kind of literature. Forced to consume what his teachers decided was worthy, he rebelled and would consume nothing. Later in the evening, while telling me about his record collection, my friend spoke with insight and fervor on the life and thought of Woody Guthrie, the American folk singer. He had learned about Guthrie on his own and knew about him all that his teachers said he should have known about Wordsworth. True, Guthrie is no literary classicist or exceptional stylist. But for my friend, Guthrie was chosen for study not because a required reading list forced the issue but because Guthrie evoked a response that led to a deep caring. A teacher's task is to light fires, nothing more. Get the young to burn with the desire for literature, to be hot with it all their lives. Get them to say, with Aldous Huxley as he was leaving Oxford: "I should like to go on forever learning. I lust for knowledge. ..."

The essays here are on men and women who have become my inner companions. To have companions of any kind—inner or outer—suggests that a journey is being made, as indeed with all of us there is. It should be a traveling toward gentleness, integrity and joyfulness, a destination all of us long for but hesitate to imagine ourselves reaching, lest on arrival we be given new obligations to love. But if we can travel with a band of inner companions, what tests can prove too demanding? It is not that the chosen companions of our interior, at least not the ones whom I have taken into my life, are meant to teach us matters of power and might—how to earn a living, how to make sense or make progress. Those are the most handily mastered of life's chores. Instead, we need them to share with us the wisdom of the obvious, to repeat and repeat for our stubborn minds what we never quite get right—that all of us are fragile, that the wealth of the planet should be shared justly and that nothing matters unless it is done with a perpetual fidelity to love. This wisdom must be absorbed into us by opening our interior lives—an intimacy of the spirit—and trusting that what results is not an invasion of our privacy but an expansion of our awareness. Jung believed, "Only the man who can consciously assent to the power of the inner voice becomes a personality. . . . That is the great and liberating thing about any genuine personality: he voluntarily sacrifices himself to his vocation, and consciously translates into his own individual reality what would only lead to ruin if it were lived unconsciously by the group."

Americans have trouble with the idea of the inner life. On one hand, anyone who talks about it is suspected of going on an inward bliss-out, of preferring a few safe feelgood jollies rather than continuing the effort toward wholeheartedness that is often a dry struggle. On the other, the idea of an inner life is dismissed because it doesn't produce any marketable goods, the way our working lives do. "If only those damned inner companions of yours"—a father says to his son or daughter, a husband or wife to each other, teachers to students—"put some money into your pocket or gave you a name in the neighborhood, well, then it might be worth it." We live among sounds like this, as we live among too many phones, televisions, radios, doorbells, horns, all of these megaphonics pounding so heavily at our consciousness—a carpet-bombing of the spirit—that we have little room within for anything but the clutter. The alienation of the self hasn't become a national disease by accident. How can a self—mind, soul, emotions, spirit—be kept intact if no interior adhesiveness exists? Small wonder that the disunified person is not satisfied by life; he seldom experiences it. "Pull yourself together" is the grand American phrase, and it is exactly right. But the pulling is all but impossible if the fake props within us have not been cleared out. Our personalities become like homes in which all floor and air space is consumed by furniture, and if any items of worth are there, they sit like bric-a-brac on the unused shelf of consciousness. It is not as though we were born with this clutter within us, and thus have still another excuse to lay it on our parents for messing us up. In fact, it is the opposite. The country priest of Bernanos wrote in his diary: "It is rare for a child not to have known any inner life . . . however embryonic the form. One day or another all young lives are stirred by an urge which seems to compel; every pure young breast has depths which are raised to heroism. Not very urgently perhaps, but just strongly enough to show the little creature a glimpse, which sometimes he half-consciously accepts, of the huge risk that salvation entails, and gives to human life all its divinity."

None of the pieces here are intended to be the last word or the only word. Nearly all my companions have spoken for themselves, and many are served in worthy biographies or long studies that a diligent seeker can find. I am trying to serve the reader in a more modest way: by arousing tastes more than satisfying hungers. It would be a disappointment to me if this book becomes an ending rather than a beginning. I am an introducer: you two should know each other. To open the dialogue is my role, to keep it going is yours. My hope is that a deep commitment will be made by the reader to some of those included here, all of whom have made commitments to us through the excellence of their writing or the passions of their lives.

It is important that the reader stay with one thinker at a time—after going through and making choices among the ones here—rather than flicking the dial among them to catch only a small part of each show. "Books," Thoreau said in Walden, "must be read as deliberately and reservedly as they were written." It is possible to spend a whole year reading, say, the stories of Flannery O'Connor or the essays of E. B. White. For diversion during that time, one can easily find commentaries on each. Some scoutwork in the library will uncover some rich finds.

Go through the *Reader's Guide*—those thick green books—for magazine pieces. Browse through the low-circulation journals, such as the *Virginia Quarterly Review, Modern Age, Commonweal, Katallagete*. Visit dusty bookshops. Keep a bibliography of your own; I have included selected ones here as a start. Begin a journal; write in it of your discoveries about your new companion and how you are getting on with him or her.

All this involves a measure of discipline, of being able to set aside time each day or week when nothing else takes priority but the dialogue with your inner companion, when "the mind's passion to know," as Aristotle said, is honored. Often the evidence suggests that we would rather honor not the mind but the mindless. Every year, I am amazed at what Mr. Gallup, the asker, discovers about the people Americans "most admire." The most recent top ten includes Gerald Ford, Henry Kissinger, Billy Graham, Barry Goldwater, Henry Jackson, George Wallace and Ronald Reagan. Could Gallup have gotten his findings wrong? I would think those names would be on America's list of least admired men. I wish the pollsters would knock at my door for some selections. I'd give them George Seldes, Harry Caudill, Denise Levertov, E. B. White, Dorothy Day, Josephine Johnson, J. F. Powers (all of these Americans are living and included here) as well as others: Herblock, Sargent and Eunice Shriver, I. F. Stone, Lili

Hahn, Louise Dunlap, Denis McCarthy. These are heroes of mine and the next time I am in Gallupland in Princeton, New Jersey, I will drop in to see how many other votes my candidates received.

The discipline needed to read is not some abstraction for which no model exists. Take to the street at any time of day and what will be seen if not the radio crazies, people walking along with hand radios pressed to their ear? Never mind the bilge being pumped into their minds; instead, marvel at such devotion and enthusiasm—not missing a minute of their medium, keeping all else outside. Yet how seldom do we see anyone walking along paying such fervid attention to a book? I have been walking this way for years along the streets of Washington—getting off the bus (after reading there) and walking six blocks to the *Post*. Friends tell me to be careful, that I risk bumping into lamp posts or other people. It has never happened, thanks; one develops an extra sense, the way the blind know the secrets of side-walk navigation. If I do take sight of anything other than my book, it is, again, the radio people. So pleased with garbage, what would they be like if they were afire with words and ideas? Presumably, their listening time on the street is only a fraction of what is heard at home. *The Washington Post* carried a story about the study habits of some high school seniors; several said that they were psychologically unable to study without the radio and the stereo playing. It is as if silence is feared, an enemy to be dumped upon by noise, sound, collisions.

We hear now of America's polificacy but it refers to the natural resources we have thrown away: oil, coal, land, air and water. But the spillage of our inner resources—our inner lives—may be even greater, the immeasurable hours most of us waste on the banal and meaningless. It is a form of self-contempt: I think so little of myself that this match-up of my mind and spirit to the worthless is fitting. The insults from our enemies are nothing compared to the demean-ings we inflict on ourselves.

All the companions here reflect my own leanings, pleasures and needs. Sometimes I fantasize about what a time would be had if all of them could be put in a large room together for an evening of friendliness. Imagine the conversation between St. Teresa and Florida Scott-Maxwell, women of different centuries and cultures but time-less in their mutual intensity about what is eternally luminous. What serenity Rabbi Heschel would enjoy from some moments with Charles de Foucald, both of them contemplatives who fevered for the Absolute. As the host for this gathering, a trespasser on wisdom's property, I would try to keep some guests apart—Emma Goldman, say, from Edwin Arlington Robinson—lest their headstrong compulsions for despair turn the evening gloomy. As for controlling the conversation, that would be impossible, confirming what Eugene Delacroix believed: "What makes men of genius, or rather, what they make, is not new ideas; it is the idea by which they are obsessed that what has been said still has not been said enough."

I have satisfaction and deep contentment in doing the work for these pieces—reading, jotting excerpts, sending a letter to someone to suggest they read this or that writer (get to the library immediately!), looking up obscure commentaries, re-reading, discussing it with family and friends, writing and re-writing. It has been said that the test of a vocation is whether you would embrace it whether you were paid or not. The work of this book has been play, the kind that I would be doing whether salaried or not. That I have been able to do it as part of my contribution to *The Washington Post*—the first and only paper I have served—is an ongoing pleasure. It is also a responsibility and a hope, the latter being that the men and women I have chosen as my inner companions also become yours. All of us have ample room within ourselves. As for those we invite for this intimacy of the mind and spirit, we can be sure they want it also. Why else did they bother to take their thoughts and feelings to paper, if they didn't wish us to take them to heart?

Colman McCarthy

Washington, D.C

The Writing Life

REPORTS FROM HIGH SCHOOLS AND COLLEGES *regularly note that more students than ever have signed up for courses in creative writing. Some colleges, as creative as their creative writing students, offer it as a major to meet the growing market among young people thirsting to write. Apparently, writers symbolize a currently fashionable style of freedom: they need not suffer the nine-to-five martyrdom, they can make their own game plan, they can hole up in the East Village with other writers or in the inevitable Big Sur commune with neighbors like Henry Miller, they can be involved in the great issues by using their words to move the movers.*

The illusion of a writer enjoying such enormous freedom is not one the writing courses will break in a year, even if it is desirable that they should.

This is the healthy illusion of young people who have yet to face the social enslavements of earning a living, getting on with the neighbors—even a happy one like Henry Miller—paying taxes, facing death.

The more dangerous illusion that a good writing course will try to shatter is that creative writing is teachable. Writing is; creating isn't. The most a writing course can do is expose the future writer to rules, techniques, habits, styles and ideas that make it easier to be taught by oneself, not by another, how to create.

Having oneself for a teacher in an art like writing is not the folly it would be in one of the sciences or social disciplines, because the first and deepest fact about writing is that it should come from within. The within of a writer is the only source of style that belongs to him and no one else. Although the line from Faust is true, that "the highest beauty is not external but within," the difficulty of many people who try to write is that they have never seized possession of their interior life. As a result, what they put on paper, and perhaps slip past an editor, is not writing but only notes on experience or memos from the brain. They are secretaries, not writers.

Paul Engle, the wise teacher at the State University of Iowa, says that before anything else a "work of art is work." No one who has ever seen a writer trying to join passion, clarity and style with a selection from the eleven million words in the English language could fail to see the trying labor of it. No one ever spent a harder day's work than Oscar Wilde when he came from his room beat and sweaty, saying, "I spent all morning putting in a comma and all afternoon taking it out." Flaubert had the same agony. "I have just spent a good week," he wrote to a friend midway in Madame Bovary, "alone like a hermit and calm as a god. I abandoned myself to a frenzy of literature. I got up at midday, I went to bed at four in the morning; I have written eight pages."

Writing is like walking blindfold: instinct will carry you far, but not always where you want to go. Before long, the instinct-guided writer, like the blinded walker, bumps into things. Like the hard question of when to write. Everyone knows that Hemingway liked to write in the morning, Mark Twain when he was lying down, H. L. Mencken when he sniffed a deadline and Norman Mailer whenever he gets punched in the mouth. Many who have yet to be terrorized by the writer's natural enemy, the blank page, say the time to write is when you feel like it. But feelings are unreliable, a roving muse who will not become a kept muse.

What is least understandable about writing is style. Even after it is acquired, style is almost impossible to define, unless vaguely; it is the way a writer gets language to enjoy itself. But even here, the

24

enjoyment is relative. One reader's taste may water at the style of Thomas Wolfe, who liked big words and big woods. Another prefers the style of Ralph Ellison, who was more concerned about social awareness than language awareness.

Readers found style three hundred years ago in the line of Molière, "The greater the obstacle, the more glory we have in overcoming it." Today, the wording of that seems flat, almost preachy. More stylish is the same thought as phrased by the Spanish writer Unamuno: "Strive after the impossible, because the possible you achieve will scarcely be worth the effort."

How does one get style in his writing? One answer is in the remark a few years ago of Katherine Anne Porter, a Washingtonian whose stories in Noon Wine and Pale Horse, Pale Rider flow with pure language. "The style is you," she said. "Oh, you can cultivate a style, I suppose, if you like. But . . . it remains a cultivated style. It remains artificial and imposed, and I don't think it deceives anyone. (In the end), you do not create a style. You work, and develop yourself; your style is an emanation from your own being."

Sooner or later, people who write must face the question: What do I do with what I have just put to paper? Publish it, says one person. Send it to a friend, says another. Put it in a drawer, says an Emily Dickinson. But the writer who wants his words to live for more than a day neither publishes, mails or buries what he has just written; instead, he rewrites it. With the kind of courage that only he will know about, he cuts whatever words are useless or false, whatever thoughts are vague or stale. He reads it over and over like a sniffling editor who has an allergy to weak language. He asks questions: Is this really worth writing, have I said it well, will it stand in print as well as it stands in my ego? If the answers are yes to the hard questions, he has learned a basic fact: writing is rewriting what you have already rewritten.

Discipline is needed to write well, from the discipline of avoiding worn-out columnists to that of developing the habit of using the dictionary. Perhaps this is one reason why few students can write with a style and with clarity. Too often, they are children of open marriages who were sent to permissive classrooms; who talks of discipline among all these blessings of the new openness? Norman Mailer once told of a friend "who always has a terrible time writing.

He once complained with great anguish about the unspeakable difficulties he was having with a novel. And I asked him, 'Why do you do it? You can do many other things well. Why do you bother with it?' I really meant this. Because he suffered when writing like no one I know. He looked up in surprise and said, 'Oh, but this is the only way one can ever find the truth. The only time I know that something is true is at the moment I discover it in the act of writing.'"

An irony of discipline is its relationship to freedom; the two are not opposite blacks and whites but are part of the same gray. The sprinter disciplines his muscles with years of running around a track so that those muscles will gain the freedom to run fast. Writing is similar. One disciplines the mind by repeatedly running over the rules of grammar, style and syntax so that the mind will gain the freedom of clear thinking. Learn the fundamentals and you are free for the nuances, subtleties and shadings, a source of pleasure not only in writing and reading but in all life. More crucial, you are free from the thought control and political control of the sloganeers, ones who reactively avoid nuances and subtlety. They don't want to engage the intellect, they want to engage the instincts and the senses. Products are easier to sell that way, elections easier to win.

English teachers have bravery, at least the ones who stick it out year after year. Faced with ignorance and laziness piled as high as mountains, they keep climbing nevertheless. "We must not silently let our students accept, as many of them do accept," Professor J. Mitchell Morse wrote in his instructive book The Irrelevant English Teacher, "the reactionary notion that they are innately incapable of successful intellectual effort. . . . That is how we, as English teachers, can work to change a repressive society into one that must respect personal freedom." Is the professor a dreamer, a man with bugs in his eyes from seeing too many blackboards? Hardly. His vision is only too clear. The rest of us may have been looking at the problems, but his eye has been on one of the causes.

All those authors included in this section have produced writing that will last for as long as pure language is honored. Most are Americans, which may surprise some readers. Sadly, we tend to ignore or forget the breadth of our country's literary richness. Whether it is because we are still waiting for an American Shakespeare to appear or because we are shamed by the vulgarity of the commercials and

26

advertisements that we allow to lure us, we have little awareness of the magnificence of American writing. A friend who teaches English in a large university told me that she asked some members of her class to talk about their heroes. "It was amazing," my friend said, "they had no heroes. Even the idea that someone should have heroes struck them as strange."

I don't know what to do about that, short of suggesting that the writers included here are heroes of mine, that I couldn't get along without them, and I am more than happy to share them with whoever cares to join me in my studies.

Denise Levertov

DURING THE LENGTH OF AMERICA'S Vietnam involvement—still not ended, because we have not yet begun to make restitution—many of those who saw the deceit in our justifications for napalm, defoliation and mass-bombing first felt the shame of these horrors in the poems of Denise Levertov. Consistently and gracefully, she wrote poetry that illuminated both what prisoners of untruth many Americans had become and what senselessness the war had for the Vietnamese peasants. Her resistance poetry was not polemical—what is more pointless than bullhorn verse?—but instead was a forceful joining of common images with themes necessary for the integrity of the nation. She wrote in the poem "Art":

> The gods die every day
> but sovereign poems go on breathing
>   in a counter-rhythm that mocks
> the frenzy of weapons, their impudent power.
> Incise, invent, file to poignance;
> make your elusive dream
>   seal itself
> in the resistant mass of crude substance.

Levertov's war resistance poems are only a part of her work, going back through eight volumes of exceptional verse to 1946, all published by New Directions. But, for many, these poems were the means of introduction to the rarest kind of poet, one of moral consciousness who produces living language as part of a moral commitment. In a 1970 essay (included in *The Poet in the World,* the recent New Directions collection of Levertov prose), she said: "The spring sunshine, the new leaves: (poets) still see them, still love them; but in what poignant contrast is their beauty and simple goodness to the evil we are conscious of day and night . . . As corrupt and self-seeking politicians erode the Constitution and bring us daily closer to

28

outright fascism, the poet is turned away from his impulse to sing, to testify in patterns of words to the miracle of life, and is driven willy-nilly to warn, to curse, to gnash the teeth of language; and at the same time, living always in the war shadow, to celebrate the courage and high spirit of all who dare to struggle. . . ." The poet, she insisted, cannot separate politics from his life.

This non-separation of powers has meant that Levertov's poems move with a distinct freeness, poems different from each other in the way each human life has a different identity and rhythm. A poetic risk is involved, because the poem's excellence must be established on its own, independent of what she called "metric molds." One Levertov poem might be a mere six lines, another six stanzas and another six pages, each with an organic movement that creates its own attentiveness. She wrote that "form *as means* should never obtrude, whether from intention or carelessness, between the reader and the essential force of the poem, it must be so fused with that force."

Levertov's style of organic poetry could easily be abused by a lax hand, and she is sufficiently sure of her own mastery to issue a warning to pretenders. "The would-be poet who looks on language merely as something to be used, as the bad farmer or the rapacious industrialist looks on the soil or on rivers merely as things to be used, will not discover a deep poetry; he will only . . . construct a counterfeit more or less acceptable—a subpoetry, at best efficiently representative of his thought or feeling—a reference, not an incarnation. And he will be contributing, even if not in any immediately apparent way, to the erosion of language, just as the irresponsible, irreverent farmer and industrialist erode the land and pollute the rivers."

Denise Levertov is in her fifties, lives in Somerville, Massachusetts, and has served as poetry editor of the *Nation*. As a child in England—her mother Welsh and her father a Russian Jew who became an Anglican priest—she was taught at home by her parents. They read stories and novels to her, from Tolstoy and Conrad to Dickens and Cather; she and her sister read poems to each other. Such a style of childhood is almost unknown today, most children's imaginations exposed early to electronic communication, and few parents with any sense of vocation about being a father or mother.

Critics have traced the Hasidic legends in some of Levertov's poetry to her father's telling the tales in their home. She has recalled their influence: "Hasidism has given me since childhood a sense of marvels, of wonder . . . The Hasidim were a bit like the Franciscans;

29

although in both movements there was also a very great strain of asceticism, yet along with it there was a recognition and joy in the physical world. And a sense of wonder at creation, and I think, I've always felt something like that . . . I think that's what poems are all about." As a poet, Levertov has acknowledged a debt to William Carlos Williams, saying she was influenced by the New Jersey physician's "sharp eye for the material world and the keen ear for vernacular which characterize his earlier and shorter poems."

Poets are always contemplatives, so when they open their lives to new people and ideas, what they learn can be more self-revealing than their poetry. In a long and quietly joyful essay, "The Untaught Teacher," we see Denise Levertov in the classroom at several colleges, a teacher showing uncommon affection toward her students. "My hope was not to teach anybody to write poetry—indeed, I had deep suspicions of the very idea of poetry workshops—but to attempt to bring each one to a clearer sense of what his own voice and range might be and to give him some standards by which to evaluate his own work." At one university, students came to her home whenever possible—to read poetry together and break through the anonymity that large schools—and even the smaller ones—often impose on people. Levertov's teaching was non-authoritarian—"I was not out to prepare anyone for graduate school or help make scholars"—but was in a friendly and approachable style students long remember. In the backgrounds of most writers, whether a master or only a newspaper reporter on a temporarily dull beat, there is usually a former teacher like Denise Levertov who once exposed a student's imagination to the beauties of language, a matter less of setting a person straight than setting him on fire. Writing is a flame that burns a lifetime, and nothing else a teacher does is worth more.

The worth of Denise Levertov's poetry and prose is that, like her teaching, it is natural, clear and without pretension. Above all, the last: What is there to pretend, when one has used language with care and honesty and has embraced the rest of life with the same standard of intensity?

SELECTED BIBLIOGRAPHY OF DENISE LEVERTOV

Footprints. New York: New Directions, 1972.
Jacob's Ladder. New York: New Directions, 1961.
O Taste and See. New York: New Directions, 1964.
The Poet in the World. New York: New Directions, 1973.
Relearning the Alphabet. New York: New Directions, 1970.

The Sorrow Dance. New York: New Directions, 1967.

To Stay Alive. New York: New Directions, 1971.

With Eyes at the Back of Our Heads. New York: New Directions, 1960.

The Craft of Poetry. New York: Doubleday, Packard, William, ed. Contains an interview with Denise Levertov.

The Real Paper, Boston. Denise Levertov is a regular contributor.

Reed Whittemore

WHO IS OUR BRAVEST POET, our stoutest, one who still insists that language is better than lingo? One nominee is Reed Whittemore. He is put forward for the poetry and essays he has been writing with sensibility and fresh gayety since 1945 but also—here is the bravery—for writing much of it from Washington. He came here in 1965 as the consultant in poetry to the Library of Congress. Rather than meekly consult with the librarians and then hightail back to his Minnesota woodland before the capital's speeches, memos, orations, press briefings, press releases and press conferences could miff or addle him, Whittemore stayed on. For nearly a decade now, for whatever else it lacks—a voting congressman, coordinated traffic lights, enforceable dog laws—the District of Columbia has had a major poet within its borders, and he is neither straining to leave nor flinching while he remains. Instead, he has lived the poet's life while avoiding the poet's role, standing by himself amid the postures of imposters who overflow with words to make laws or make history—all the while humming requiems for the language they help deaden.

A Whittemore sympathizer has said that being a poet in Washington must be "a difficult and tenuous life." But this suggests that the city's people are unstomachable. The people are fine, Whittemore wrote in a poem; the poses get to him.

> I look around around me
> and inside,
> and am ashamed, mostly
> Not by country, not by Congressmen
> (Them I'll put in the book),
> But by the spectacle of the self, the

pompous self,
The minuscule godlet strutting behind the wall
And with unmitigated gall
Surviving, thriving, bragging, beating
his chest, despite all.
Dear God, could you bless him?

Why waste time on godlets is a question raised by that poem. And a poet's wasted time at that. But Reed Whittemore is a poet of his culture, with godlets—saps and boobs—as worthy of his attention as sunsets were of Wordsworth's. We can get away from neither, no matter what clouds of unknowing fly over. This explains much of the richness in Whittemore's poetry—his generosity in giving himself to subjects that other poets might ignore as unpoetic. His last collection—*The Mother's Breast and the Father's House* (Houghton Mifflin)—examines high school bands, clamming, New York, money, gossip, marriage. In "Clamming," Whittemore writes with wryness about a temporal event in his life while artfully revealing its spirituality.

I go digging for clams once every two or three years.
Just to keep my hand in (I usually cut it),
And whenever I do so I tell the same story
Of how at the age of four I was trapped by the tide
As I clammed a sandbar. It's no story at all
But I tell it and tell it; it serves my small lust
To be thought of as someone who's lived.
I've a war too to fall back on, and some years of flying,
As well as a high quota of drunken parties,
A wife and children; but somehow the clamming thing
Gives me an image of me that soothes my psyche
Like none of the louder events: me helpless,
Alone with my sandpail,
As fate in the form of soupy Long Island Sound
Comes stalking me . . .
The self, what a brute it is. It wants, wants.
It will not let go of its even most fictional grandeur
But must grope, grope down in the muck of its past
For some little squirting life and bring it up tenderly
To the lo and behold of death, that it may weep
And pass on the weeping, keep the thing going.

Whittemore is fifty-five. After his year at the Library, he taught at the University of Maryland. This continued his long affection for students that developed when he taught for nearly twenty years at Carleton College in Minnesota. He has made room in his life for other incorrigibles—politicians. When Eugene McCarthy displayed

33

leadership in 1968, Whittemore offered to write speeches. The sena-tor was grateful for the effort but he came to rely on the poet not for his genius but for his gentleness—of language and spirit. McCarthy has written of Whittemore's respect for the mystery of the person. "I have seen this most clearly in his attitude toward children—his own and others. He speaks to children always with a touch of special reverence and surprise, and always, even when children are not present, as though children were listening and he were on guard against giving scandal to the little ones. He writes also with something of that same care, as though not knowing who will read what he has written, and not knowing the innocence and simplicity with which readers may come to his text."

Many of Whittemore's readers cannot decide whether, as one critic put it, he is grimly merry or merrily grim. His poetry appeals to the mind but it also plays with our emotions, this playfulness helping loosen the stiffness of somber thoughts that poetry is mistakenly meant to evoke. So much of contemporary wit is little more than kidding around in print, produced by standup comics sitting down before a typewriter. The laughs they produce are safe, derision directed at others, while the genuine masters of whimsy and lightness, such as Whittemore in many of his poems and essays, evoke laughter about ourselves. His wit is circular, moving around and around until it hits center, with himself often standing there too. "I am one of those," he wrote in an essay, "But Seriously," who, "when I look at history, literary and social, find that I side pretty steadily with history's eccentrics. I don't mean all the mad astrologists and mystics—the best satirists have not, I think, gravitated toward exotic ideals and idealisms—but simply the mundane eccentrics who have stood on the sidelines with the game in progress, and made frosty remarks instead of cheering. The kings and noblemen and high churchmen, the generals and the senators and big-league pundits—all these responsible gentlemen who have had and continue to have the burdens of the world upon their shoulders make less of an impression upon me than the fools (like Lear's fool) and the Hamlets and the Falstaffs, the Sancho Panzas and Huck Finns and Holden Caulfields. It is in this sense that I suppose I have the disposition, the temperament of a humorist."

Whittemore's humor—in such books as *The Boy from Iowa* and *The Fascination of the Abomination*—roots around in his own eccentricity as much as others'. Bicycle stores ought to hand out copies of his 10-speed essay, "How I Bicycled Seventeen Miles No-Handed on

34

Cape Cod," because few texts better exude the romance of this handlebar machine. When I last visited him, working at home amid his children and wife—she is a noted paperhanger—Whittemore was completing a biography of William Carlos Williams. Among poets, Whittemore passes a test that most others flunk: his fellow writers speak of him not in cold praise—that is easy to give, because nothing personal is involved—but with feelings of affection. If he walks into a group of writers, the room gets warmer. The chill leaves because here is a citizen of intensity, but with the grace and sense to be relaxed about it, whether among eccentrics, politicians or claims.

SELECTED BIBLIOGRAPHY OF REED WHITTEMORE

An American Takes a Walk. Minneapolis: University of Minnesota Press, 1956.

The Boy from Iowa: Poems and Essays. New York: Macmillan, 1962.

The Fascination of the Abomination: Poems, Stories and Essays. New York: Macmillan, 1963.

Fifty Poems Fifty. Minneapolis: University of Minnesota Press, 1970.

From Zero to the Absolute. New York: Crown, 1967.

Literary Lectures. Washington, D.C.: Library of Congress, 1973, pp. 587-602.

The Mother's Breast and the Father's House. Boston: Houghton Mifflin, 1974.

Poems, New and Selected. Minneapolis: University of Minnesota Press, 1967.

The Self-Made Man. New York: Macmillan, 1959.

Voyages, A National Literary Magazine, a Reed Whittemore issue, Spring 1970, Washington, D.C.

Michele Murray

MICHELE MURRAY IS NOT LISTED in the highest ranks of American letters—her rise was prevented by many forces—but for a group of her followers she was unique as a human being and as an artist. She died in March 1974, at forty, tormented by cancer, death coming in her home with her husband offering final mercies and thoughts. The last hours of her life, amid her family and the books of her home library where she studied and wrote, were a stirring resistance against the tyranny of death. Perhaps if she had died the conventional American death—stuck in a hospital room, ministered to by strangers and kept from knowing the end was coming—many of those who knew her would not now be thinking that her life and ideas also had special meaning. The beauty of her death called out for reflections on the beauty of her life and writing.

As a writer, Michele Murray was best known as a literary critic. She was one of the nation's three or four most competent and thorough book reviewers, qualities of insight that were revealed in her regular columns in the *National Observer*, where she served as book editor. She cherished the opportunity to write for the *Observer*, she said once, because its audience was independent of the New York literary shapers. But she wrote regularly also for the *Washington Post* and the *New York Times*.

In the past few years, Mrs. Murray published two novels, both drawing excellent reviews, and a book of poetry. In 1974, she edited *A House of Good Proportion: Images of Women in Literature*. (Simon and Schuster). It has had good sales, not only in the feminist market but among audiences that believe, with Mrs. Murray, that "the imagination brings to fruition infinite possibilities, it annihilates nothing, it charges all our being with meaning too rich to be fully conveyed, yet sustaining us in the operations of our life. In contrast, failure of the imagination brings about the conditions so visible around us—boredom, anomie, ugliness of relationships, inability to *see* the other in his/her wholeness."

On the morning of the day before she died, Mrs. Murray, lying on a small couch in her library, talked individually with three of her four children—David, eighteen; Jonathan, sixteen; and Sarah, thirteen. She told them she would die soon, though she didn't know when, and that she had enjoyed being their mother. And she offered, characteristically, practical advice about their lives after her death. She had a comfortable day, however, and a comfortable night as well.

By 10:00 AM of the next morning, she began losing consciousness. Her husband Jim read the Psalms to her—the joyful psalms which Mrs. Murray had learned to recite in her Jewish childhood. He recited also the poetry of Catherine deVinck, played recordings of Mozart's chamber music, kissed her and prayed with her. Alone with his dying wife—the children in school—he could do nothing now except acknowledge that an awesome mystery was occurring, the powers of fatality forcing themselves in another freedomless confrontation. Between one and two in the afternoon, she died. Mrs. Murray had declined the help of doctors in her last hours; keeping her alive was their business now past, but dying was hers.

Jim Murray called me at the office, and I went immediately to be with him. I arrived at two PM. At three, the two oldest children came home from school, and the father took them in to see the body of their mother. One son, with skills in drawing, closed the door and sketched a picture. Americans have been conditioned to avoid even thinking about death, much less looking at it, but for months this one family had been gently coached by its father not to hide from death when it came. "There is growth in silence," his wife had written in her journal.

In Michele Murray's life, the same attitude—embrace reality, don't avoid it—characterized her writing and accounted for her large following. In her long and powerful essay that prefaced *A House of Good Proportion*, Mrs. Murray wrote: "Ten years ago, I taught at Catholic University and lived nearby in a new apartment built in a barren part of Washington, all little row houses and saplings running up and down the hilly streets, none of a city's delights, no shops or theaters, no libraries, no public gathering places, only these little houses and their owners mesmerized by their separate patches of lawn, their fenced gardens. The bus stop was a piece of wasteland.

From here I went each day to teach English literature, to participate, in however humble a fashion, in the great chain of culture that circled Oxford and Cambridge, the London theaters, Dr. Johnson's essays on Shakespeare, Hopkins' poem on Purcell and Purcell's music, theories of poetry from Longinus to Eliot, Dante's unmeasured world, the Gothic architecture so badly parodied in the university buildings, and so on. What was the connection between that spacious world and the raw, narrow one I came home to? Whether these worlds were even aware of each other was problematical. To say *the same sky over them*, was it to say mere words? But I was aware of them, going back and forth, I was the connection, and any others who made that journey or similar journeys, for it is living people who transmit culture, joining together all the arcs of their days into a circle and joining all the circles into what we call a culture, a country, an era."

Late in the afternoon, I helped make funeral arrangements. On occasion, Mrs. Murray wrote columns for the *Observer* on consumer problems, so I thought it fitting that I was able to make arrangements for cremation, followed by a Catholic Mass and a memorial service, for less than $300—a true and a rare consumer victory.

In the strength of her vocation to literature, Michele Murray wrote several million words and read countless millions more. "Nourished on literature," she wrote, "it is difficult for me to accept technology or politics as more than ways of making this night at an uncomfortable inn a bit more comfortable, without sharing the illusions which feed, after all, a considerable portion of the apparatus of the modern state."

Perhaps that was part of her uniqueness: no illusions about the values of life—her family, her belief in a personal God and the community of literature were important, and little else—nor illusions about death and dying. There is no separation of the self, only a wholeness, provided there is the courage to embrace it.

When friends came together for a memorial service for Michele Murray they read one of her works called "Death Poem."

> *What will you have when you finally have me?*
> *Nothing.*
> *Nothing I have not already given*
> *freely each day I spent*
> *not waiting for you*
> *but living*
> *as if the shifting shadows of grapes*
> *and fine-pointed leaves in the shelter*

of the arbor would continue to tremble
when my eyes were absent
in memory of my seeing,
or the books fall open where I marked them
when my astonishment overflowed
at a gift come unsummoned, this love
for the open hands of poems,
earth fruit, sun soured grass, the steady
outward lapping stillness of midnight
snowfalls, an arrow of light waking me
on certain mornings with sharp wound
so secret that not even you
will have it when you have me.
You will have my fingers
but not what they touched. Some gestures
outflowing from a rooted being, the memory
of morning light case on a bed
where two lay together—
the shining curve of flesh!—
they will forever be out of your reach
whose care is with the husks.

SELECTED BIBLIOGRAPHY OF MICHELE MURRAY

The Crystal Nights. New York: Seabury, 1973.
The Great Mother and Other Poems. New York: Sheed and Ward, 1974.
A House of Good Proportion, Images of Women in Literature, ed. New York: Simon and Schuster, 1973.
Nellie Cameron. New York: Seabury, 1971.

J. F. Powers

IN THE SPRING OF 1966, the creative writing class at Smith College, Northampton, Massachusetts, was taught by J. F. Powers. The school's first writer-in-residence, Powers had won the National Book Award in 1963 for his novel *Morte D'Urban* and had a reputation as a craftsman of surplus talent. The class at Smith had only seven members—out of 2,500 students. Doesn't this rankle you, having so few students, Powers was asked. Not at all, he said. In fact, he expressed elation at the seven member class. "In the fall semester, I had only two students. So things are picking up."

Such a comment—suggesting a wry and detached mind, not at all self-consumed—illustrates a style of gentle irreverence that is in much of Powers' writing. He is one of our quality storytellers, a man of personal kindness and whose stories go far beyond the ventriloquizing that so many dummy fiction writers are allowed to get away with. Powers enjoyed a plenary year at Smith and the students—at least the few wise enough to seek him out—were grateful that he came. On leaving Smith, Powers settled with his wife and children in County Wicklow, Ireland. Many are puzzled by Powers' long absence; a few years ago, he was asked about American writers in exile abroad. You have it backwards, he reportedly said. The American writer is in exile in America.

Fiction writers, we are told, are meant to be concerned with "questions," like the Camus novels that ask why we do not commit suicide. "I stay away from idea stories," Powers has said. "Characters should have lives, should live in their own right and not simply hang like puppets from the minds of authors with ideas. That is why I find certain writers—particularly all French writers of the present day—so tiresome."

The liveliest Powers creation is Father Urban of the award-winning novel. He is "a poor man's Fulton Sheen," a priest-promoter who is the Lord's bulldozer, with opportunism that cuts wide paths through secular forests. We have had many novels—by Mauriac, Graham Greene—about whiskey priests and womanizing priests, but Urban has no problems with moral failure. The angel he wrestles with is worldly success. He has a taste for shishkebab and champagne and knows exactly which parishioners' tables will provide them. The care of souls is indeed the priestly calling but Urban prefers to do his caring among the wealthy and beautiful. He is a priest only from the waist down, avoiding the temptings of the flesh while his head and heart hotly pursue the delights of the expense account. The title of the novel—The Death of Urban—is the theme of the story; how worldiness dies in a man in whom it should never have lived.

James Farl Powers was born July 8, 1917 in Jacksonville, Illinois. The town (at Powers' birth Jacksonville was little more than a village but currently nears 22,000) is thirty-five miles west of the state capitol, Springfield, and sixty miles east of Mark Twain's Hannibal, Missouri. Powers' father, who is said to have been a child prodigy at the piano, was a manager for Swift & Company. His mother was an amateur painter.

After attending public and parochial schools in Jacksonville, Powers went north in 1935 to the Chicago campus of Northwestern University. Because he lacked money for the four-year degree program, Powers decided to struggle where it counted and took a number of English courses at night. He managed a year like this but then dropped out and looked for work. This terminated his formal education and may account for his habit of regularly interrupting himself in conversation to say, "I'm not an intellectual," or "I haven't read enough about that," or "You went to college so you can tell me about this," or "I can't go into it deeply because I don't know enough to back up my arguments." None of this is said in the blankness of self-resignation. Instead, it appears as a kind of humility similar to the operational candor of children who are unembarrassed by anything they have and too preoccupied to worry about what they lack.

Because it was still the depression, Powers failed to find decent work and settled for a series of dishwashing and packing house jobs. Finally, he gained employment in a large Chicago bookstore which occasionally doubled as a hangout for writers. Powers met Richard Wright, who was there on a Federal Writers' Project, and Nelson

Algren, who drifted in once in a while between excursions. Powers recalled that one of his diversions in the bookstore was pushing books he was moved by, particularly Algren's novel, *Never Come Morning*. Eventually, Powers began to think that possibly he himself was a writer. "Very little time, actually, passed between the time I tried to publish and succeeded in doing so," he has said. "I wasn't really knowledgeable enough to have hopes of money when I sent out my first work, and received very little. I haven't made much from my books, though I have been well paid for my stories in the *New Yorker* and have been the beneficiary of several foundations."

In 1943, the literary quarterly *Accent* published Powers' first short stories. One of these—"Lions, Harts, and Leaping Does"—was included in *O. Henry Prize Stories of 1944.* This established a credential which enabled Powers to sell his stories at higher prices to large circulation magazines and eventually to benefit from several foundation grants: a Guggenheim Fellowship, a grant from the National Institute of Arts and Letters, a Rockefeller Grant at the University of Iowa, a Writers Workshop Fellowship and a Rockefeller Kenyon Review Fellowship.

Though nearly all of Powers' short stories deal with Midwestern Catholicism and the activities of priests within that framework, no critic has ever suggested that his material is reworked. "What we have here," writer Peter De Vries explained in the *Time* edition of Powers' short stories, "are not the familiar joshing, pawky attempts to 'humanize the clergy' but the work of a mature artist quite naturally showing human nature to be no better in the green wood than in the dry. He portrays priests practicing their profession, not their religion. This is not the Church triumphant, only the Church militant, and with most of the warfare civil at that. It is the members of a spiritual family rubbing along with one another, even as you and I. With a few exceptions we are not given souls on trial, but egos—the serial nuisances and daily frets of life sufficing Mr. Powers for the delineation of character quite as well as major crises do lesser writers."

After the Second World War, Powers married Betty Wahl, also a writer. They have five children. Carrying on in the custom of many writers, Powers has been forced to earn money from outside work. This has usually been teaching—far from ideal but much better than the serfdom of corporation work or civil service. Powers confesses that during the teaching periods his fiction production tapers considerably. "I'm lazy, anyway," Powers jokes, "so teaching is a good excuse for not getting anything written."

From 1949 to 1951, Powers taught at Marquette, a Roman Catholic multiversity in Milwaukee. Previously he had taught a semester of creative writing at St. John's College, Collegeville, Minnesota. Powers declined to say whether he had originally sighted any of his fictional characters among the Benedictines at St. John's. He taught at the University of Michigan in 1956-57 but left after one semester to work in Ireland on a grant.

In 1947, Powers' first book of short stories, *Prince of Darkness,* was published by Doubleday. *The Presence of Grace,* his second collection, appeared in 1956. Powers did not reach full stride until his novel *Morte D'Urban* came out. On March 13, 1963, at New York's Americana Hotel, his career received the vote of confidence every American writer most cherishes, short of royalty checks: the National Book Award for fiction. At a post-awards dinner at Toots Shor's, Powers reflected on his accomplishment. "Awards are fine for those writers who get them," he told his audience. "What do they mean? They mean as much as any public, official recognition of a writer's work can mean. They mean that either someone has fooled a hell of a lot of people or that his work is the real thing. I think mine is the latter."

A reflective, generous man, and gifted with great perceptive power and swift insight, Powers is essentially a person who looks at the primary colors. If there is any despair in his vision, it has one mark to distinguish it from the many cults of desperation currently abroad: it is not chic. Powers stayed clear of the 1960's teach-ins, the protests and the higher-fi forms of intellectualism, chiefly because the hard, firm edge of his intelligence refused to be exploited by invitations to come to the Wailing Wall, regardless of how many commas are out of place in the world. Although his political thoughts are debatable they are not irresponsible; he has paid in full for his inclinations. A profoundly and even touchingly spiritual man, Powers' nonliterary victories have been won on orthodox lines: a happy and sharing marriage, intelligent children, fidelity to the Church, and good health. Powers' great belief is that moral laws exist and that everyone, not only the *aficionado* of religion, must pay some kind of homage to them or else suffer the ruthlessness of reality.

It is easy to wonder why Powers hasn't taken steps to withdraw from the main flow in order to maintain a grip on his artistic militancy or, at another level, retreat in the way Evelyn Waugh sought seclusion at his Gloucestershire home to protect himself from the era. From many possible answers, the most likely, is that Powers does not feel that his prime object is "to get things done." Powers seems indifferent to production. The energy for doing things is less meaningful to him than possessing the originality of soul to decide what is worth doing and what is right to do in the first place. Because of this, most trade people, particularly the overlords of the publishing business, consider J. F. Powers one of the ranking enigmas of the American literary community. "He hasn't shored up a tenth of the money he could have from his writing," an acquaintance of Powers told me, "and he has bungled chances to get his books peddled in the drugstores. But the remarkable thing is that none of this bothers him."

Powers himself has little trouble understanding his lack of commercial success. A few months before *Morte D'Urban* was published, a Catholic book club sought the novel as one of its monthly selections. Powers turned them down. He did not want his book running the risk of being categorized "Catholic." Later, the movie vendors lusted after the story of Father Urban, with one company proposing Alec Guinness for the lead, but again Powers refused. It was a difficult no, calling on something fundamental to his integrity. "I did not want Father Urban to become," Powers said at the time, "the kind of priest that Hollywood would decide the American public would buy. That was one button I'd never push."

It is a fact of contemporary fiction that the better a writer becomes the more he is forced to rule his fate like a dictator. The necessity of warding off the public cry, the book clubs, and MGM with one hand while trying to write a lasting document of fiction with the other is the eventual lot of any writer wanting to protect his superiority. When I visited him at Smith, Powers remarked to me that people write for many reasons: to make a dollar, to achieve a name or immortality, or as a means of putting on a show. "To some extent," Powers said candidly, "all these things motivate me, even the part about putting on a show. But I prefer to say it is the desire and pursuit of the whole. It is the highest form of creative activity given to men, proof that we are made in God's image. I have created a little world, with God's help."

With Minnesota roots, Powers is a product of the same midwestern culture that Abigail McCarthy has written about so well. According to biographer John V. Hagopian (whose volume is part of the Twayne series), Powers refused to serve in World War II and did a prison stretch of thirteen months rather than bear arms. Hagopian cites a sketch Powers wrote in 1945 for Dorothy Day's *Catholic Worker* newspaper, "Night in a County Jail," a narration whose truth rings even louder today: "Here I was in jail because I objected to war, and all about me were men locked up for other reasons. It seemed to me as I listened to these men, that I was surrounded by innocence. I felt old and guilty among them. These men, too, were objectors. They would know that if only they knew themselves. The mild, floundering, tender people, betrayed by leaders, themselves betrayed, the young men marching off to war with books of poetry and New Testaments in knapsacks. They were the leaven. Without them in its armies the war would collapse instantly of its own monstrous evil weight."

Powers enjoyed his year at Smith. "There are people who say you can't teach writing," he believes. "I think this is right in the sense that you can't teach surgery to people who can't slice bread. You teach writing in the way you teach surgery—use of the knife, sewing up and so on. The surgeon studies anatomy. The writer does, too, inside and out, meaning character and psychology. People who have no feel for character—who have no feel for other people except as male or female, old or young, fat or thin, good or bad—will not make writers. They can't be taught writing."

Powers supposedly has another novel coming out soon, but the supposedlys have been piling up for some time. No matter. Writers can't win; if they produce a novel every year, like Joyce Carol Oates, the ruck says they are spreading it too thin. If nothing comes for a long stretch and there is no running with the hounds, they have "lost touch." But how can that be said about Powers, even if he never produces another syllable? Instead of demanding more from this proven master, we ought to go back and read his old stories again. Once fictional characters like Urban are given life, we die long before they do.

SELECTED BIBLIOGRAPHY OF J. F. POWERS

"Dealer in Diamonds and Rhinestones," *Commonweal*, Aug. 10, 1945, reprinted in *Commonweal*, Nov. 16, 1973.
"Fairwell," *The New Yorker*, Aug. 6, 1973.
Literary Lectures, Library of Congress, carries an essay by Saul Bellow, p. 514, that discusses *Morte D'Urban*.
Morte D'Urban. New York: Doubleday, 1963 (paperback, Popular Library).
Presence of Grace. Freeport, N.Y.: Books for Libraries, 1969.
Prince of Darkness. New York: Doubleday, 1947.
Hagopian, John V. *J. F. Powers*. Boston: Twayne, 1968.

Sigrid Undset

As YET, WE HAVE SEEN NO POPULAR revival of Sigrid Undset, Norway's masterly and rapt novelist who died in 1949. Perhaps, though, a revival—a brief spell of new regard—is not what we should be looking for, because a public's appreciation of a writer often has nothing to do with a bookseller's sales chart or what is catching on with trendsetters. This statement is not offered as a donation to Sigrid Undset's defense fund but comes from an awareness that Undset has a considerable committed following and that no revival is necessary—because there has never been a letdown. Those who originally went to Undset for the perceptive portrayal or the elevated insight still go, with no prodding needed. Those new readers of Undset, who refuse to become search parties for the lost causes of so many of our contemporary novelists, go to her books for their fullness and deft force of expression. It is a force that, once felt, only the sluggish can forget.

Going back over some of her novels, which helped her win a Nobel for literature in 1928, it is clear she practiced a craft not much sold in American bookstores today: large-sweep dramas that tell stories, not psychoanalytical reports, about people. She could write about sex not because it was sexy but because men and women struggled to make it sublime. Her greatest novels—*Kristin Lavransdatter* and *The Master of Hestviken*—are filled with characters who seek redemption by allegiance to their roots, who grow not because they leave values behind but because they are spiritually restive until making a return to them. Much of the anguish in life comes from that: a failure not in getting what we want but in not recovering the valuables we once had but wasted—innocence, imagination, hope. *We squandered* will be a fitting epitaph for most of us personally and all of us collectively.

Sigrid Undset's own feeling and conduct had as much drama as in any of the lives she created. Born in 1882, the daughter of an archaeologist who interested the child in Norway's rich past, Mrs. Undset fled the Nazi's in 1940. In a language of simplicity, she wrote of her homeland and her flight from it in *Return to the Future* (Knopf, 1942). Norway is a land "from which it is so difficult and heavy a task to win a living. No wonder we have always used our strength to save precious human lives rather than to destroy lives. Heroic deeds on sea and land to rescue men in peril of death have, thanks to God, always been daily happenings in Norway, but crimes of violence have been rarer than in any other country in Europe, and they roused our terror and abhorrence; in Norway every small murder became a topic of talk among the people for years. And if we captured one or another of our murderers he could be certain of decent treatment—of examination by psychiatrists, a conscientious lawyer, and if he were sentenced, not too severe imprisonment."

Mrs. Undset's childhood in Oslo was secure and calm but uneventful. She wrote about the peacefulness of it in her reminiscence, *Eleven Years*. She recalls a visit to her grandfather's garden in Kalundborg, a summer holiday that suggests her parents gave her plenty of time for creative idleness: "One came into an air which was a surfeit of scents—bitter-sweet from the box-hedges, cool and pure from the phlox, and the rank sweaty smell from elder and ivy. . . . Then there were spiders of every shape and size, fat blue-bottles that flashed as they skimmed out of the shade into the sunshine, and the terrifying earwigs. But the gloom under the old trees and the mystical insects only made the gardens more fascinating in my eyes."

When her father died, the family was left with little money. Living near to what we now call "the poverty line," Undset writes in *Eleven Years* of her embarrassment on seeing her mother bargain-hunt in a clothing store. Undset believed "that the most joyless form of poverty is that where submission is made without protest to the opinion which considers it a shameful thing to be poor. She [her mother] did not want to submit to such an assessment of life's values, but at the same time she felt that something inside her was yielding under the pressure of circumstance. She knew that, in a way, she too would have dearly liked to be invited to the 'fine rich houses,' though she knew she would never enjoy herself in them, the people were so boring. And she was ashamed of herself because she had become the same as they."

To earn her living after her father died, Undset went to secretarial school to learn a craft. For ten years after she worked in an office. It was hardly a joy, fighting the battles of in-basket dullness, but like a root that needs time and stillness to borrow, Undset found herself going deep into Oslo, making it a part of her consciousness. "It was after I had settled down in the office and had come to feel myself on equal terms with the people I met there, that I realized I was at home in my own town. I had roots everywhere in this earth which I had trodden all the while I was growing up, roots in all the suburban streets where I had lived as a child and played in the open space, in gloomy Keysers Street and in Pilestraede where I spent some wretched years, in Vestre Aker where I wandered when I was small, and in towards Frognersaeteraasen and Vetakollen and up through Nordmark, penetrating further and further as I grew older, in the blue anemones' season, in the burning summer sun, in November's pouring rain, over the hard snow of winter and the slushy snow of spring." Some parallels exist between Undset's rooted years in an office and Simone Weil's shorter periods of work in factories. Both women who spoke of roots were profoundly changed by closely experiencing the lives of citizens who are mostly passed over.

During this period, Undset was saving string, to be unwound later in the stories she wrote about the working class and middle class. In *The Happy Age*, one of her earlier novels—she tried a long historical novel at this time but a publisher rejected it, advising her to stick with what she knew—a character speaks what Undset herself could have expressed: "I wanted to write about the town. You know—all these half-lovely districts we respectable drudges live in. The wet dirty streets and the worn paving-stones, small apartments and small shops—I should really love to write about the windows of such shops—shops selling chemists' sundries, and toyshops with dolls and sewing-boxes and glass necklaces, where children stand outside in clusters and say 'Bags I that one'. . . . I could love and make use of all the worn-out little words which we all let fall so carelessly—words we use when we drop in on someone, words that go with some sign of love, words whispered in grief or in the surprise of some small joy. . . . I could write a book about you or about myself or about any office-worms. We carry on and find a job which allows us to live—we can't live *for* it."

In 1909, when she was twenty-seven and had worked ten years and had written enough stories and novels to be self-confident, Undset left her secretary's job and travelled. The evidence suggests she was a lively and sparkling woman, as much taken with long and talkative evenings among friends in Germany, Rome and Paris, as with her deepening studies of medieval life. In 1912, with another novel—*Jenny*—added to her reputation, Undset married A. C. Svarstad, a painter with three children from an earlier marriage. During this period of early marriage, when she had two sons of her own as well as doing most of the caring for her three stepchildren, Undset also wrote criticism and commentary. The original women's liberation movement was beginning at this point—women like Jeanette Rankin and Emma Goldman were among its leaders in America in the second decade of this century—but Undset's intellectual independence earned her attacks from both sides. *Jenny* created the inevitable furor because it suggested, among other bold notions, that a woman's sexual needs were as valid as a man's. A. H. Winsnes reports a conversation Undset had: "A rather patronising lady asked, 'I hear that you are an authoress, Miss Undset. Tell me, in what genre do you write?' Sigrid Undset answered, in the most matter-of-fact tone, 'In the immoral.' "

At the same time, Undset refused to get in line with the argument that motherhood is an obstacle to a woman's fulfillment. "Any woman," she wrote, "who becomes a good mother is greater than most ministers of state, for she is indispensable in her work, whereas very many ministers can be replaced with advantage."

In her middle life, at fifty-two, Undset embraced Christianity and Catholicism. She wrote that "only supernatural intervention can save us from ourselves," but there was more to her conversion than that. As a passionate student—not a school student but one who pursues studies because truth is at the end of the journey—she had learned what Christianity meant to so many in the historical past; finally, understanding what it meant to others, she embraced its meaning for herself. Knowledge led to faith. A few months after "taking instructions," as the expression went, and joining the Church, Undset was in Rome. She describes her religious experience during services at Monte Casino: "All these tens of thousands in the church, believers and doubters and unbelievers, the prayerful and the curious, good Catholics and bad Catholics—the first pope in his tomb and all the popes who are at rest around him, and the last pope who kneels in prayer, while around him now prayers rise up from this church like the flood-tide. The prayers spread themselves like an atmosphere over those who pray and those who do not pray, as does the cry that mounts up to all those who have gone before, innumerable myriads of dead Christians, begging that they too will pray with us. I cannot explain it properly: it is, I feel, as if the names of ideas which I accepted purely with my intellect were suddenly illuminated by an object-lesson. The Christian congregation, the catholicity of the Church, the communion of the saints, the relative reality of time and space and, outside the eggshell, the absolute reality of eternity, the untold souls who have lived through the ages, each of them imprisoned in the ravelled net of his own self, from which no doctrine can set us free, only God, and He only by dying on a cross. One can recognize it as the only thing which makes sense in the end: one can understand it, but sometimes it seems as if one can *see* it. . . . Something of the kind I can see this evening also—the fleetingness of time and every event, the reality of eternity and of the spirit; but actually I see it bare of ceremony, as a sober truth—even so, it is no less overwhelming."

Kristin Lavransdatter, the daughter of Lavrans, lives in fourteenth century Norway, a period well before the Renaissance and shortly before feudalism. The novel is a trilogy, the whole life of Kristin from childhood to death in the Northern woods. The first part, *The Bridal Wreath*, appeared in 1920, and in successive years *The Mistress of Husaby* and *The Cross* were published. To understand Kristin, it is important to see the father Undset has created for her. Lavrans, a landholder of wealth who "liked well to come among the small folk who lived on clearings and leaseholdings high up on the outskirts of the parish," came from a prominent family, builders, and loyalists to the king. Kristin saw Lavrans as "the comeliest man far around; he looked like a knight, standing there among his men, though his dress was much of the farmer fashion, such as he wore at home for daily use." In his home, secure among wife and daughters, Lavrans was a whole house of a man, with east and west wings crammed full of faith in the Lord and strong emotions toward his children. His piety was such that he romanticized the monastic life, and on hearing the bells of a local monastery thinks "there exists no worthier occupation for a man, who has been given the grace to understand a little of God's mercy, than to serve Him and watch and pray for those who still go with the darkness of the world's affairs before their eyes." Actually, Lavrans' lay eyes were not totally darkened, because he kept a close watch on the local clergy, particularly when his prized daughter was involved; he "was not so pleased when the priest sometimes likened his daughter to an unblemished, silken-coated filly."

This, to Lavrans' paternal thinking, was a right reserved for him. Like the Norse knights, he owned land, he owned ideals and he

50

believed he owned Kristin too. By tradition, he arranged a marriage for her. At first, Kristin went along with the choice—a landowner, kindly but older than Kristin and somewhat of a bumbler. But then, second and third thoughts came. "Of a sudden she thought with dislike of Simon's round, red face and small laughing eyes—of his jaunty gait—he bounced like a ball, it came to her all at once; of his bantering talk, that made her feel awkward and foolish. Twas no such glory either to get him, and move with him just down to Formo. Still she would rather have him than be sent to a convent." Or at least sent to a convent for good. As a stall, she agrees with Lavrans that a year in the nunnery at Oslo would "give her a little time to get back her peace of mind before they drank the betrothal ale."

Instead of finding peace of mind, Kristin found Erlend Nikolaussen. Passions between them immediately stirred, ones that saw no sense in the tradition of arranged marriages. Kristin replaced her father's choice of a man with her own. Erlend was young, defiant and a breaker of customs, and one who knew when his power had swept away a woman. Unlike the man she had been committed to, Erlend had little in common with Lavrans. The dissimilarity did not cause sorrow with Kristin; instead, "she had only that strange new feeling that she was cut off from all the ties that she had felt binding on her before."

This is the sweeping theme of Undset's greatest novel. Kristin, in marriage to Erlend, was never to be free of feeling the pull of emotional ropes, ones of doubt, of grieving for the past. Like many contemporary women, she sought liberation not fully knowing what she wanted to be liberated for. It may be hard to imagine a modern daughter grieving about defying a father—women today, we're told, are tough about such quaint concepts as family ties—but Sigrid Undset was depicting as much a modern woman as a medieval one. Wives who have no sense of their fathers often fight calamitously to make sense of their husbands. This fate befell Kristin. Erlend was not changed by marriage—what man ever is, though women keep hoping—and soon Kristin had to endure him, not love him. In time Erlend had enough of family life. He longed to taste strife and war, roll them around on his tongue and swallow them like the proteins of manhood.

If the main drama of *Kristin Lavransdatter* is a woman who has cut her ties, the greatness of the novel is also in the number of other levels of action that Undset sustains in detail. First, there is the

51

religious passion of Kristin. It is not a soft piety, the kind her father practiced and which was closer to religiosity than religion, but a stern kind, an awareness that the strength of faith is often interlocked with the weakness of the believer. As a girl, Kristin is influenced by a monk, Brother Edvin, much in the way that Alyosha, in *The Brothers Karamazov,* learned wisdom from a monk. Echoing St. Augustine, Brother Edvin tells Kristin: "There is no man nor woman who does not love and fear God, but it is because our hearts are divided between love of God and fear of the devil and fondness for the world and the flesh, that we are unhappy in life and death. For if a man had not any yearning after God and God's being, then should he thrive in hell, and it would be we alone who would not understand that there he had gotten what his heart desired. For there the fire would not burn him if he did not long for coolness, nor would he feel the torment of the serpent's pit, if he knew not the yearning after peace." Years later, in anguish over her doubts, she cries out to the memory of her childhood monk: "Brother Edvin, if in truth thou art a holy saint, if thou standest before the face of God, pray for me now."

A second undercurrent of action is Kristin's relationship with her father. "Tell them at home," she says to Erlend as he leaves his own house for a cross-mountain journey to the estate of Lavrans, "that, everyday since I left, I have longed to fall at the feet of Mother and Father and beg their forgiveness." Kristin's break with her father was not a defiant rejection of his values but a moving away from them, a departure more subtle because Kristin believed she would find a replacement for what she moved from. It is not easy to return to her father's home even for a family visit. Few scenes in the literature of fathers and daughters compare with Undset's description of Kristin's parting from Lavrans at Hjerkinn. Lavrans says: "Grieve no more for what you have to repent toward me, Kristin. But remember it, when your children grow big, and you may deem that they bear them not towards you or towards their father as you might think was right. And remember then, too, what I said to you of my youth. Faithful is your love to them, I know it well; but you are most stubborn where you love most, and I have marked that in these boys of yours dwells self-will enough."

As a portrait of Medieval Scandinavia—reverence for the land, the centrality of the Church—few historians can tell us more than Sigrid Undset in *Kristin Lavransdatter.* Americans know little about other cultures, much less past cultures, and the loss is revealed in the shallowness of our own. Post-moral America draws on no richness. Without romanticizing the past—"everything was better back then" is as false as the view that "things are bound to be better tomorrow"— Undset suggests that the hunt for authenticity is hard enough in a small group like the family without trying to do it alone. The world soon enough tries to throw us on the periphery; why lunge for it ourselves?

In his biography *Sigrid Undset: A Study in Christian Realism* (Sheed & Ward, 1953), A. H. Winsnes wrote about the historical fidelity of *Kristin Lavransdatter:* "Sigrid Undset spared no effort in acquiring as much factual knowledge as possible of religious life in the Catholic period of Norwegian history. She was not content with the story told by the visible relics—architecture, churches, monasteries, pictorial art—of the magnificence, brilliance and beauty which went with the Church's expansion. Her penetrating glance was directed . . . to the life of the common people and their relationship with religion. In this connection, unexpectedly revealing glimpses into the life of the common people were given by literature of religious edification. In the aristocratic family sagas, common life is either ignored or touched on only by accident, but in religious writings its appearance is not due merely to chance. There it results from a new value set on humanity, from a brotherhood between men unknown in the family-society. There was no lack of evidence to show that people understood that they belonged to a society whose bounds stretched far beyond life and the visible world. Old folk beliefs and customs showed how tenacious of life the heathen conceptions continued to be, but they are equally indicative of the power which the new attitude to life and death had won over the thoughts, feelings and conduct of the people."

Undset's first novel after joining the Church was *The Master* of *Hestviken*, in four volumes. As broad and as gripping a saga as *Kristin Lavransdatter*, the dominant story here—also set in medieval Norway—is not of a person reconciling herself with old values, but of reconciliation with new values. Olav Audunsson of Hestviken disobeys the God he accepted only recently. His disobedience is the secret murder of a student who seduces the woman Olav was to marry. In the pagan culture from which he came, Olav would have carried no guilt for the vengeful killing, and would have even been hailed for his manliness. But his new Christianity has different ideas about the worth of human life. In the last part of the novel—it runs to 994 pages—Olav's children discuss their father whose death has brought them together. "You are right, brother—Father was more of a man than we guessed. And yet . . . for half his lifetime he bore the guilt of an unshriven slaying—and when he would make amends for it at last, God took judgment into his own hand." The brother replies: "We may not inquire into such things—God's hidden counsels. But never will I believe it fell upon him because Father's sin was worse than most men's. Mayhap it was done to show forth an example—the rest of us take so little heed of our misdeeds. And God made choice of Father to do full penance, since He knew his heart—stronger and more faithful than we poor wretches who would not be able to swallow one drop of his justice."

The importance of the story of Olav Audunsson is its statement about being true to one's conscience. Undset is saying that this is often the easiest of acts; much harder is to be true to the search for new ideas and visions that may demand from the conscience a braver stand. Undset probably had Olav in mind when she wrote in one of her essays that "the Catholic Church confirmed much of the pre-Christian pagan way of thinking; because this had already grasped something of the individual's profound connection with his fellow men meant not only the family, the class, and the tribe, but the community of the living and the dead. Protestantism was from the first . . . in alliance with the individualism of a dechristianized generation. In referring people to their own consciences, without any infallible authority with which the decisions of conscience could be confronted, Protestantism made it far too easy for men . . . to take the impulses of egoism for the voice of conscience—till it became a tacitly accepted maxim that the self is the first consideration."

Although it is inaccurate to say that Undset was now making the case for Christianity, she was emphatically writing from a Christian viewpoint. Her essays reflect this. The religion that replaced Norway's pagan cults was not a mystic vision, she believed, but was founded "by a Man whose life and death could be reckoned in time, and of whom there are written records; the faith was passed on from age to age and from nation to nation, by apostles, martyrs and bishops, and professed by men and women in spite of persecutions, perils and the sentence of death—the saints of whose life and death men also had written evidence." Although not a social activist in the sense that we know that term today—with wheel-spinning often much a part of it—Undset insisted that the Gospel had as much to do with this world as the next one. "That element of democracy which is in Christianity is the only one which cannot be argued out of

54

existence. Against all talk of equality, there remains the irrefutable objection that human beings are not equal—one is coin of copper, another of silver. Christianity meets this objection by maintaining that all of them are minted with the kings' picture on them."

In 1935, seeing the clouds that were coming, she began writing against Nazism, a denunciation that would last until Hitler's defeat. In *Return To The Future,* the book that tells of her exile—she went first to Sweden, then Moscow, across Siberia, to Japan and then to America—she notes the characteristics of a deluded national leader. She spoke of Hitler but other politicians came to mind. "The gifted psychopath has again and again in the course of history found the solution for the hostile attitude toward man—as war lord or revolutionary." There is one thing "which psychopaths cannot possibly do: that is to establish a peaceful and satisfactory relation to their fellow men. Psychopaths are constitutionally unpeaceful, spiteful, obsessed by grudges against real or imagined antagonists." In an essay in *Men, Women and Places,* (Knopf, 1939) a similar thought appears. "Hatred is a far more uniform and rallying emotion (than love). . . . Every demagogue and dictator knows that nothing is so useful as hatred for kneading people into a mass under his hands."

As a Nobel winner, Undset was welcomed by the American intellectual community, even to the point of being invited to stay at the Algonquin Hotel in Manhattan. She did for a time but then moved to the more quiet Columbia Heights section in Brooklyn. From there, she wrote for newspapers and magazines—including the *New York Times Book Review* and *America*—contributed essays to anti-Nazi anthologies and lectured on almost any available platform. Occasionally, her fierce loathing of Hitler's Germany led her to extravagancies. "Not that I think the doctors are infallible any more than other people," she wrote in *Return To The Future,* ". . . but if it becomes possible to diagnose Hitlers' Goerings and Goebbelses while they are still very young, place them under medical care, or isolate them if they are incurable, then certainly much unhappiness could be prevented." She was also excessive when saying that "it will be useless to go on believing that there is no fundamental difference between the German people's nature and the nature of all European nations." Such statements as these, whose pitch seems shrill now, were said at a time when the menace of Nazism was in full force, and should be understood in that way. When the war ended, Undset returned to Norway and her village of Lillehammer. In 1947, she was awarded by the King of Norway the nation's highest honor, the

Grand Cross of the Order of St. Olav.

Governments seldom have the sense of daring to honor writers while they live, and even less so when they die. Better these unpredictables be avoided on either occasion. Norway's distinction was not only to honor Sigrid Undset while she lived but to pay her unusual homage at her death. In June 1949, burying her from a country church in Hamar, the Norwegian Parliament, in unshowy mourning, voted that her burial be at public expense. This gift from the grateful living—bread coming back on the waters to people who now needed it—was both a gesture of personal affection for a storyteller and a display of reverence for the stories themselves. Norway does not have a long list of genius worldknown writers—Ibsen, Knut Hamsun, Bjornson, Undset—but when one comes along the citizens of that mostly barren land know enough to know.

SELECTED BIBLIOGRAPHY OF SIGRID UNDSET

Four Stories. New York: Knopf, 1959.
Jenny. New York: Fertig, 1974, (reprint).
Kristin Lavransdatter. New York: Knopf, 1935.
The Master of Hestviken. New York: Knopf, 1952 (four volumes in one).
Men, Women and Places. New York: Knopf, 1939.
Winsness, A. H., *Sigrid Undset: A Study in Christian Realism.* New York: Sheed and Ward, 1953.

E. B. White

THE SAVING GRACE ABOUT COMMON SENSE is that it's uncommon. Baloney, guff, hokum—as hard as these hamburgers are to swallow, we need them if only to savor the juicier meats of common sense when someone serves them up. E. B. White, a headwaiter of clear thinking, has been doing this as long as the younger ones among us can remember and ever since the older ones knew that a writer who exposed foolishness had more effect than one who merely damned it. He is a master of the language and the essay, and has been joining the two since the mid-1920s when he and the *New Yorker* magazine started out. Befitting the harvest years, he hauled in a money-crop prize of $5,000 awarded in New York as the 1972 winner of the National Medal for Literature. He's won other prizes, too—the private Nobels that grateful readers award when a writer satisfies the longing for clear truth.

"Old age is a special problem for me," he said on his seventieth birthday to a *New York Times* legman who visited the White farm in North Brooklin, Maine. "I've never been able to shed the mental image of myself—a lad of about 19." How should one adjust to age? "In principle, one shouldn't adjust. In fact, one does—I gaze into the faces of our senior citizens in our Southern cities, and they wear a sad look that disturbs me. I am sorry for all those who agreed to grow old. I haven't agreed yet."

Nor has E. B. White agreed to sit still for any number of other social handcuffs that American life clamps on us. Rebellion is in nearly all of his essays, collected in such books as *Second Tree from the Corner, One Man's Meat, The Points of My Compass.* But it is rebellion with neither seethe nor sweat, so that what is rebelled against is not shaped by the wild wrath of the protestor's emotions but by his controlled logic, always the deadliest of weapons. Among the better examples of White's rebellion against grossness came in the essay "On a Florida Key"; like all of us, he is aghast at what the commercialists—with their dyes and water hoses—have done to oranges and orange juice. But few have made the indictment against this felony with more calm assurance. "In the kitchen cabinet," he wrote about a visit to a Florida cottage, "is a bag of oranges for morning juice. Each orange is stamped 'Color Added.' The dyeing of an orange, to make it orange, is Man's most impudent gesture to date. It is really an appalling piece of effrontery, carrying the clear implication that Nature doesn't know what she is up to. I think an orange, dyed orange, is as repulsive as a pine cone painted green. I think it is about as ugly a thing as I have ever seen, and it seems hard to believe that here, within ten miles, probably, of the trees which bore the fruit, I can't buy an orange which somebody hasn't smeared with paint. But I doubt there are many who feel that way about it, because fraudulence has become a national virtue. . . . In the past twenty-four hours, I see by this morning's paper, 126 cars of oranges have been shipped. There are probably millions of children today who have never seen a natural orange—only an artificially colored one. If they should see a natural orange they might think something had gone wrong with it."

In gentle understatement—easy-flowing language as though moving to music—White has essayed on both the hard issues of the day and the soft awes that measure our personal lives. He lost an animal once—from illness—and memorably wrote of the event in "Death of a Pig." The first line read: "I spent several days and nights in mid-September with an ailing pig and I feel driven to account for this stretch of time, more particularly since the pig died at last and I lived, and things might easily have gone the other way round and none left to do the accounting." Cows, farming, trees, telephones, couches, railroads were other subjects, all appearing on the pages as though they were sighs of enjoyment interrupting the daily heavy-breathing of fearsome issues. He didn't avoid pondering the latter, though he did avoid sounding ponderous. On diplomacy for example, he believed it to be "the lowest form of politeness because it misquotes the greatest number of people. A nation, like an individual, if it has anything to say, should simply say it. This will be hard on editorial writers and news commentators, who are always glad to have diplomatic notes to interpret; but it will be better for the people."

That elbow in the ribs of editorial writers as he passed by was only a minor lapse in White's grace; he should be pardoned and forgiven. Understood, also. White himself wrote for many years under the anonymous "we" of the *New Yorker's* "Notes and Comments." Those who know that the best reading is often between the lines could recognize the White style tucked away in the folds of anonymity. A favorite of many—the piece should be pasted on the wall of every Washington big shot and little shot—was the note "Impasse in the Business World." "While waiting in the antechamber of a business firm, where we had gone to seek our fortune, we overheard through a thin partition a brigadier general of industry trying to establish telephone contact with another brigadier general, and they reached, these two men, what seemed to us a most healthy impasse. The phone rang in Mr. Auchincloss's office and we heard his secretary take the call. It was Mr. Birstein's secretary, saying that Mr. Birstein would like to speak to Mr. Auchincloss. 'All right, put him on,' said Mr. Auchincloss's well-drilled secretary, 'and I'll give him Mr. Auchincloss.' 'No,' the other girl apparently replied, 'you put Mr. Auchincloss on, and I'll give him Mr. Birstein.' 'Not at all,' countered the girl behind the partition. 'I wouldn't dream of keeping Mr. Auchincloss waiting.' This battle of the Titans, conducted by their leftenants to determine which titan's time was more valuable, raged for five or ten minutes, during which interval the Titan's themselves were presumably just sitting around picking their teeth. . . ."

Perhaps the widest read of E. B. White's books is one he didn't entirely write but only had a hand in—*The Elements of Style*, co-authored with his old professor at Cornell, Will Strunk. Freshman English teachers, or at least those who want to skirt trouble ahead, automatically pass out the slim volume in the first class of fall. Crumbled and tattered copies of it have been seen on the desks of veteran journalists who still care about a true hone in their English. The book details, with prickly guidance, how to write a declarative sentence that communicates something, the hardest of all the arts. "When you consider that there are a thousand ways to express even the simplest idea," White has said, "it is no wonder writers are under great strain. Writers care how a thing is said—it makes all the difference. So they are constantly faced with too many choices and must make too many decisions."

As Charles Karault would say from his eternal road, not many write like E. B. White anymore. Perhaps not; the thing to do then, if one has run through all the White books, is to start over. One man's meat is every man's meal. For sheer surprise, there is nothing to beat a new thought springing from an old insight. White has plenty.

SELECTED BIBLIOGRAPHY OF E. B. WHITE

Charlotte's Web. New York: Dell, 1967.
The Elements of Style, with Will Strunk. New York: Macmillan, 1962.
Here Is New York. New York: Harper and Row, 1949.
Is Sex Necessary? with James Thurber. New York: Harper and Row, 1973.
One Man's Meat. New York: Harper and Row, 1944.
Points of My Compass. New York: Harper and Row, 1962.
Second Tree from the Corner. New York: Harper and Row, 1954.
Stuart Little. New York: Dell, 1967.
Bradford, Robert W. and Watt, William W., eds. *E.B. White Reader.* New York: Harper and Row, 1966.
Gill, Brendan. *Here at The New Yorker.* New York: Random House, 1975. Has twenty-one references to White.
Kramer, Dale. *Ross and The New Yorker.* New York: Doubleday, 1951. Has nineteen references to E.B.White.

Claude McKay

IN A SEPTEMBER 1971 COVER STORY on the Attica State Prison Revolt, *Time* magazine said the inmates had often smuggled banned books into their cells and "passed around clandestine writings of their own: among them was a poem written by an unknown prisoner, crude but touching in its would-be heroic style." The first lines of the poem read:

> *If we must die—let it not be like hogs*
> *Hunted and penned in an inglorious*
>   *spot,*
> *While round us bark the mad and*
>   *hungry dogs,*
> *Making their mock at our accursed lot.*

The poem the prisoners shared among themselves actually was not from the hand of an anonymous inmate but was by Claude McKay, published in 1919. A black writer who died lonely, weary and poor in Chicago in 1948 at age fifty-nine, McKay is best identified with the Harlem Renaissance of the 1920s. But the identification has been hardly strong, as the error by the editors of *Time* suggests, in the failure not only to recognize one of McKay's poems but also to let it off as "crude but touching."

This wasn't the first negative review McKay suffered, either as a poet or a person. In 1926, while staying with literary friends in the south of France, another house guest was F. Scott Fitzgerald; at first he took McKay for a servant. The black writer easily rose above this unintended slight, but his misfortunes as a poet, novelist and essayist were bitter and severe, demoralizing his spirit and forcing him at one period to seek refuge in an upstate New York welfare camp for homeless men. Some of his books received harsh reviews while others were either critical successes but made no money or—the universal complaint of authors—were poorly promoted by the publishers. Defiled but not defeated, he wrote in his 1937 autobiography, *A Long Way from Home* that "All my life I have been a troubadour wanderer, nourishing myself mainly on the poetry of existence. And all I offer here is the distilled poetry of my experience." Such a summation may be too romantic to capture the hardness of his life, and it is best joined with his comments about some of his picaresque characters from his novels *Home to Harlem* and *Banana Bottom.* Like McKay, these characters were citizens who would not "go down and disappear under the serried crush of trampling white feet."

Thanks to several recent reissues of McKay's novels, poems and his autobiography, he is now being read with the seriousness that might have made his life a little easier, and his wallet a little fatter, if such a public came to him while he lived. Broadside Press of Detroit published a McKay biography in 1972 and *The Passion of Claude McKay* (Schocken) is a new collection of his works edited by Wayne Cooper, both volumes offering broad and useful looks at this artist who had a sacramental view of race and blackness. Unlike Fanon, Ellison or Baldwin, who came later in the struggle and could write with power because they were expanding black consciousness rather than trying to define it, McKay could not capitalize on dramatic events to present his thoughts. His first works were verses written in Jamaican dialect, recollections of his boyhood among the black peasantry of his Caribbean birthplace. He was twenty-three when these poems came and still lived in a society where British class discrimination prevailed more than racial oppression. McKay discovered the latter when he came to the United States, first as a student in Alabama and Kansas, and then for many years in Harlem. He became a porter, houseman, janitor, butler, railroad worker. In America, he wrote, he found "strong white men, splendid types, of better physique than any I had ever seen, exhibiting the most primitive animal hatred towards their weaker black brothers. In the South, daily murders of a nature most hideous and revolting, in the North silent acquiescence, deep hate half-hidden under a puritan respectability, oft flaming up into an occasional lynching—this ugly raw sore in the body of a great nation. At first I was horrified, my spirit revolted against the ignoble cruelty and blindness of it all. Then I soon found myself hating in return but this feeling couldn't last long for to hate is to be miserable."

In its place, McKay began to write from feelings of creative bitterness. His poem "If We Must Die," later adopted by the Attica prisoners, comes from this period. It had wide popularity among black workers, but the black critics dismissed McKay as an angry propagandist. He was put in the pressured position of being misunderstood by the constituency he might have depended on—what he called "the colored elite." In an essay, "A Negro Writer to his Critics," he wrote that "the feeling of bitterness is a natural part of the black man's birthright as the feeling of superiority is of the white man's. It matters not so much that one has had an experience of bitterness, but rather how one has developed out of it. To ask the Negro to render up his bitterness is asking him to part with his soul. For out of his bitterness he has bloomed and created his spirituals and blues and conserved his racial attributes—his humor and ripe laughter and particular rhythm of life."

Weary of American racism, McKay traveled abroad. He stayed in such places as Russia, France and Africa for twelve years. Upon return, he began writing for the Nation and the New Leader, laying out a philosophy of community organization that is similar to what we are hearing today from Jesse Jackson. "Any group-conscious Negro," he wrote, "should be interested in the intensive development and advancement of his community. . . . That is the real issue the Negro has to face—the economic issue upon which integration depends. Negro leaders who evade the practical issue of group organization and development to shibboleth the empty slogan of 'integration' without being able to demonstrate a practical plan of integration are not only betrayers but lynchers of the soul of the race."

This was black nationalism to many in McKay's audience, and he was dismissed as lightly as he had been when he insisted on bringing black bitterness to people's attention. Thus, McKay, in his refusal to whitewash his outrage, was forced to carry it himself. Wayne Cooper, in his excellent introduction to his McKay sourcebook, notes that "his volatile temperament and complex ideas were more feared than understood by those best situated to help him gain a secure position within the Harlem community."

Near his end, McKay had a religious conversion, though by current standards a strange one because he didn't prattle to the press about the sweetness of Jesus. Instead, with humility, he confided to a friend: "I have had a hard time but I have also had some superb moments and in spite of my chronic illness I don't want to go sour on humanity, even after living in this awful U.S.A. I still like to think of people with wonder and love as I did as a boy in Jamaica."

SELECTED BIBLIOGRAPHY OF CLAUDE McKAY

Selected Poems of Claude McKay. Boston: Twayne, 1953.
Cooper, Wayne F., ed. *The Passion of Claude McKay.* New York: Schocken Books, 1973.

Mary Lavin

WHO TELLS BETTER STORIES than the Irish, and who among Ireland's living writers tells them better—with more strength, more grace—than Mary Lavin? She is known in this country for the purity of her fiction alone, meaning she hasn't attracted a following who relish Irish writers more for their escapades than their talents. Not only has Mary Lavin avoided marching in the personality parade that Irish writers—honorary grand marshals—so often love to lead, but she has avoided any kind of nonfiction: she never writes reviews, essays or journalism, nor has she been involved in lecturing. Her only vocation is stories. A small shelf carries them, books of excellence that go back to 1942—*Tales from Bective Bridge* to the 1973 *Memories and Other Stories* (Houghton Mifflin). V.S. Pritchett wrote of Mary Lavin: "I cannot think of any Irish writer who has gone so profoundly without fear into the Irish heart."

One of these hearts belongs to a woman in the title story of *Happiness and Other Stories.* She had lost her husband and was left in widowhood with two daughters. Years later she tells them of their father's dying in a Dublin hospital and her last mercies to him by bringing in mounds of daffodils. "Why, I could hardly see over them as I came up the steps; I kept tripping. But when I came into the hall, that nun—I told you about her—that nun come up to me, sprang out of nowhere it seemed, although I know now that she was waiting for me, knowing that somebody had to bring me to my senses. But the way she did it! Reached out and grabbed the flowers, letting lots of them fall—I remember them getting stood on. 'Where are you going with those foolish flowers, you foolish woman? she said. 'Don't you know your husband is dying? Your prayers are all you can give him now!' " But the mother tells her daughters: "She was right. I was

65

foolish. But I wasn't cured."

Lavin characters are inevitably incurables of one breed or another—one with the infirmity of opinionating (the severest of all Irish ailments), another with rue, another with possessiveness (as among Irish sisters who resent the other actually marrying a man), some with going through life with huge emotional straps across the back, needed to carry weighty grudges to the edge of the next world, and whole families full of pride who keep their egos in one basket. Her characters are the farm people of the Irish midlands, or the fishing villages of the seacoast, strong widows, listless husbands, girls in pained courtship, priests, children, the old and the dying. They are the earth's menials without being mediocre. Lavin cares nothing about expositions of human depravity, the easiest of all fiction because only floodlight prose is needed to reveal it; Lavin prefers the nightlight, a small power that keeps watch at the outlines of darkness and shadows that dominate (but should not destroy) the inner life. Her stories—exploring emotions in characters whose provincial lives seem outwardly emotionless—depend on similar settings and themes, but in true brilliance, in none of this sameness is there repetition.

In many of Lavin's stories, as in all Irish lives, the comic and tragic rub close. In "Brigid," the husband and wife have been quarreling for years. Brigid is the other woman in the husband's life, but with the rope of wryness twisted tight, Brigid is not a lover but an older sister. It's an old theme in Irish marriages: relatives are the home-wreckers, not adulterers. In "Brigid," the argument is whether to put the sister in a home, as the wife wants for the sake of stopping the town gossip and getting the daughters married off. "Is any man," she asks, "going to marry a girl when he hears her aunt is a poor half-witted creature, soft in the head, and living in a poke of a hut, doing nothing all day but sitting looking into the fire? . . . Men don't like marrying into a family that has the like of her in it. . . . You know the way Matty Monaghan gave up Rossie after dancing with her all night at a dance in the Town Hall last year. Why did he do that, do you suppose?"

The husband, who had promised his mother "never to have hand or part in putting the poor creature away," is less worried of town tongues with Brigid present than with Brigid banished. "There'd be a lot more talk if the poor creature was put away. Let me tell you that, if you don't know it for yourself! It's one thing to have a poor creature, doing no one any harm, living quiet, all by herself, up at the end of a boreen. . . . It's another thing altogether to

66

have her taken away in a car and everyone running to the window to see the car pass and talking about her and telling stories from one to another till in no time at all they'd be letting on she was twice as bad as she is. . . ."

The husband leaves the argument and the house, walking across the fields to visit Brigid. We aren't shown the scene in the hut but, apparently after a stroke, the husband falls dead into the hearth. Brigid is powerless to help. Three hours later, the wife comes and finds him cold and stiff. The end of the story—in a powerful climax after the wife thinks to herself: "I always failed him, I never loved him like he loved me"—comes when the wife returns to the hut. "Something will have to be done about (Brigid) now all right," says a villager. The wife agrees: "Sitting on the side of the bed, all alone, she saw Brigid. 'Get your hat and coat, Brigid,' she said, 'You're coming home with me.' "

Mary Lavin lives in County Meath, in Bective on a farm on the Boyne River near the ruins of a twelfth century Cistercian Abbey. She was born in East Walpole, Massachusetts, and moved to Ireland at age ten when her father came to look after the castle of a rich American. She married a solicitor with whom she had three daughters before being widowed in 1954. In 1968 she married a Dublin educator. Over the years, Miss Lavin has had a share of grant money—two Guggenheims—but her main support has come from her fiction. The *Atlantic* and the *New Yorker* have been outlets. "It is in the short story," she has written, "that a writer distills the essence of his thought. I believe this because the short story, shape as well as matter, is determined by the writer's own character. Both are one. Short-story writing—for me—is only looking closer than normal into the human heart."

Nothing suggests that Mary Lavin is anywhere near writing her last story. Words are the heritage of the Irish, and beautiful language is the country's leading export. Mary Lavin has built up a world trade, supplying us characters and themes that the smallest Irish village is filled with. It is not in the fury of cities where life is found but in the fury of emotions, and these, as Mary Lavin is telling us, are found anywhere.

SELECTED BIBLIOGRAPHY OF MARY LAVIN

Collected Stories. Boston: Houghton Mifflin, 1971.
Happiness. Boston: Houghton Mifflin, 1970.
In the Middle of the Fields. New York: Macmillan, 1969.

A Memory and Other Stories. Boston: Houghton Mifflin, 1972.
The Second-Best Children in the World. Boston: Houghton Mifflin, 1972.

Edwin Arlington Robinson

THE TERM "STARVING POET" is a part of our language, but who among our major poets actually did starve for The Word? Not Dickinson, nor Frost, Williams, Whitman or Jeffers. When the pack is thinned, one of the few poets who truly did share a bed with the muse of hunger was Edwin Arlington Robinson. For a long period of his life—he died in 1935 at age sixty-six—a good day meant having fifty cents for food. Dinner was often a piece of bread. He would go to restaurants and instead of tipping the waiters, they would give *him* money. As if this knot was not tight enough, his poetry was strangled by other forces. No publisher would take his first manuscript so he printed it himself, only to see the book barely noticed. He sent off another manuscript. It was accepted at first but then the publisher changed his mind, adding that he'd lost the poems. Months later, the madam of a brothel found them where the editor had forgotten them one night.

With such battles—against poverty and editors, as if poetry was not already painful—it is not a surprise that Robinson's different kind of poetry received little recognition until his fiftieth year. Even then, many contemporaries dismissed him as "the dry New England psychologist." We know better today. One current biographer believes that Robinson "gives us a general statement of the meaning of life that will stand with those of Milton and Blake, of Wordsworth, Shelley and Whitman." Most of us remember Edwin Arlington Robinson from his inclusion in our high school English class anthologies where poems like "Miniver Cheevy" or "Richard Cory" were standards. How strange, it seemed, to come upon a poet who wrote of bizarre characters, mired in the earth, while other poets soared skyward with verses about wind-swept meadows or the lilts of songbirds.

But were Robinson's characters bizarre? The factories, offices, markets and homes of common life are kept going or kept back by the citizens of Robinson's poetry, from Leffingwell and his lies or "Clavering, who died because he couldn't laugh" or "Lingard with his eerie joy." These people are not bizarre; they are us. Robinson, who liked to feed his reader "some word that hurts your tongue," explained: "I prefer men and women who live, breathe, talk, fight, make love, or go to the devil after the manner of human beings. Art is only valuable to me when it reflects humanity or at least human emotions." The poetic value of Robinson's work is not only that it produced a distinct style that moved amid an entourage of possibilities, but that the content of his poems is also the content of life that we see and feel daily. Who does not know a Bewick Finzer, the money monger who had much but in pushing for everything wound up with nothing. For Robinson, and for us, Finzer is "Familiar as an old mistake/And futile as regret."

Although many of Robinson's characters were stoics, losers, mindfoggers or other sufferers of interior confusion, he saw his ruins with compassion, believing that life—"God's joke"—kicks everyone around but that some bruise easier than others. Asked once what he was trying to say—what a torment for writers to be asked that question, as if to answer in a fly's minute what they have been working to communicate in a lifetime—Robinson graciously replied: "I suppose that a part of it might be described as a faint hope of making a few of us understand our fellow creatures a little better, and to realize what a small difference there is, after all, between ourselves, as we are, and ourselves, not only as we might have been but would have been if our physical and temperamental makeup and our environment had been a little different." Most of us live as though good luck is owed us, and that some distant force is forever sending us pleasant delights but others—husband or wife, the boss, the kids—keep getting in the way when delivery is imminent. Robinson knew this delusion; he portrays men and women—a considerable census in fifteen hundred pages of the *Collected Poems*—who were better off when they were content with a modest share of life's blessings instead of haunted by useless hoping and longing for a better share.

Robinson's environment was Maine. The last of three sons of a highborn family—the wealth was not to last—he saw both older brothers become drug addicts: one to alcohol, the other to morphine. Many characters later to be a part of his poetic world were originally the citizens of Gardiner, Maine, Robinson's home village.

He knew early that "there is poetry in all kinds of humanity—even in lawyers and horse-jockeys." Quiet, fervent, contemplative in his root qualities, Robinson went to Harvard but washed out after a year. He preferred his education not to be thrown at him; ducking, he went back to Gardiner. During this period, he developed a dislike for competition among individuals, and he loathed it even more when he saw it in the marketplace. He wrote: "Dollars are a convenient thing to have . . . but this diabolic, dirty race that men are running after them disgusts me. I shall probably outgrow this idea, but until I do I shall labor quite contented under the delusions that [there] is something to life outside of 'business.' Business be damned." Much later, when he had seen how many men and women were left unfilled by wealth and power, he wrote his famous rejection of materialism: ". . . It is true that we have acquired a great deal of knowledge in recent years, but so far as knowledge of the truth itself is concerned, I cannot see that we are any nearer to it now than our less imaginative ancestors were when they cracked each other's skulls with stone hatchets, that we know any more than they knew of what happened to the soul that escaped in the process. It is easy, and just now rather fashionable to say that there is no soul, but we do not know. . . . The cocksureness of the modern 'mechanist' means nothing to me; and I doubt if it means any more to him when he pauses really to think. His position is not entirely unlike that of an intrepid explorer standing on a promontory in a fog, looking through the newest thing in the way of glasses for an ocean that he cannot see, and shouting to his mechanistic friends behind him that he has found the end of the world."

A number of women were in and out of Robinson's life but he never married. Although a solitary man, he had a personal completeness that kept him from being a loner. For most of his adult life, he had a quiet affection for his sister-in-law. Twice she rejected Robinson, once before she married his brother and again after the brother died. Some of Robinson's poems about women have a special quality that few American poets have achieved. He understood that few American men get beyond the most simplistic notions of captivating a woman. A Robinson female says to her male: "Somewhere in me there's a woman if you know the way to find her."

Where the Light Falls (Macmillan) by Chard Powers Smith is an excellent biography of Robinson. James Dickey has written a meticulous examination of the verse in the introduction to *Selected Poems of Edwin Arlington Robinson* (Macmillan). It is doubtful that

Robinson's powerful originality will ever be duplicated, this Maine citizen "always hungry for the nameless." Near the end of his life, he told a biographer, "I could never have done anything but write poetry." For certain, if Robinson had done anything else, he couldn't have written poetry of such purity and light.

SELECTED BIBLIOGRAPHY OF EDWIN ARLINGTON ROBINSON

Collected Poems. New York: Macmillan, 1937.

Literary Lectures, Library of Congress, 1973, pp. 527-551, contains an essay on Robinson by Louis Untermeyer.

Smith, Chard Powers. *Where the Light Falls: A Portrait of Edwin Arlington Robinson.* New York, Macmillan, 1965.

Sutcliffe, Denham, ed. *Untriangulated Stars: Letters of Edwin Arlington Robinson to Harry de Forest Smith.* Westport, Conn.: Greenwood, 1947.

Brendan Behan

HE SWIGGED HIS FIRST LIQUOR at age seven and his last at forty-one, with a sea of swallowed poison in between. Yet to the Irish who loved him, and who understood the weakness in all men—particularly in this one who had so much of it—Brendan Behan really had no trouble with the bottle. One can hear the low-life Dubliners (as against the clubroom Irish who would as soon forget him), saying that Brendan never lifted the glass as much as people say. "In fact, lads, he only drank on two occasions—by himself or with someone."

Behan, born in 1923, was not among Ireland's heavier thinkers—a Joyce or Yeats—but what he did ponder and put to paper was guided by the same compass of the heart that has led all the noblest Irishmen to search for ways of easing the weariness and cruelty of life. His main personal trait, after one fended off the larkiness, was unconditional care—for his family, his proven friends, the working people, the stepped on and pushed around. Drinking, clowning and wandering were his defenses against the frustration that inevitably stalls caring idealists on their forced marches to a reformed world. Yet his credo remained simple: "I respect kindness to human beings first of all, and kindness to animals. I don't respect the law; I have a total irreverence for anything connected with society except that which makes the roads safer, the beer stronger, the food cheaper, and old men and old women warmer in the winter and happier in the summer."

As happened in America during these past years—with pacifists and war resisters being slapped into jail—Ireland often imprisoned its citizens not because of crimes but because of patriotism. As an infant, Brendan was taken to meet his Irish nationalist father in Kilmainham prison; a cellmate of the elder Behan was the future

73

president of Ireland, Sean T. O'Kelley. When sixteen, after a childhood spent learning why the 1916 uprising fell short and needed to be risen more, Brendan got three years in the Borstal reformatory for his tricks with the outlawed Irish Republican Army. It was the first of many stretches in prison. None broke him.

Borstal Boy resulted from the earliest term. Though structurally loose and chattery, the novel can be placed either among the literature of prison books or among the classic novels of adolescence. The second grouping might be more apt. Like Huck Finn or Holden Caulfield, the hero of *Borstal Boy* insists on his right to stay out of step if he wishes. That is always the delicate thing about youthful stances: resisting the shams of society in such a style that your own protest does not become a sham also. The Irish gift for wryness helps, as illustrated in this Behan description of Holy Joe clergymen: "Such is the condition of man in this old world and we better learn to put up with it, for I never saw much hurry among parish priests in getting to the next one, nor among parsons or rabbis, for the matter of that; and as they are all supposed to be the experts on the next world, we can take it that they have heard something very unpleasant about it which makes them prefer to stick it out in this one for as long as they can."

A devil's advocate for devils already eloquent enough themselves, Behan's plays *The Hostage* and *The Quare Fellow* depicted satirically the grim but often laughing lives of Ireland's outcasts. The feisty plays do not give us the Ireland of tour guides or Barry Fitzgerald movies but, as critic Benedict Kiely wrote, of "romantic, idealistic Ireland fallen on sordid, materialistic days . . . heroic Ireland down in the dumps." The plays, unsurprisingly, fell flat in Dublin, and needed critics elsewhere to honor them. Small wonder the natives felt insulted, when with jarring frankness Behan wrote in *The Hostage:*

Pat: . . . Your real trouble when you go to prison as a patriot, do you know what it will be?

Officer: The loss of liberty.

Pat: No, the other Irish patriots, in along with you.

Professor Ted E. Boyle, in a study of Behan in the Twayne series of authors, praised *The Hostage* not for what it said about Ireland but what it proclaimed about all of us. "The Irish and the English, in fact all mankind, says Behan, enslave themselves with hollow, selfish systems which would stamp out life itself and everything that is beautiful in life. Whether man kills his fellow man out of

sheer viciousness, foolish pride or mere bumbling makes little difference. He follows his penchant for paying attention to the nonessen-
tials of his existence, and he causes untold suffering—all the more
horrible because it is needless."

Aside from the novels and the plays, Behan also wrote memorable short stories, old shoe tales cobbled together from scraps and
pieces of the tough-hide Gaelic poor. For a time, in his early thirties, he worked hard as a writer, rarely looking up from the rough
drafts. But suddenly he realized people were calling him famous, and,
in Irish simplicity, Behan made the mistake of listening to them.
Come entertain us, said cafe society in London and New York, our
court needs a jester.

With no brush-off skills, and not sensing his talent needed
guarding, Brendan did entertain them—performing looped on the
BBC, cutting up in New York watering holes, wasting his wit in
drawing rooms, glad to be anybody's dial-a-drunk. During the late
fifties and early sixties, the crowds called him a high-roller, but
nearer the truth, he was a sick man, the way alcoholics are called that
now. His friends tried drying him out in hospitals, but as for writing
again, or ever rubbing together the grating ideas that had once struck
showers of sparks as they flew from his mind, well, raise a glass to
that memory. Behan never left the dark world of alcoholism. Yet, he
could be light about that, too. "As regards drink," he wrote, "I can
only say that in Dublin, during the depression when I was growing
up, drunkenness was not regarded as a social disgrace. To get enough
to eat was regarded as an achievement. To get drunk was a victory."
He died in March 1964 in Dublin's Meath hospital. How much future
writing was buried with him is only a guess; wittily, he remarked
once about *Borstal Boy*: "There's more where that came from, as the
mother of twenty said."

In 1961, Behan celebrated St. Patrick's Day by trying to march
in the New York parade. The grand marshall barred him, saying the
Dubliner was "disorderly." Behan crossed the river to Jersey City
and walked the streets there, forming his own parade and calling
himself "the leader of the banned." A reporter for *Newsweek* caught
the following comments:

New York's Irish—"They're always giving you advice. And
they're always asking you how the people are back in Ireland, like
they were stuck with the bloody plague or famine or in the Congo,
or something."

Swimming—"A great cure for a hangover. I'm not of course a

75

good swimmer. More like an Irish cop, you might say. Stupid but willing."

The professional Irish—"All terribly anxious to pass as middle-class Englishmen."

New York fire engines—"I think they all must be driven by Micks from the mountains who were fed up with all that silence and like to make a lot of noise."

Ireland—"We don't have leprechauns, paddys in top hats and magic mists. We're proud of our hydroelectric plants, our transport, and our housing, none of which are run by leprechauns. We are now wiping out tuberculosis, and we're prouder of that than all the blather about Glocca Morra."

SELECTED BIBLIOGRAPHY OF BRENDAN BEHAN

Borstal Boy. New York: Knopf, 1959.
Confessions of an Irish Rebel. New York: Lancer, 1971 (paperback).
The Quare Fellow. New York: Grove, 1965. Includes *The Hostage.*
Behan, Beatrice. *My Life with Brendan.* Los Angeles: Nash, 1974.
Behan, Dominic. *My Brother Brendan.* New York: Simon and Schuster, 1971.

William Carlos Williams

O NE SUMMER EVENING in 1909, a young man of twenty-six rode a streetcar down New York's Tenth Avenue, heading for the Nursery and Child's Hospital at Sixty-first Street in Hell's Kitchen, the city's most wretched neighborhood. He carried a suitcase. Inside was a dead infant, the victim a few hours before of infectious gastro-enteritis. The bearer of death was a pediatrics intern at Nursery and Child's, a place considered lower on misery's ladder than even Belle-vue. Years later, William Carlos Williams, by now one of America's most consequential poets, would write of such scenes in an autobiog-raphy of deep refinement and revelation. Only a man who simulta-neously practiced medicine and searched for clear language could write such poetry:

> *It is difficult*
> *to get the news from poems*
> *yet men die miserably every day*
> *for lack*
> *of what is found there...*

At his death in March 1963, William Carlos Williams had pro-duced such a full literature on American consciousness that he had a place not just in the sun but in one of his own making. His poetry was of a universe. The public made Robert Frost their poet—he looked like one, which helped—but Williams earned a rarer tribute: devotion from other poets, ones who also knew the torments of the Word. Webster Schott called him "an American original" and James Dickey asked, "Has any other poet in American history been so actually useful, usable, and influential?" In all, Williams wrote six-hundred poems, four plays, four novels, fifty-two short stories, essays and criticism, an opera, and finally a biography of his mother. All of it contained precise words and images, snapped pictures of reality from a mental camera restless to miss nothing.

On leaving Hell's Kitchen, Williams sought the quietness of a general practice. He began in rural Rutherford, New Jersey, in 1910. Until retirement in 1951, he estimated he delivered two thousand babies and had seen more than a million patients. This was a time when American medicine had not yet been dominated by answering services or blind faith in drug company advertising. Even after he won fame as a major poet, Williams had a standard reply for the question all writers of experience are asked, what influenced you most. Medical case histories, he would say. American medicine has many doctors whose concern is only tinkering with the body, like auto mechanics forever giving lube jobs to get the squeaks out, but Williams heard the cries of his Rutherford women as soundings of far greater mystery than mere physical breakdown. He wrote in the autobiography: "My medicine was the thing that gained me entrance to . . . [the] secret gardens of the self. It lay there, another world, in the self. I was permitted by my medical badge to follow the poor, defeated body into those gulfs and grottos. And the astonishing thing is that at such times and in such places—foul as they may be with the stinking ischio-rectal abscesses of our comings and goings—just there, the thing, in all its greatest beauty, may for a moment be freed to fly guiltily about the room. In illness, in the permission I as a physician have had to be present at deaths and births, at the tormented battles between daughter and diabolic mother, shattered by a gone brain—just there—for a split second, from one side or the other, it has fluttered before me in a moment. . . ."

Perhaps because his education was medical, not liberal arts—how wasteful that medical schools require no courses in poetry, creative writing or painting—Williams was into his forties before reaching full poetic energy. His major work was "Paterson," called his "personal epic." Its purity of language fulfilled the rarest achievement of poetry; showing us what we see. Many Americans have little taste for poetry because we resent exactly that: being told we lack talents for seeing. But it's true: we watch everything, and see little.

About the poem, which as much as Eliot's "Wasteland" or Pound's "Cantos" was a model of liberation from meter and rhyme, Williams said, "I wanted, if I was to write in a larger way than of the birds and flowers, to write about the people close about me: to know in detail, minutely what I was talking about—to the whites of their eyes, to their very smells. That is the poet's business. Not to talk in vague categories but to write particularly, as a physician works, upon a patient, upon the thing before him, in the particular to discover the universal. . . ." On the notion of watching but not seeing, Williams wrote in the prologue to *Kora in Hell*: ". . . The thing that stands eternally in the way of really good writing is always one: the virtual impossibility of lifting to the imagination those things which lie under the direct scrutiny of the senses, close to the nose. . . . He who even nicks the solidity of this apparition does a piece of work superior to that of Hercules when he cleaned the Augean stables."

Williams had friendship with other poets—Ezra Pound, Marianne Moore, Wallace Stevens. Williams knew the common truth that only artists can bear other artists as friends. "I could never take him as a steady diet," he wrote of Pound, "never. He was often brilliant but an ass. But I never—so long as I kept away—got tired of him, or for a fact, ceased to love him. He had to be loved, even if he kicked you in the teeth for it." Williams often visited Pound in St. Elizabeths. In the autobiography, a description of one of these visits tells us as much about mental health as some of the touted texts of Freud. In a comic but revealing scene, Williams records the conversation with a taxi driver on a ride from St. Elizabeths to downtown, a dialogue suggesting that insanity is often undefinable and incarceration arbitrary. After telling the driver of Pound's "illness," the driver exclaimed, "he ain't crazy. He just talk too much."

Many of Dr. Williams' patients were the inarticulate and uneducated. But he rejoiced in them because a clarity of communication tied the doctor and the patient together. "These are the matters which obsess me so that I cannot stop writing. I can recall many from the past, boys and girls, bad pupils, renegades, dirty minded and fisted, that I miss keenly. When some old woman tells me of her daughter now happily married to a handicapper at the Garden City track, that she has two fine boys, I want to sing and dance. I am happy. I am stimulated. She is still alive." Several of Williams' short stories are little more than candid dialogues between a doctor and patient, or a doctor and the family. In telling of a woman dying from toxic neuritis induced by opium abuse, Williams writes: "I had no right to keep what I knew from her husband any longer." In another story, the ordeal of a difficult birth is told. This time it is the patient who speaks with candor. Not only does she benefit from the exchange but so does the doctor: "It was I who was being comforted and soothed."

Dr. Williams, for whom "the practice of medicine has become

the pursuit of a rare element which may appear at any time, at any place, at a glance," believed that "the relationship between physician and patient, if it were literally followed, would give us a world of extraordinary fertility of the imagination. . . ." Yet, he knew also how difficult communication is. "Do we not see that we are inarticulate? That is what defeats us. It is our inability to communicate to another how we are locked within ourselves, unable to say the simplest thing of importance to one another, any of us, even the most valuable, that makes our lives like those of a litter of kittens in a wood-pile. That gives the physician . . . his opportunity . . . the physician enjoys a wonderful opportunity actually to witness the words being born. Their actual colors and shapes are laid before him carrying their tiny burdens which he is privileged to take into his care with their unspoiled newness . . . no one else is present but the speaker and ourselves, we have the word's very parents. Nothing is more moving."

Because so many of his patients were women, some of Williams' finest writing goes deep into the mentality and emotions of womanhood. At the moment, for example, many doctors are criticized for the lack of understanding of women who are rape victims. Myths—accepted, even fostered by some doctors—persist that the woman "really enjoyed it," that the victim should have "resisted a little more" and that rape is only a physical assault and never mind the psychological damage. With an estimated quarter to half million annual rape victims, the issue can hardly be ignored by the medical community. A poem by Williams—"The Raper from Passenack"—suggests that his special interest in the subject was perceptive.

> *The Raper from Passenack*
>
> *was very kind. When she regained*
> *her wits, he said, It's all right, kid,*
> *I took care of you.*
>
> *What a mess she was in. Then he added,*
> *You'll never forget me now.*
> *And drove her home.*
>
> *Only a man who is sick, she said*
> *would do a thing like that.*
> *It must be so.*

The poem goes on, the woman wishing that "I could shoot him." It ends with her calling him "every vile name I could think of. I was so glad to be taken home."

I suppose its my mind—the fear of
infection. I'd rather a million times
have been got pregnant.

But its the foulness of it can't
be cured. And hatred, hatred of all men
—and disgust.

Dr. Williams did not write whether or not he had ever treated rape victims, but the insight of the poem suggests he did, often. In a short story, he shows another depth of understanding about women. In "The Burden of Loveliness," two men in a gas station—one a doctor, the other an attendant—are discussing women from the usual machismo view when a "classy babe" pulls into the station. The pair ogle at her, and Williams has them talk on. Gradually, though, the two begin to realize that although a woman's beauty may make a man happy, it can have the opposite effect on the woman: her beauty may be a burden. "It must be tough," the doctor says, "being that good looking. A fellow never thinks of it that way. But when you look at it from a woman's side, they don't have it so easy." The dialogue of Williams' short stories has been compared to that in Hemingway's, but no Hemingway male ever looked at life's anguish from a woman's view.

As with most doctors, Williams had daily contact with women who were nurses. Their "discipline is rigid," he wrote. "I have long listened to their stories." The nurses of Dr. Williams "are women, they are young women, they are for the most part intelligent young women and frequently, in their crisp and becoming uniforms, they appear as beautiful young women with whom the distresses of mankind have little to do directly. It is their own backgrounds out of which the 'call' comes to serve humanity that determine their lives."

"Serving humanity," Dr. Williams believed, was a lofty calling but he insisted, at least for himself, that such a notion was an abstraction. A patient in the office is not "humanity," he is a person in pain who wants relief or cure. "The cured man," he wrote, "is no different from any other. It is a trivial business unless you add the zest . . . to the picture. That's how I came to find writing such a necessity, to relieve me from such a dilemma. I found by practice, by trial and error, that to treat a man as something to which surgery, drugs and voodoo applied was an indifferent matter; to treat him as material for a work of art made him somehow come alive for me."

Perhaps this astounding view of his patients—as "materials for a work of art"— is the strongest reason for the relevance of Dr.

Williams. Large numbers of patients, not only the poor or the lower classes but many of the wealthy, complain that their doctor is machine-like, that he treats the body not the person. Dr. Williams insisted that the doctor-patient relationship be a personal relationship; enthusiasm for the skill of medicine was as crucial as the skill itself. "Obviously enough," he wrote, "the entire world today is a hospital so that, one thing cancelling the other, that makes the hospital a very normal environment. It is only incidentally concerned with illness: quite casually, to itself, it measures, with some indifference, the decay of flesh, its excreta, bad odors and even its ecstasies of birth and cure. Cure to a physician is a pure accident, to the pathologist in his laboratory almost a disappointment. The real thing is the excitement of the chase, the opportunity for exercise of precise talents, the occasion for batting down a rival to supersede him, to strut, to boast and get on with one's fellows. Discovery is the great goal. . . ."

It is natural, with decades of practice, that Williams had something to say about his associates. "There are good doctors and bad doctors: you can't tell them by their names; thieves, even murderers, with the most respectable names. On the other hand there are the most painstaking and humane priests of healing whose names show their origin to have been the ghettos of Poland or Sicily's stricken villages. . . . It's strange how many phases go into the making of a good serviceable physician. Some have hands, just good surgeon's hands, and if by luck they have a head and a heart to go with them, they can reach the heights. Others are a menace to the community they inhabit. How are you going to tell them apart? Most of their fellows know them. But the human animal is an untrustworthy self-seeker, and the worst doctors know how to make themselves attractive. They are usually popular."

Williams died at seventy-nine, after a series of strokes. He was occasionally grouchy in his daily medical practice—he had a right to be, a million ailing patients coming in for forty-one years—but he was ever approachable by young writers. One recalled that "a personal relationship, even with a stranger this way, held sacred meaning for Williams, as did any vivid experience." The poet wrote of it:

> So let us love
> confident as is the light
> in its struggle with darkness
> that there is as much to say
> and more
> for the one side
> and that not the darker

What is this morning's news from William Carlos Williams? Many items, for sure, all worth a headline. AWARENESS, that's one. How can we feel each other if so many of our aware moments are slept through, in open-eye blindness? For Williams, to be aware— through imagination, language—was to pay heavily. But payment bought the treasured return—touch.

SELECTED BIBLIOGRAPHY OF WILLIAM CARLOS WILLIAMS

Autobiography of William Carlos Williams. London: MacGibbon & Kee, 1968.

Collected Earlier Poems: Before Nineteen Forty. London: MacGibbon & Key, 1967.

Collected Later Poems. New York: New Directions, 1962.

Farmers' daughters: Collected Short Stories. New York: New Directions, 1961.

In the American Grain. London: MacGibbon & Key, 1966.

Selected Essays. New York: New Directions, 1969.

Yes, Mrs. Williams: A Personal Record of My Mother. Stamford, Conn.: Astor-Honor, 1959.

Whittemore, Reed. *The Happy Genius of the Household.* Boston: Houghton Mifflin, 1975.

Willa Cather

WHY HAS WILLA CATHER BEEN ignored? Is it because she wrote about the glory of the American soil and we would rather forget about this part of our past now that we are either paving over the land or desecrating it with strip mines? Or is it because she could write about ethnics and women in Nebraska, when everyone knows that we male eastern WASPS and WILCS (White Irish Liberal Catholics) are the only fit subjects for novels? "The history of every country," she wrote in *O Pioneers!*, begins "in the heart of a man or a woman," and we know where our hearts are. The stories spun from this pure strand have often been dismissed as sentimentalism; but the sentiment is as firm and durable as any truth we have. On Willa Cather's tombstone in the village of East Jaffrey, New Hampshire—where she wrote *My Antonia*—the words appear: "That is happiness; to be dissolved into something complete and great." Her stories have plots that simple: women and men trying to keep their appointments with dissolvement.

Although identified with the prairies, Willa Cather was born—in 1873—in Back Creek Valley, Virginia, an area near Winchester in what is now called northern Virginia's horse country. The Cather family was large, both in children and in the number of aunts, uncles and relatives. In her girlhood, Willa Cather saved string on her impressions of this multi-generational family, later unwinding it in the details of her fiction. *One of Ours* was such a story, a novel she wrote in 1922 based on her cousin. He was killed in World War I, and on reading his introspective and graceful letters sent to his mother on the farm, Cather said, "I never knew he was that kind of a fellow. He revealed himself in his letters." The book won a Pulitzer, though such critics as Louis Auchincloss now call it "her worst novel." But Cather defended it: "Any story of youth, struggle and defeat can't be as smooth in outline and perfect in form as just a portrait. When you have an articulate young man butting his way through the world you can't pay that much attention to form."

When she was ten, her family (she was named after her two grandfathers, both Williams) moved to Nebraska. The soil and air were better, and hopes were higher. Willa, a child who was loved by both parents, enjoyed the new location; she described it some forty years later in a Cather story, "Old Mrs. Harris." She "was no longer living in a feudal society, where there were plenty of landless people glad to render service to the more fortunate, but in a snappy little Western democracy, where every man was as good as his neighbor and out to prove it."

As a young woman, Cather recalled that she had roamed "all over the country then, on foot, on horseback and in our farm wagons. My nose went poking into nearly everything . . . I always intended to write." The families in the Republican Valley—an area named for the river, not the party—were Czechs, Swedes, Germans, Norwegians, Russians and other Old Country stock. Sturdied by the richness of this informal education, Cather left her town of Red Cloud at eighteen for the formal kind at the university. She did well, was known as a non-follower and began writing drama criticism in a Lincoln newspaper. Already, though, she had seen enough Nebraska primary colors to know they were the only ones worth describing; the past was too important to let go, even if it meant resisting the future. One biographer reports that Cather had grown up hating change—"change in herself, in her family, her hometown, in the countryside. She mourned the old 'board walks' which were replaced by cement sidewalks. She missed every tree that died, every land-mark that had been destroyed."

This theme was to dominate her novels. In letters and conversations, she made clear that it was not the road to progress that she wanted torn up but the desolate places such a road takes us: to standardization, conformity, disarray. "New things are always ugly," she wrote. ". . . A house can never be beautiful until it has been lived in for a long time. An old house built in miserable taste is more beautiful than a new house built and furnished in correct taste." Even in 1925, America had someone who could say, "I like horses better than automobiles" and practice this belief by avoiding the dangerous and dirty vehicles. She was saddened by second and third generation Nebraskans who shook off the manners of their pioneer and immigrant parents, as though rough hands, flawed speech and head handkerchiefs should be left for the servant's quarters. One sad result, Cather believed, of the new ways was the miseducation being handed out. "The one education which amounts to anything is learning how to do something well, whether it is to make a bookcase or write a book. If I could get a carpenter to make me some good bookcases, I would have as much respect for him as I have for the people whose books I want to put on them. Making something well is the principal end of education. I wish we could go back, but I am afraid we are only going to become more and more mechanical."

In her mid-20s, Cather took the familiar route of sending off stories to magazines. Editors liked them and asked for more. She came East in 1908 to work on *McClure's* magazine as managing editor. But reporting the events of New York had none of the powerful pull of Cather's remembrances of Nebraska. "My deepest feelings were rooted in this country because one's strongest emotions and one's most vivid mental pictures are acquired before one is fifteen. I had searched for books telling about the beauty of the country I loved, its romance, its heroism and strength and courage of its people that had been plowed into the very furrows of its soil and I did not find them. And so I wrote *O Pioneers!*"

The novel was a success and still a better one followed, *My Antonia*. The heroine, a Bohemian primeval of the plains named Shimerda, is described: "She had only to stand in the orchard, to put her hand on a little crab tree and look up at the apples, to make you feel the goodness of planting and tending and harvesting at last. . . . She was a rich mine of life, like the founders of early races."

Cather regularly shuttled between East and West—"Whenever I crossed the Missouri River coming into Nebraska the very smell of the soil tore me to pieces. I could not decide which was the real and which the fake me." She traveled to the Southwest and in her middle life—fifty-four—wrote *Death Comes for the Archbishop*. Many see this novel as Cather's greatest. In it she created a psychic world in which the soul of the land is one of the rewards sustaining the soul of the spiritual seeker. Physically old and dying, the archbishop "in New Mexico . . . always awoke a young man; not until he rose and began to shave did he realize that he was growing older. His first consciousness was a sense of the light dry wind blowing in through the windows, with the scent of hot sun and sage-brush and sweet clover; a wind that made one's body feel light and one's heart cry 'today, today,' like a child's."

Willa Cather never married, nor did she take on anything else she considered an inconvenience. She never adapted to cars, radios or intruding promoters wanting to make movies out of her books. She died in 1947 in New York. Two friends—Edith Lewis and Elizabeth Sergeant—have written faithfully detailed accounts of their friendship with Willa Cather. These books, together with a growing body of Cather scholarship, suggest that perhaps among those for whom the past is valuable Cather is not being ignored so much as studied quietly. This is fitting because another modern terror to which Cather never adjusted was noise.

SELECTED BIBLIOGRAPHY OF WILLA CATHER

Death Comes for the Archbishop. New York: Knopf, 1927; New York: Random House, 1971.

A Lost Lady. New York: Knopf, 1973 (new edition).

My Antonia. New York: Houghton Mifflin, 1961.

My Mortal Enemy. New York: Vintage Books, 1961.

O Pioneers! New York: Houghton Mifflin, 1953.

Sapphira and the Slave Girl. New York: Knopf, 1940.

Willa Cather on Writing. New York: Knopf, 1949.

Willa Cather's Collected Short Fiction. Lincoln: University of Nebraska Press, 1970.

Slote, Bernice, ed. *Kingdom of Art: Willa Cather's First Principles and Critical Statements.* Lincoln: University of Nebraska Press, 1967.

Flannery O'Connor

ONE OF THE REVEALING STORIES told about Flannery O'Connor is one she told herself many times. It was on the way she practiced her craft, the slow desk-work of writing from which came some of the best short stories of our day. "Every morning it's the same," she would say in a Georgia voice too quick for a drawl but still noticeably paced to the South. "I go into my room to write from nine to twelve. I put a blank paper before me, and then wait. Writing comes hard to me. Often, three hours later, at noon, the paper is still blank. But I do it every day. The important thing is not that I get a lot written, but that I am there in the room before the page. If an idea does come to me between those hours of nine and twelve, well, I'm ready for it."

There must have been many days of blank pages. Her output of fiction was not large, totalling two novels and two collections of short stories. Yet almost every character she created was a large silhouette of reality, figures cast against the turmoil shadows of mystery and redemption. No conversation is more spirited than when two Flannery O'Connor readers meet up. They talk about her characters—Tarwater, Hazel Motes, the Misfit, the Greenleafs—as friends from a common hometown, discussing their troubles not as records of pain but as people who couldn't be mellowed. That's all of us, we like to think.

Grotesque became the word critics liked to use about O'Connor fiction, with the term having an accuracy obvious in the first paragraphs of her stories. Grungy Bible salesmen, mean grandmothers, wily farmers, suffering Jobs too proud or too baffled to leave the ash heap—Miss O'Connor wrote about the Southern pile of white trash because she believed these people, so lowly, were the most fit to rise and converge. They were capable of redemption because they were capable of majestic evil; unlike the sterile captives of the cities, these rural grotesques at least had something to be redeemed from. She explained: "Whenever I'm asked why Southern writers particularly have a penchant for writing about freaks, I say it is because we are still able to recognize one. To be able to recognize a freak, you have to have some conception of the whole man. . . ."

Unlike many writers who haul themselves around to colleges for give-and-take lectures—give talk and take money—Miss O'Connor visited the campuses almost from a compulsion to explain to audiences the writing craft. Some of these talks were gathered into *Mystery and Manners,* a valuable book edited by Robert and Sally Fitzgerald a few years after their friend's death—from lupus—in 1964. Many authors with well-conditioned airs have reflected on the mechanics of writing, but few match the grace and wit of Flannery O'Connor; her thoughts are topical because of all the creative writing courses which are now given in the schools.

Flannery O'Connor on seemingly negative writers. "People are always complaining that the modern novelist has no hope and that the picture he paints of the world is unbearable. The only answer to this is that people without hope do not write novels. Writing a novel is a terrible experience, during which the hair often falls out and the teeth decay. I'm always irritated by people who imply that writing fiction is an escape from reality. It is a plunge into reality and it's very shocking to the system."

On why she wrote. "Last spring I talked here, and one of the girls asked me, 'Miss O'Connor, why do you write?' and I said, 'Because I'm good at it,' and at once I felt a considerable disapproval in the atmosphere. I felt that this was not thought by the majority to be a high-minded answer; but it was the only answer I could give. I had not been asked why I write the way I do, but why I write at all—and to that question there is only one legitimate answer . . . A gift of any kind is a considerable responsibility. It is a mystery in itself, something gratuitous and wholly undeserved, something whose real uses will probably always be hidden from us."

On hacks. "Everywhere I go I'm asked if I think the universities stifle writers. My opinion is that they don't stifle enough of them. There's many a best-seller that could have been prevented by a good teacher."

On meaning. "People have a habit of saying, 'What is the theme of your story?' and they expect you to give them a statement: 'The theme of my story is the economic pressure of the machine on the middle class'—or some such absurdity. And when they've got a statement like that, they go off happy and feel it is no longer necessary to read the story."

Flannery O'Connor lived with her mother in Milledgeville, Georgia, a small community in the central part of the state. Her roots were sunk deep into the region and like William Faulkner's fiction before her and now Cormac McCarthy's after, it was ever stretching into the earth-richness of rural people. Her mother and aunts, proper Southern ladies whose branches were the sturdiest of the family tree, could never understand how their mild and innocent "Mary Flannery" could produce such disturbing stories of turmoil and pity. Miss O'Connor often commented wryly about her perplexed kin. "I have an aunt," she wrote, "who thinks that nothing happens in a story unless somebody gets married or shot at the end of it." The aunt rarely "got" what her niece's stories were saying. Yet for all of her family's slowness in understanding literature or even the backwoods culture of her Baldwin County neighbors, she preferred them to the intellectuals in the city. "The trouble with these people," she once said at a cocktail party in Manhattan, "is that they aren't from anyplace." It was hardly coincidence that intellectuals and world-savers appeared in many of her stories; they were model fools.

Miss O'Connor bore down hard on her creations. Choose any one of her characters—say Raber in "The Violent Bear It Away"—and he will be more blooded than a dozen people of a writer like John O'Hara, long fiction's most well-shined display case of mediocrity. Among the many visitors to the O'Connor home in Milledgeville were hopeful writers, including a group of Catholic sisters from Atlanta. They belonged to an order devoted to what is perhaps the least rewarding of all the great work done by sisters—caring for poor people who have incurable cancer. The group wanted the story of a patient to be told to the world, a girl of twelve who had died of a cancer tumor on the face. Miss O'Connor was the one to write the story, they said; but like a wrong tree being barked up, she stood still until the siege passed. No, she said, you write it, and I'll help you. "A Memoir of Mary Ann" resulted, with a moving introduction by Flannery O'Connor. Writing in *Saturday Review* a few years ago, one of the sisters recalled one of the many pulls on the bridle Miss O'Connor applied to her runaway enthusiasm: "Don't get poetic when you are writing prose. Don't even get poetic when you are writing poetry. Only bad poets are poetic."

Plugged into the darker sockets of Southern consciousness, Miss O'Connor's stories are about the complex wiring systems of her characters; but they also describe a region, one that many Northerners still don't understand, nor, it often seems, care to. "We in the South live in a society that is rich in contradiction, rich in irony, rich in contrast, and particularly rich in its speech." Miss O'Connor handled this wealth with care, whether sharing it through talks with audiences, or investing in it to produce her stories, or only by sweating over it every morning from nine to twelve.

SELECTED BIBLIOGRAPHY OF FLANNERY O'CONNOR

The Complete Stories of Flannery O'Connor. New York: Farrar, Straus and Giroux, 1971; paperback, 1972.

Eggenschwiler, David. *The Christian Humanism of Flannery O'Connor.* Detroit: Wayne State University Press, 1972.

Fitzgerald, Robert and Sally. *Mystery and Manners: Occasional Prose.* New York: Farrar, Straus and Giroux, 1969; paperback, 1970.

Jean Toomer

DURING THE PAST FEW YEARS, when an intensity of interest has been felt regarding Negro writing, such novelists as Ralph Ellison and Richard Wright were pursued again, with a new trust of intimacy created by the imaginations of these powerful writers. Some of this new interest sprung from the "black studies" movement on the campuses. But it is a movement that now appears to be slowing, even stopping, and perhaps the movement was never more than a sentimental journey taken by travelers wanting to hop the express line to the past and return quickly to rise with the latest jumps of fashion. But many of those who care about Negro literature have not returned; they have stayed behind, penetrating deeper, wanting something more than mere skimmings of the masters. One of the obscure but profound Negro writers currently being rediscovered is Jean Toomer. He is a writer who stationed himself in the Harlem Renaissance of the 1920s, and his joinings of image and mood are convincing portrayals of Negro life, of peasants in rural Georgia whose courage was to stare into misery and not be blinded, of the captives of the ghetto in the Washington, D.C., of fifty years ago.

Jean Toomer produced one book, *Cane.* Boni and Liveright, a quality house, originally published it in 1923, and Harper and Row republished it in 1969 in its "Perennial Classic" series as a ninety-five-cent paperback. Although *Cane* was Toomer's only book, it was a production written in the fever of genius and torment. *Cane* mixes prose, poetry, mood, mysticism and sketches into a common fund of wisdom. Not many writers have conveyed the anguish of the ghetto as Toomer did in his sketch, "Seventh Street," even though the modern ghetto as it lays rotting today was decades away: "Seventh Street is a bastard of Prohibition, of the War. A crude-boned, soft-skinned wedge of nigger life breathing its loafer air, jazz songs and love, thrusting unconscious rhythms, black reddish blood into the white and whitewashed wood of Washington. Stale soggy wood of Washington. Wedges rust in soggy wood ... Split it! In two! Again! Shred it! The sun. Wedges are brilliant in the sun; ribbons of wet wood dry and blow away. Black reddish blood. Pouring for crude-boned soft-skinned life, who set you flowing? Blood suckers of the War would spin in a frenzy of dizziness if they drank your blood. Prohibition would put a stop to it. Who set you flowing? White and whitewash disappear in blood. Who set you flowing? Flowing down the smooth asphalt of Seventh Street, in shanties, brick office buildings, theaters, drug stores, restaurants and cabarets? Eddying on the corners? Swirling like a blood-red smoke up where the buzzards fly in heaven? God would not dare suck black red blood. A Nigger God! He would duck his head in shame and call for the Judgment Day. Who set you flowing?"

Such scenes were cooly and tightly recorded. Toomer seldom broke into the narrative with his personal leanings, preferring not to impose a forgery of his own feelings on the solid genuineness of the scenes he described. Toomer knew there was enough force in telling us about the despair of Seventh Street without adding in his own despair. This is often the hardest and least practiced writing of all, to throw oneself into the complexity of words yet maintain a simplicity of language. Toomer never confused frenetic writing with skilled, passionate writing, the latter being in the command of few, while styles of frenzy sell wholesale cheap. In one of his sketches of rural Georgia women—how delicately these superior women are defined—Toomer writes of Becky, the white woman who "had one Negro son. Who gave it to her? Damn buck nigger, said the white folks' mouths. She couldn't tell. Common, God-forsaken, insane white shameless wench, said the white folks' mouths. Her eyes were sunken, her neck stingy, her breasts fallen, till then. Taking their words, they filled her, like a bubble rising—then she broke. Mouth setting in a twist that held her eyes, harsh, vacant, staring ... Who gave it to her? Low down nigger with no self-respect, said the black folks' mouths. She wouldn't tell. Poor Catholic poor-white crazy woman, said the black folks' mouths. White folks and black folks built her cabin, fed her and her growing baby, prayed secretly to God who'd put His cross upon her and cast her out."

Toomer's Negroes are of the earth. He does not create this earthiness as an imposition of glamor, but pays homage to it because the land and the soil dominated the lives and feelings of his people. The critic Saunders Redding in *To Make a Poet Black* called *Cane* a "revolutionary book," a "lesson in emotional release and freedom." Toomer, writing of the earth, displayed such qualities in his poetry:

> *O land and soil, red soil and sweet-*
> *gum tree,*
> *So scant of grass, so profligate of*
> *pines,*
> *Now just before an epoch's sun de-*
> *clines,*
> *Thy son, in time I have returned*
> *to thee,*
> *Thy son, I have in time returned*
> *to thee.*

When *Cane* appeared in 1923, other critics from Langston Hughes to Allen Tate, joyously welcomed Toomer—then only twenty-nine—as a comrade in literature. But strangely, Toomer was not stirred to further writing, and published almost nothing again. Why this dimming of a light once so bright? Arna Bontemps tells of Toomer's travels to such scenes as France, Wisconsin and New Mexico, seeking the secrets of his own consciousness. After a second marriage in 1934, Bontemps writes, Toomer "appeared to vanish from literature among the tolerant Quakers of Bucks County, Pa. When next heard from, he was writing for the "Friends Intelligencer," sometimes calling himself by his father's first name, lecturing piously to Friends' meetings. . . ."

Toomer, who was born in Washington, once wrote of himself that "a visit to Georgia (in 1921) was the starting point of almost everything of worth that I have done. I heard folk-songs come from the lips of Negro peasants. I saw the rich dusk beauty that I had heard many false accents about, and of which till then, I was somewhat skeptical. And a deep part of my nature, a part that I had repressed, sprang suddenly to life and responded to them. Now, I cannot conceive of myself as aloof and separated. My point of view has not changed; it has deepened, it has widened. Personally, my life has been torturous and dispersed."

Jean Toomer died in 1967 in Philadelphia at seventy-three. He vanished almost as a lost person, with obituaries in neither the *Washington Post* or *New York Times*, nor any later inclusion in encyclopedias. These omissions—silence for a man who lived silent for forty-five years—suggest less a deliberate snub than common forgetfulness; he didn't do anything lately for us, did he? So we are left to wonder why Toomer wrote *Cane* and no other book. But we do know, in the most fundamental way, that if knowledge of the feelings, beauty and tragedy of Negro life fifty years ago is our interest, then no other book is needed. What praise is greater for a writer—that he said it well when he said it once.

SELECTED BIBLIOGRAPHY OF JEAN TOOMER

Cane. New York: Liveright, 1971 (reprint of 1923 edition); New York: Harper and Row, 1969 (paperback).

Turner, Darwin, ed. *The Wayward and the Seeking: A Miscellany of Writings*. Wash., D.C.: Howard University Press, 1974.

Richard McKenna

EVERY SPRING, THE COLLEGES AND HIGH SCHOOLS turn loose their graduates—citizens we now call "educated." They aren't, of course. The only educated graduates are the few who realize that genuine learning begins only now, when there is no teacher to please, no exam to bluff through and no safety net of a classroom to break the falls sure to come. When he went to sea at age eighteen, Richard McKenna thought his education was behind him, back in a desert town in Idaho where he grew up. At his death in 1964, at fifty-one, McKenna was an American original, a man who put his shoulder to the wheel and pushed it to the deepest understanding of self-education.

In the public mind, McKenna is known for his thick novel, *The Sand Pebbles*, a 1962 hit that made money and made the movies. But a thin book, *New Eyes for Old*, put together in part by his widow and published in 1972 by John F. Blair (Winston-Salem, N.C.), carries a full portion of his thought. McKenna stayed at sea for twenty-two years, as a machinist's mate who served on gunboats in China and troop transports everywhere. On leaving the Navy, he enrolled as a forty-year-old freshman—majoring in English—at the University of North Carolina at Chapel Hill. He graduated in four years, married a librarian and began wrestling with words and forcing some of them to their knees.

New Eyes for Old contains ten essays, all but one originally given as speeches. The audiences for these clear and stubbornly fresh talks were not lecture circuit crowds who have heard it all anyway, but North Carolina groups, kinds that are easily passed over by the big talkers. They included a teacher's association, a woman's club and a gathering of librarians. To this last group, he pays poignant

96

tribute to libraries and their devoted keepers. On his first boyhood visit to the stacks, "Suddenly it seemed to me that a library was like a town with thousands of movies all showing at once, and you could go to any one you wished at any time or place that pleased you . . . and best of all, it did not cost anything. I felt suddenly free and wealthy, as if I had found my way into a cave full of treasure."

In his lucky youth, McKenna recalls, he barely knew about distinctions of worth between books. He told his North Carolina librarians "that any book, however trashy and ephemeral, is good for a child if he finds pleasure in reading it. Any book that helps him to form a habit of reading, that helps to make reading one of his deep and continuing needs, is good for him. Discrimination will come naturally in time, perhaps in college years. An attempt to instill it too early in life may well put a youngster off books altogether and rob him of one of the chief advantages of being human." McKenna believed that a government or town could be measured by its libraries. What a hard judgment he would have made on the Nixon administration's proposed budget cuts for libraries and increased funding of weapons.

While in the Navy, McKenna heavily consumed books. "Finding them in my trips ashore was one of my chief enjoyments. . . . I would hide books away in crannies all over the engineering spaces the way a squirrel hides acorns." For a time, he believed that would do it, except he kept meeting books beyond him. "The ideas would appear on the printed page only as a casual reference or a literary allusion, yet a full knowledge of them was necessary to follow the author's argument. I began to understand it as a kind of shorthand of thought which permitted the author to convey to the initiated clearly on one page what might require fifty pages to make clear to my more limited comprehension. It was not enough to be literate in letters; one had also to be literate in ideas. When I had learned that the hard way, I decided I must attend a university before retiring to my desert Walden."

At Chapel Hill, unlike many English majors, McKenna embraced the physical sciences also. From a course on botany, for example, "I discovered the whole world of meaningful form and color, of beauty and wonder, that lies beyond the reach of natural human vision." Under the microscope of his love of learning, McKenna observed his fellow students, most half his age. "Overwhelmingly, my impression was of passiveness. Some of the boys seemed dutifully to sit there expecting the professors to give them an education much as they would expect a barber to give them a haircut. Others sat braced as grimly as they might in a dentist's chair. They were finding it unpleasant, but they were going to sweat it out. Whatever the emotional tone, however, the attitude seemed predominantly passive. They were undergoing an education, not undertaking it."

What would McKenna have students do? He went before one college audience to offer advice and spoke about creative energy. He believed that "we all begin life with a vast fund of creative energy and lose it along the way at rates which vary between individuals." Mistakenly, many believe that creative energy is only used to produce art. "Not nearly enough people understand that it can also power every aspect of daily living and make the difference between dispirited boredom and a life that is vividly exciting regardless of external circumstances." For a man who spent years confined physically to a small shipboard world but whose mind roamed in wide freedom, McKenna encouraged others to be roamers too. "In the realm of thought wear custom like a decent garment, but never let it come to lie upon you heavy as frost. . . . Then, when you are alone or in congenial company, you can cast it off and go adventuring. Men all around you will be living in stony thought-worlds sometimes sculptured grandly into Grecian architectural forms. Visit them there, for they are often good men. Do not disturb them with your freedom, for that would not be good manners. But if you feel your garment of custom beginning to cleave to your flesh, if you can detect a certain stoniness creeping about your ankles, make your excuses politely and get out fast."

It is true that McKenna had home court advantage when speaking to friends and neighbors in North Carolina. But his ideas hold value for another reason. While commercialists and publicists shout from the house-tops that appearances mean everything, here is a citizen in a lower window saying calmly that appearances are nothing, they can never satisfy us. The person who can thrill to a quiet library may feel more of life than those mighties who work fourteen and sixteen hour days to get the newest and buy the latest. McKenna was neither a buyer or seller; he believed he already owned everything when his desire to learn took possession of him.

John Blair of Winston-Salem—his firm puts out only five titles a year—is owed credit for gathering McKenna's speeches. (Like small libraries, small publishers are often storehouses for excellence.) McKenna died at fifty-one, in full sweat on another novel. That is an early age to die, and barely time to lay down more than a few skidmarks on the road to fame and fortune. Most of us think our education ends at ages eighteen or twenty-two, but as McKenna knew, it should end only when we do.

SELECTED BIBLIOGRAPHY OF RICHARD McKENNA

The Sand Pebbles. New York: Harper and Row, 1962.
The Sons of Martha and Other Stories. New York: Harper and Row, 1967.
McKenna, Eva Grace and Cochrane, Shirley Graves, eds. *New Eyes for Old: Nonfiction Writings.* Winston-Salem, N.C.: Blair, 1972.

Heinrich Boll

HOW DO YOU TELL STORIES about the common man without producing common tripe? There is nothing in the outward dullness of most lives worth wasting ink on, other than what the phone companies use up listing the names and addresses of the faceless. Outwardly, we are all the same, lined up in a forced march to the hothouse to be fertilized with a common anonymity. But inside, in each person's interior life, it is something else. There, even the dullest clod, is full of experiences and emotions that have passed through all the daily ambushes survival sets for us. Some of the characters in the stories of Heinrich Böll don't even rate a phone listing, yet his style of fiction cultivates their interior lives like a great garden always flowering.

Böll is best known and read in America for his stories about the postwar German conscience. On this subject he is forceful and looming, a story teller who crawled free from the wreckage of his homeland not embittered but purified. "About the war, the present, we had said all we had to say," a German soldier reflects in one short story. "Too often and too intimately had we seen the bared teeth in its hideous face, too often had its nauseating breath set our hearts quivering as we listened on dark nights to the wounded pleading in two languages between the lines. We loathed it too deeply to be able to believe in the cant sent up like soap bubbles by the riffraff on both sides to invest it with the virtues of a 'mission.' "

Tirade writing is common to antiwar literature, as if the eye of realism must be blinked in quick fury to see all the absurdity. Böll is different. Some of the stories are written in a deliberately flat style, suggesting that Böll knows well a basic truth of fiction, even journalism: the unbelievable is often better believed if understated. In "My

Expensive Leg," a short story from *Children Are Civilians Too*, an ex-soldier goes down to the Department and asks for a higher pension. His right leg was blown off in the war. The bureaucrat argues that the leg is already costing the state plenty—seventy marks a year—without spending any more tax funds on it. The ex-soldier agrees his ex-leg is expensive, even in ways the pension office never dreamed. "Just as I was going to clear out," he says about his accident in the trenches, "this business of my leg happened. And because I had to go on lying there anyway, I thought I might as well pass on the word, and they all scrammed, first the divisional staff, then the regimental, then the battalion, and so on, one after another. The silly part was, you see, they were in such a hurry, they forgot to take me along. It was really too silly for words, because if I hadn't lost my leg they would all be dead, the general, the colonel, the major and so on down, and you wouldn't have to pay them any pensions. Now just figure out what my leg is costing you. The general is 52, the colonel 48, and the major 50, and with the military life they lead they'll live to be at least 80, like Hindenburg. Figure it out for yourself . . . My leg's become a damned expensive leg, one of the most expensive legs I can think of." The pension officer offers the ex-soldier a job shining shoes in Republic Square, but being a one-legged shoe shiner has no appeal. He recalls a fellow soldier in the trench when the battle began. "At first, there were two of us, but they shot the other fellow, he's not costing you a cent now . . . He was a real bargain. He'd been only a soldier for a month, all he cost was a post card and a few bread rations. There's a good soldier for you, at least he let himself be killed off."

Böll himself was in the German war machine, though hardly a significant part—only a corporal. After the war, he spoke of the "almost total senselessness of the military life," with himself in the "frightful fate of being a soldier and having to wish that the war might be lost." As with many Germans, the concentration camps were not on his mind during the war, but they were after. In "And Where Were You, Adam?", Böll's most incisive attack on militarism, S.S. Captain Filskeit ran a small death camp where "the important thing, after all, was not whether one liked carrying out orders but to realize their necessity, to respect them, and to see that they were carried out. . . ." To throw light into the darker shadows of depravity, Böll describes Filskeit as the good German who loved art and music. In the camp, Filskeit discovers he can serve both the goals of the high command and his own passion for choral music. "He had quickly discovered the enormous latent fund of musical talent among the prisoners: he was surprised to find this among Jews, and he applied the selective principle by ordering each new arrival to undergo a singing test and by recording each one's vocal capacity on an index card, with marks ranging from 0 to 10. Very few were given 10—those were assigned immediately to the camp choir, and those who got zero had little prospect of remaining alive for more than two days. When required to supply batches of prisoners for removal, he chose them in such a way as to retain a nucleus of good male and female voices so that his choir always remained complete."

From a lower middle-class family himself, Böll depicts many characters who are smalltown workers, romantics who burn out early, the rest of their lives sent up in the smoke of boredom. Their careers are always in doubt, and some are glad to have it exactly there. One of these is a statistician, a drone whose job is to count other worker bees as they cross the new town bridge back and forth from the hive. The work is senseless but the statistician keeps his spirit alive by the enjoyment of privately juggling the figures. "Secretly it gives me pleasure to do them (the chief statistician's office) out of one pedestrian every so often, and then again, when I feel sorry for them, to throw in a few extra." "At the Bridge" is a wry classic, a sardonic bite into the flesh of tedium that all workers must chew. It is a story that all of Washington's GS 9s and under should read, not only to have confirmed the hunch that much of their bosses' paper work is limitless nonsense but to know that everyone needs some style of personal resistance.

Böll lives in Cologne and has been chairman of the International PEN club. One of his best known novels in America is *The Clown*, an apt story for this country because it depicts an agnostic youth whose moral sense is far deeper than that of the adult moralizers around him. Among the least known of Böll's works is his lightest—*Irish Journal* (McGraw-Hill). It is hard to imagine a German understanding the Irish—the Irish themselves can barely do it—but Böll is cheerful and affectionate to the small towns he visits and the large souls in them. *Irish Journal* is from 1955, and the innocence of Connemara, Galway and Limerick has long vanished, so the book is now a history text. The ancient past of a mid-1950s Irish village is described, and where can you find it now? "It had seemed blasphemous when someone once said to me in Germany, the road belongs to the automobile. In Ireland I was often tempted to say: the road belongs to the cow. Indeed, cows are sent as freely to pasture as children to school: they fill the road with their herds, turn around haughtily when you blow your horn, and the driver has a chance to show a sense of humor, behave calmly and test his skill. . . . He would never be able to coin a snobbish slogan such as, the road belongs to the automobile. Ireland is a long way from deciding who the road belongs to."

Böll has returned often to Ireland, so he knows how much life has gone out of the country since it became "modern." But he has not written about it. No doubt, the demands of writing about the Germans, and their problems of conscience, is sufficient to the day.

SELECTED BIBLIOGRAPHY OF HEINRICH BÖLL

Absent Without Leave. New York: McGraw-Hill, 1965.
Adam and the Train. New York: McGraw-Hill, 1970.
Billiards at Half-Past Nine. New York: McGraw-Hill, 1973.
Children Are Civilians, Too. New York: McGraw-Hill, 1970.
Eighteen Stories. New York: McGraw-Hill, 1966.
Group Portrait with a Lady. New York: McGraw-Hill, 1973.
Irish Journal. New York: McGraw-Hill, 1967.
Schwartz, Wilhelm J. *Heinrich Böll, Teller of Tales.* New York: Ungar.

Sean O'Casey

THE ENDEARING TRAIT of the Irish is their remembrance of roots. In conversations, many of the sons and daughters of pig farmers, for example, happily recall how their father farmed pigs, others recall their father as a skilled barkeep, carpenter, bricklayer or picklock. No matter how hoarse an Irishman gets shouting to the world of his self-importance, there is seldom a low-voiced denial of his rooted origins. In contrast, who can recall meeting an American or Englishman who tells company his father was a pig farmer? Such children must exist, the ham industry being as pervasive as it is. But the rough roots of Americans are usually licked smooth by the countless kisses from social propriety and image.

It is good to go to Sean O'Casey if only to be reminded that the manual laborers among us—Irish or not—often understand life in undeceiving ways as few intellectuals ever do. O'Casey, a worker's son from the slums of Dublin who reached thirteen before he could read or write—why not, what's the hurry?—returned again and again in his prose to the similarities between manual and mental work. He wrote in "The Green Crow" that "the writer should not encourage the thought that his work is more important than the worker in wood, in metal, or the weaver of textiles from the spinning thread. ... The delicate pencil and paintbrush, the sculptor's searching chisel, or the potent pen is no more than the plumb line and the spirit level, the jack-plane and saw, or the hammer beating out utilitarian shapes from metal." People often wrote letters to O'Casey seeking advice on how to become a writer. He usually wrote back warning them to get work on a farm, a factory or a workshop, and to stay there as long as they could. In this way, they might learn not only the proper ways of knocking at the door of literature but also learn that other rooms than the writer's are worth entering. "Too many metal workers and carpenters," he wrote, "want to be writers and painters, seeing with foolish eyes a glow around authorship that never was on sea or land . . . We shouldn't abandon a craft we do well for one which we shall do but badly; nor should we set aside our craft to do trivial things. Only the other day, I got a letter from a man who lives in Calumet City, Ill. He begged me to send him used Irish stamps, adding as a hint to me that, as well, he collected coins, matchbox covers, beer-bottle caps, auto-club emblems, catalogues and buttons, all of which he had five hundred. Casually, he mentions that he is a carpenter, abandoning the calm and really beautiful art of carpentry for the feverish collection of rubbish."

Many of the better known plays of O'Casey are about wrecked Irish families in wrecked Ireland. *Juno and the Paycock* is one of these, with its famous line from the heroine (a line still unheeded today in Ireland, as the latest of the world's religious wars rages): "Sacred Heart o' Jesus, take away our hearts o' stone, and give us hearts o' flesh! Take away this murdherin' hate, an' give us Thine own eternal love!" A less known play was *The Silver Tassie*, written when O'Casey no longer had to moonlight as a janitor for bread money. The play was about the effect of war on those ordered to wage it, the bright young men sent off by politicians to dark graves. O'Casey was a pacifist and saw no problem in using the theater to portray the useless stupidities of war, organized legal murder. O'Casey was less concerned with the politics of war—both sides always have deft arguments to justify their killing—than with the immense suffering that follows. The play was rejected by the Abbey Theater and by W.B. Yeats. In *The Green and the Red*, a useful study of O'Casey, Jules Koslow notes that "we have here one of several cases in literary history in which a humorous criticism of society— *Juno and the Paycock*—is accepted, but a serious and biting criticism of society—*The Silver Tassie*—meets with opposition." The result of this panning was the development of O'Casey's skills for grudge-bearing, a perennial Irish trait. Go ahead, he advised young dramatists, "and don't bother about the critics. They are no use to you. They don't know their own minds." He also scorned hacks in his own trade, as illustrated by the taut wit in this appraisal of a suicide director: "The poor fellow's gone now, making his exit by way of a gas oven, giving in a kitchen a better production than he ever gave on a stage."

Like most Irish males, O'Casey married late, but unlike many he married happily. "From the first afternoon I met him until his death 38 years later, I don't suppose I ever lost him," his widow wrote in her gentle biography, *Sean* (Coward-McCann). The couple suffered the harshest cruelty of any marriage, the death of a child; O'Casey, a man filled with feeling anyway, never recovered. Another ache was money. Often, the pain was not only in having little, but in knowing that it could easily be the other way, via the sellout. In 1944, a Hollywood film agent wrote O'Casey, promising $100,000 if he would do a screenplay. Sarcastically snorting that the offer "was a temptation for more than an hour" before remembering what Hollywood was, O'Casey later wrote: "In spite of powers thrusting big money before an author for work he doesn't want to do . . . it is better for him to go his own way, even if it be with a limp. It is not a happy way, but it is his only way if he wishes to remain true to himself and right with God." The small daily gains of integrity are often the only profit an Irishman shows in life. Or cares to show.

O'Casey followers often argue like Kilkenny cats about which of the six volumes of their man's autobiography is best. There is no settling the account, but the last chapter of the last book—"Sunset and Evening Star"—is easily one of the twentieth century's finest statements for pacifism. "The generals . . . love guns as kids love candies. They call upon people to get ready for war as if they were calling upon them to get ready for a walk. 'The sight gladdens my old eyes,' a general is alleged to have said, when he saw a heap of Korean dead; forgetting that where there are Korean dead, there will be American dead, British dead, and maybe, Irish dead too. . . . If generals had their way, the tide of the third World War would sweep over all before men had a real chance to see what the last war looked like. So we hang together as best we may, going through a life that has become a corridor of war memorials, built in honour of the young who gave their lives gallantly, for his nib's sake; with obeliskan officers standing at every corner shouting: Prepare to fight, prepare to die, prepare to meet your enemy. Aw, go to hell, and leave our little world alone; our little lives rounded with a little sleep; our little streets, our little homes; we want them all, we love them all—we'll die in our beds, you tabb'd and uniformed sons of bitches!"

O'Casey did die in his bed, at age eighty-four, holding his wife's hand and holding his spirit proud. The Irish, lucky in their saints and legends, are nevertheless a mourning people these days, burying their bloodied dead in the needless Northern curse. They need the ground-shift of O'Casey's thinking, if only to rise with the earthy uplift of

O'Casey's last written words: the world "is full of disappointments, and too many of us have to suffer the loss of a beloved child, a world that aches bitterly till our time here ends. Yet even so, each of us one time or another, can ride a white horse, can have rings on our fingers and bells on our toes, and if we keep our senses open to the scents, sounds, and sights all around us, we shall have music wherever we go."

SELECTED BIBLIOGRAPHY OF SEAN O'CASEY

Collected Plays (four volumes). New York: St. Martin's, 1949.
Letters of Sean O'Casey. New York: Macmillan, 1975.
Benstock, Bernard. *Sean O'Casey.* Cranbury, N.J.: Bucknell University Press, 1971.
Krause, David. *Sean O'Casey: The Man and His Work.* New York: Macmillan, 1975.
O'Casey, Eileen. *Sean.* New York: Coward-McCann, 1972.

The Committed Life

MUCH OF THE EVIDENCE AROUND us suggests that we live in a time of collapse. The world's oceans, needed to sustain life on earth, face destruction from oil spills by giant tankers. Scientists warn that gases from aerosol cans accumulate in the upper stratosphere and are harming the crucial layers of ozone that shield the earth from lethal ultra-violet radiation. A thousand acres are ravaged each week by strip miners. And then, as if this destruction to the air, water and land were not enough, the United States and Russia have enough nuclear bombs to destroy human life many times over. Amid all this, why do anything? Can our capacity for hope, for social improvement, go beyond what Albert Camus believed? "The important thing is not to be cured but to live with one's ailments."

It is true that the signs of collapse engulf us, but a case can be made that time is not running out, it is running on. Those who say disaster is coming are practicing the kind of hubris that is historically common. Every age thinks it is the worst ever because every recorded century has had its tyrants ready to do in the planet to achieve their ends; and every age has had its observers warning about such tyrants. Those in the doom business today agree that the previous forecasts have been wrong, but this, they argue, is because all the earlier threats to humanity came in the form of social disasters affecting a few—a plague, a famine, a war between kings—and never as technological disasters affecting everyone.

The trouble with such an argument is that, like the theologians who condemned Galileo because he said the earth was not the center of the universe, the twentieth century is not centered in a fixed point in time. In 1974, it was estimated that the earth is part of a universe 16 billion years old. The number is too awesome to imagine, but this does not excuse the silly pride that puts the twentieth century as the most important yet to appear nor does it justify saying that if we collapse, that's the end.

Scientists use the analogy of a twenty-four hour clock to explain that the twentieth century is a mere part of a time measurement that is running on, not running out. If the beginnings of the planet occurred 16 billion years ago, a time scale of twenty-four hours would put the era of the Peking man—650,000 years ago—at about 11:55 P.M. Neanderthal man appeared at two minutes to midnight and homo sapiens only about a minute ago. The thoughts of Moses, Jesus and Buddha have been around for less than a second.

This unimaginable slowness of time, and man's recent appearance in it, suggests that the damage done by oil spills, aerosol cans and nuclear bombs—not to mention the trouble with OPEC, on Wall Street—is but a minor foul-up. It leads to the conclusion that we are still in the most primitive beginnings of evolution, that "modern" man is no more the finished product than was the cave man. When he wrote about twentieth century awareness, Carl Jung referred to the problem of "inflated consciousness." Applying to nations as well as people, this inflation is always "egocentric and conscious of nothing but its own existence. It is incapable of learning from the past, incapable of understanding contemporary events, and incapable of drawing right conclusions about the future. It is hypnotized by itself and cannot be argued with. It inevitably dooms itself to calamities that must strike it dead."

The demoralization now is caused less by the calamities than by the slowly rising level of intelligence that is able to see, however faintly, alternatives to the world's violence and chaos. In an earlier period of evolution, say 400,000 years ago, men may have lived by compulsive violence—with no options for other behavior because their wills and emotions were still forming. Today there is at least a consciousness that alternatives to violence exist—the peace treaty, the handshake—though it may be another 400,000 years before the treaties and handshakes mean anything. No doubt, citizens 400,000 years hence will look back on us in the pitying way we look back on the coarseness of the Neanderthals: pathetic savages, we say, using a phrase that we are doing much to earn ourselves.

What is deceiving about the twentieth century is that science has made many believe that positive change is a rapid process, not a slow one. A goal is set to land on the moon, for example, and ten years later the scientists get us there. A few years after, the moon-shots began to bore us. But what if 6,000 years ago, when men first began carving symbols on walls, someone announced that the whole world would be literate in ten years? Compared with reaching the moon, an idea like literacy—the simple act of deciphering basic symbols—should have posed no special challenge. Yet, 6,000 years since reading began, large parts of the global tribe are still illiterate. Campaigns against illiteracy are waged regularly, but since 1950 the number of illiterates has increased by 100 million.

If it has taken this long time to get only this far with an idea of stark simplicity—reading symbols—how much longer will be needed before such complex ideas as justice, sharing the wealth and civil honesty take hold? Surely it will not be anytime soon, even if the impossible happened and everyone could agree on a definition of soon: 100,000 years, 500,000, perhaps another 16 billion?

These numbers are beyond understanding. As an instrument of measuring, the mind is powerless to imagine anything beyond its own experience, as Voltaire could not imagine how sea shells were discovered on mountain peaks in Switzerland. They were there when, eons ago, the Zermatts and Matterhorns were under water.

The men and women in this section of Inner Companions—some still working at their commitment—have understood the slowness of social reform. All have had the passion of a single conviction. They have avoided what is seen all too often, especially in Washington: cause-jumping. One year, it might be prison reform, the next year women's rights, perhaps saving the bald eagle the year before, now the knees jerk to the need for day care centers, farmworkers (let's have a party in Easthampton!), consumer protection. It's like taking a new wife or husband every year, ever a honeymoon of feelings but never much of a confronting of reality.

Only a few stay with one effort, seeing it through not to the

111

end but at least to the end of their strength. It is the least practiced style of social reform—full of tedium and plodding, few thrills and few results—but is any other more effective? What my companions here are telling us is that the most important idea since evolution may be the realization that evolution is still going on. Thornton Wilder called it the eighth day of creation, now that the first seven days are ended. Now that the firmament, the heavens and water have been created, we can set about with the creation of justice, sharing the wealth and love. As for what will come of the work of those who lead committed lives, what can we know. We have only Jung's assertion that "nobody can say where man ends. That is the beauty of it."

Dorothy Day

T
HE YEARS ARE PILING UP; in her seventies now, she moves with a cane, and the body is arthritic. Her hair is yellow-white, braided over the top the way it was when Dwight McDonald wrote the memorable *New Yorker* profile in 1956, the way it was when she began working with the poor in the 1920s, the simple way it has always been throughout the full-giving and daring life of Dorothy Day. For nearly five decades, she has been on the right side of all the crucial battles; for non-violence (the pure kind) and against wars, for the workers and against board room exploiters, for the hungry and homeless and against the blindly comfortable. The last is where Dorothy Day's most measurable success has come—in the houses of hospitality now run by her followers in about a dozen inner-cities. The best known is Manhattan's Bowery, the dead-end dumping ground of society's wrecked. "It is a strange vocation," she recalled four years ago, "to love the destitute and dissolute, those people sleeping in doorways, foul with the filth of the gutter, dying of drunkenness and malnutrition, fever and cold. We have known many such deaths (on Chrystie Street) and have witnessed the depths of misery around us. Only last month a group of schoolchildren, early teen-agers, poured kerosene on three such men, sleeping in a doorway, and set fire to them. This act of horror gives witness to the all too prevalent attitude to these men—'They are only bums,' one child said, and the mother of another, 'Someone ought to do something about these bums.' Yet they are found in every corner of the city, in vacant buildings, in the shadow of warehouses in neighborhoods deserted at night."

Caring about ideals that reasonable men long ago gave up as lost, Dorothy Day can easily seem out of touch to the pushers of today's many bell-bottomed causes. She recently addressed a women's lib conference in Westchester. With Betty Friedan there gunning everyone down and after a black sister read her absurd "Bitch Manifesto," Dorothy Day spoke. A report in *Commonweal* described her as "perhaps the oldest person in the room, the most personally courageous, and in action and in practice already the most liberated." In Miss Day's talk, "she said nothing about women's liberation, never mentioned the words, never stated her views on the subjects of economic equality, careers, chores, society's institutions. Instead she reminisced about her life, her daughter, the families she has known, the poor, the work she'd done, in jail, in the streets, in her houses of hospitality."

No one definition offers fair description of the Catholic Worker, which Dorothy Day founded—with Peter Maurin in 1932. For more than forty years it has been serving the destitute by offering food, clothing and shelter. But it also publishes a monthly newspaper—still a penny a copy, still discussing pacifism and the need to share the wealth—and it is a place for students, teachers, clergy, men and women who need a port in one storm or another. They can stay an hour, a day, a year, perhaps for good, doing what they can to serve others or perhaps regain their own strength. For all of this, the Catholic Worker is not a movement, nor an organization, mission or institution. It has parts of all those, but on the most visible level—as the door opens and the homeless poor are asked in with dignity—the Catholic Worker may best be described as a spirit of active wisdom, a rare kind that takes the initiative to reduce in immediate ways the scandalously large amounts of poverty and injustice that the world's powerful allow to persist.

I have never gone to New York without a visit to the tenement where the Catholic Worker operates. I come from the distant ranks of the comfortable and secure, but the hospitality of 36 East First Street—St. Joseph's House—can accept those limitations as easily as the wounds of the poor. As with the latter, I go to the Catholic Worker to get something: a confirmation that the works of mercy and solace still comprise the most esteemed of all vocations, and unless homage is paid to that truth, no other can make sense.

Radicalism is now a cheapened word, but no better radicalism exists than the kind practiced by Dorothy Day—the wild, extreme notion that Christianity is a workable system, the bizarre idea that religion means what you do more than what you believe.

As with most vocations that stay singular in purpose over long periods of time, Dorothy Day came to hers the long way around. In her early twenties, she lived on the cheap as a reporter in New York. She liked the work, but the itch for action competed with the job of reporting the action. With an unbribed heart that sought out the rich experiences where self-identity is created automatically as one goes along, her circle included Malcolm Crowley, John Dos Passos, Allen Tate, and Caroline Gordon, all starting out then in Greenwich Village. One of Dorothy Day's fondest memories is the evenings spent in the back room of a Fourth Street saloon where Eugene O'Neill would recite for her "The Hound of Heaven." Moved by this poem of faith, and by longing that could not be satisfied by conventional activism, she eventually embraced Christianity. With a child from a common-law marriage—over quickly—she met in 1932 Peter Maurin. He came on easy with a hard message, a drifting reformer always bobbing up at the scenes of injustice to tell people how to build a "society in which it is easier for people to be good." Together with Dorothy Day, he founded the *Catholic Worker* newspaper. In its pages for the last forty years, it has been like a prowling animal outside the doors of America's deaf and lazy institutions. Danilo Dolci, the Berrigans, Jacques Maritain, Thomas Merton, Martin Buber, Gordon Zahn have written for its pages. In the introduction to a valuable collection of articles from the *Worker—A Penny a Copy, Readings from the Catholic Worker,* edited by Thomas C. Cornell and James H. Forest and published by Macmillan—the editors write "that some would like to consign this volume to the racks as a memento to the thirties. Let it be a thorn in the side of our parents. But that cannot be. For it is still going on, and to tell the truth the misery is deeper and the frustration more bitter, the apocalypse closer and each present moment more acute. Wars and rumors of war, race war, class war. Wars of liberation and wars to liberate the liberated. And as always the same victims. The people. The vast majority of the people, poor and hungry, sick unto death of liberators, whose cry is 'peace and bread.' The Body of Christ bleeding from a billion wounds. And still the Catholic Worker movement, poor among the poor, a quiet leaven, a bowl of soup, an oddly dated monthly, still a penny a copy, bringing news that is so old it looks like new."

Many of the war resisters who went to prison or who left the country rather than bear arms, first learned about pacifism and civil disobedience (but not civil destruction) from reading Dorothy Day or going to her meetings in the

Bowery. A recent article in the *Catholic Worker*—all articles there are "recent"—noted that "the younger men working here are conscientiously opposed to war. Perhaps after having seen the victims of the class war in this country sleeping forgotten on the Bowery, running up and down the steps of crumbling tenements, or staring wide-eyed and alone in mental hospitals, they do not want to fight for a materialistic system that cripples so many of its citizens. ... These are young men who have learned well one historical fact—that you can never win over an ideology by killing the men who have the idea. The job at hand is that of a peacemaker performing the works of mercy, not the works of wars."

One reason so many professional journalists know Dorothy Day is because her newspaper is an exceptional achievement. Easily, it is the only paper in the country to have kept so long to one editorial line, to one typographical tradition, and to one price. In paying homage to this rarity, Dwight Macdonald wrote in the introduction to a collection of *Catholic Workers,* each given in its entirety, published in 1970 by the Greenwood Reprint Corporation: "The thirty-sixth anniversary issue of the *Catholic Worker*—May 1969, Vol. XXXVII, No. 1—looks, reads, and costs the same as that of May 1, 1933, Vol. I, No. 1. Only the *New York Times,* another of our few stable institutions though its editorial line is jittery compared to the *Worker's,* has a longer typographical tradition (by some thirty years). Unlike the *Times,* the *Worker* costs the same now as it did in 1933: a penny a copy, 25 cents a year—the only periodical in journalistic history that costs twice as much by the year as by the issue." When Macdonald's piece was excerpted in the *New York Review of Books,* the editors footnoted it with the customary "it appears here by permission of the publisher and the author." They went on to add: "The volumes included in this edition are 1 through 27, 1933 to 1961. The price will be $435.00. If a foresighted collector had bought these numbers on the street and stashed them away, he would have paid $3.48 for the lot (29 years at 12¢). A considerable saving—$431.52, to be exact." On the newspaper itself, Miss Day recalled that the first issue run in May 1933 "was 2500 copies. Within three or four months the circulation bounded to 25,000, and it was cheaper to bring it out as an eight-page tabloid on newsprint rather than the smaller-sized edition on better paper we had started with. By the end of the year we had a circulation of 100,000 and by 1936 it was 150,000. It was certainly a mushroom growth. It was not only that some parishes subscribed for the paper all over the country

116

in bundles of 400 or more. Zealous young people took the paper out in the streets and sold it, and when they could not sell it even at one cent a copy, they gave free copies and left them in streetcars, buses, barber shops, dentists' and doctors' offices. We got letters from all parts of the country from people who said they had picked up the paper on trains, in rooming houses. One letter came from the state of Sonora in Mexico and we read with amazement that the reader had tossed in an uncomfortable bed on a hot night until he got up to turn over the mattress and under it found a copy of the *Catholic Worker.* A miner found a copy five miles underground in an old mine that stretched out under the Atlantic Ocean off Nova Scotia. A seminarian said that he had sent out his shoes to be half-soled in Rome and they came back to him wrapped in a copy of the *Catholic Worker.* These letters thrilled and inspired the young people who came to help. . . ."

A typical issue of the paper, which can be subscribed to at 36 East First Street, New York, New York 10003, usually has a woodcut on page one, often a scene of oppression or perhaps a depiction of a hero. Carried in the eight pages will be a report from one or two sites of injustice—a migrant labor camp, perhaps, or maybe a hospital ward in a city "health" center—an appeal for winter clothing, an easygoing column by an old-time member—Deane Mary Mowrer's "A Farm with a View," written from the Catholic Worker farm in Tivoli—a news story about an editor being arrested for refusing military induction (how many of these stories there have been), a couple of book reviews—and always the important books, too, such as Gordon Zahn's *War, Conscience and Dissent,* or Danilo Dolci's *The Man Who Plays Alone*—a long essay or two on nonviolence or welfare reform, a lively "Letters to the Editor" column (lively not because nutty letters are printed, but because such nutty ideas as peace, sharing the wealth, serving the sick, reforming the government are discussed and debated), column-end fillers—something from Bernanos perhaps, or Solzhenitsyn, often *Tales of the Hasidim*—and always Miss Day's column "On Pilgrimage."

"I am home again with a handful of colorful postals," she wrote after returning from her trip to Russia during the summer of 1971, "including reproductions of ikons and a folder of picture postals of Lenin's exile in Siberia, where he lived, where he studied, where he taught his peasant neighbors and their children, where he fished and hunted and rested in the forest. How I wish we had such a Siberia where the Fathers Berrigan and all the prisoners of conscience could

117

go and meditate and study and prepare for a new social order 'wherein peace and justice dwell.' "

Dorothy Day's autobiography is *The Long Loneliness,* a treasure in the tradition of Augustine's *Confessions* or Merton's *Seven Storey Mountain.* It is a moving book, the classic story of someone seeking a piece of earth of which to be the salt. The prose is clear, unpretentious, and conversational, much the way Miss Day is in daily relationships. A humility is present in her style of writing soldered together with the humility in her own life. Repeatedly, she refers to Charles Peguy, Ignazio Silone, Eric Gill, Piotr Kropotkin. The thoughts of these men are not abruptly plunked into Miss Day's text like fall-out from Bartlett's, in the manner of hack politicians wanting the eloquent sound. Instead, attracted by the play of ideas, Miss Day delights in passing on the genius of others, a servant of truth who gladly carries the tray that holds the treasures of others. Among those she leans on are William James. Tellingly, she included in her autobiography: "One afternoon as I sat on the beach, I read a book of James' essays and came on these lines: 'Poverty is indeed the strenuous life—without brass bands or uniforms or hysteric popular applause or lies or circumlocutions: and when one sees the way in which wealth-getting enters as an ideal into the very bone and marrow of our generation, one wonders whether the revival of the belief that poverty is a worthy religious vocation may not be the transformation of military courage, and the spiritual reform which our time stands most in need of.

" 'Among us English-speaking peoples especially do the praises of poverty need once more to be boldly sung. We have grown literally afraid to be poor. We despise anyone who elects to be poor in order to simplify and save his inner life. If he does not join the general scramble, we deem him spiritless and lacking in ambition. We have lost the power even of imagining what the ancient realization of poverty could have meant; the liberation from material attachments, the unbought soul, the manlier indifference, the paying our way by what we are and not by what we have, the right to fling away our life at any moment irresponsibly. . . .' "

How willingly poor has Dorothy Day lived? One example might be from a quiet event in 1960 when she sent back a large sum of money to the treasurer of the city of New York. The letter tells much about the soul and the beliefs of Dorothy Day and her refusal to adjust. "Dear Sir," she wrote. "We are returning to you a check for $3579.39 which represents interest on the $68,700 which we

118

were awarded by the city as payment for the property at 223 Chrystie Street which we owned and lived in for almost ten years, and used as a community for the poor. We did not voluntarily give up the property—it was taken from us by right of eminent domain for the extension of the subway which the city deemed necessary. We had to wait almost a year and a half for the money owed us, although the city permitted us to receive two thirds of the assessed valuation of the property in advance so that we could relocate. Property owning having been made impossible for us by city regulations, we are now renting and continuing our work.

"We are returning the interest on the money we have received because we don't believe in 'money lending' at interest. As Catholics, we are acquainted with the early teaching of the Church. All the early councils forbade it and in various decrees ordered that profit so obtained was to be restored. In the Christian emphasis on the duty of charity, we are commanded to lend gratuitously, to give freely, even in the case of confiscation, as in our own case—not to resist but to accept cheerfully.

"We do not believe in the profit system, and so we cannot take profit or interest on our money. People who take a materialistic view of human service wish to make a profit but we are trying to do our duty by our service without wages to our brothers as Jesus commanded in the Gospel (Matt. 25). Loaning money at interest is deemed by one Franciscan as the principal scourge of civilization. Eric Gill, the English artist and writer, calls usury and war the two great problems of our time. Since we have dealt with these problems in every issue of the *Catholic Worker* since 1933—man's freedom, war and peace, man and the state, man and his work—and since Scripture says that the love of money is the root of all evil, we are taking this opportunity to live in practice of this belief, and make a gesture of overcoming that love of money by returning to you the interest."

Unlike many who care for the poor and other discards of our system, Dorothy Day has not merely given until it hurts, she has given until after it hurts. She owns nothing herself, knowing that the teaching of voluntary poverty is a sham if she does not also live it. Had she been less austere on herself over the years—not sleeping in cold rooms, eating on the run, traveling on Greyhound buses— perhaps the physical hurt of old age would also be less. But what is a little thorn in the side? she asked once. "It seems to me we might begin to equal a little bit of the courage of the Communists. One of

119

the ways my American Communist friends taunt me is by saying, in effect: 'People who are religious believe in everlasting life, and yet look how cowardly they are. And we who believe only in this life, see how hard we work and how much we sacrifice.' "

Despite bishops and priests who condone war and lead the government at prayer time, Dorothy Day has never judged such men or left the institutional Church. It is probably because she is still loyal to this rich and highly organized body that she can say: "Why worry about empty schools, seminars and even rectories? Maybe the Lord is giving us a little reminder that there has been too much building going on, and that it is time to use some of these facilities for the poor, for families." In a column entitled "Meditation on the Death of the Rosenbergs," she expressed what many have felt on seeing Cardinal Spellman troop off "to be with the boys" or Cardinal Cooke show up at a White House prayer service to be court chaplain to Richard Nixon: "What a confusion we have gotten into when Christian prelates sprinkle holy water on scrap metal, to be used for obliteration bombing, and name bombers for the Holy Innocents, for Our Lady of Mercy; who bless a man about to press a button which releases death to fifty thousand human beings, including little babies, children, the sick, the aged, the innocent as well as the guilty."

Valuing communal living long before communes came into fashion, Dorothy Day has always had farms in the country for her companions. Tivoli, New York, is the current site, overlooking the Hudson River and complete with vegetable gardens and flowers. No stranger has ever been turned away, much less old friends. The lonely and confused come back loaded with problems, to retreat awhile and talk with Dorothy. She feeds them first, like Jesus and the five thousand. And in the winter at Christmas in the Bowery, the strays who come to her get a little wine with the meal. Why not? They are human beings, in need of joy and mercy, like everyone else.

SELECTED BIBLIOGRAPHY OF DOROTHY DAY.

Loaves and Fishes. Philadelphia: Curtis, 1972 (paperback).
The Long Loneliness. Philadelphia: Curtis, 1972 (paperback).
On Pilgrimage: The Sixties. Philadelphia: Curtis, 1972 (paperback).
Coles, Robert and Erikson, Jon. *A Spectacle unto the World.* New York: Viking, 1974.
Cornell, Thomas and Forest, James, eds. *A Penny a Copy.* New York: Macmillan, 1968.
Miller, William D. *A Harsh and Dreadful Love: Dorothy Day and The Catholic Worker Movement.* New York: Liveright, 1974.
The Catholic Worker newspaper, 36 E. First St., New York, N.Y.

Danilo Dolci

THE WORK OF DANILO DOLCI, begun in the 1950s in the no-hope country of Sicily, is well known in Europe but only lately has it attracted wide attention in America. Nominated for the Nobel peace prize several times, Dolci has succeeded in organizing the illiterate peasants of western Sicily—*gli-ultima,* the lowest—into informal communities of progress. On stony, good-for-nothing land, his followers have built houses, sewers, roads, dams and health centers. As sure proof that his work is producing change, over the years Dolci has been jailed by the government, denounced by the church and shot at by the rich. In common with Gandhi, Camus, Schweitzer and other complex men who simplified life by making it sacred, Dolci is unintelligible to many of the intelligent.

Thanks to the Fellowship of Reconciliation, Dolci has made visits to lecture in the United States. His philosophy is needed in this country because he insists that peaceful change is possible from within and from below. In the early days of the Peace Corps, when still planned by President Kennedy, a Dolci book, *To Feed the Hungry*, was a prime source of inspiration.

The early years of Dolci, son of a stationmaster, were spent in northern Italy. "After I turned sixteen," he has written, "the need to read, to acquaint myself through the printed word with the experience and thought of men who had lived before me, became so strong that if I had not found books in my immediate surroundings . . . I would have stolen them." Dolci read so much that his family nickname was "let-me-finish-the-chapter."

His values were formed by the Bible, the Upanishads, the dialogues of Buddha, by writers from Dante to Tolstoi. Dolci refused to fight in World War II, a choice that led to prison but also to a

121

stronger belief in nonviolence. On release, he went to Nomadelfia, a community where the orphans of war were cared for. His education from books was now reinforced by direct experience. "Hoeing weeds," he recalled in 1967 in Saturday Review's "What I Have Learned" series, "building latrines in the camps, living with orphans, former petty thieves, many of them sick, I discovered what it means to grow together; after several months of common endeavor, even abysmally stupid faces become more human and sometimes beautiful."

A few years later, with affectionate farewells, Dolci left northern Italy "for the most wretched piece of country I have ever seen"—Sicily. The indirect violence caused by poverty and ignorance was matched only by the direct violence of the Mafia, the criminal substate whose ambassadors are so well received in America.

Dolci settled in and became part of the misery. In time, he bought a piece of land, and with volunteers built a home for impoverished children and old people. In the style of reformers who quickly move beyond the romance of "saving people," Dolci bore down hard on reachable social objectives. Build a house, fix a road, clear a field, put up a dam; soon, you are not only tampering with physical structures but also social structures.

Dolci's writing, backed by years of his own sweat and frustration, constantly explores the importance of immediate objectives and the individual's self-awareness as a true source of power.

● "There can be no development unless men have an opportunity to work for it and take part according to their own needs and convictions."

● "It was essential to broaden contacts among individuals, to organize these largely isolated men and families into research and action groups increasingly aware of the need to develop resources by developing themselves."

● "To build a dam was important because the water would bring to the parched land, along with bread, the green shoots of experience, the proof that it is possible to change the face of the earth; but it was important also because the building of the dam meant a worker's union, a democratic management of the irrigation system, grape growers' and other agricultural cooperatives. In other words, it meant the organization of chaos; it meant the beginnings of true democratic planning."

Dolci's ideas, though applied in Sicily, have a familiar sound. By coincidence, they are the basis for much of what has worked in the hundreds of community action programs across this country. Somebody woke up the poor, convinced them they were important and said that self-help was better than self-pity. This rarely led to neat and tidy social change, neither in Sicily nor here. Predictably, politicians in both places preferred it the old way when the poor were silent and colonial.

Dolci, who knows the world too well to have illusions, has often been jailed or beaten for his work. He wrote: "Those who want things to remain as they are, to preserve the present 'order,' will try to put out of the running anyone who promotes change. That is how things are; and those of us who have been thrown into prison, labeled as criminals, denounced over and over again, know it well, as do all those who are striving toward a new life anywhere in the world. It is naive to be surprised or shocked by it."

At many American colleges and universities, and places where people still hope without embarrassment, Dolci's philosophy is intensely studied. In his lecture tours the crowds have been large, and far into the night has Dolci talked privately with students. Part of his popularity comes from his passion for non-violence. With Martin Luther King and Thomas Merton dead, and Dorothy Day now slowing, Dolci's voice is one of the few that totally renounces arms and violence. "In a world weary of murders, betrayals and useless death, a more direct relationship can be established between the human conscience and the movement for change, provided this movement is as forceful as it is non-violent."

How is this done? "The powerful, the exploiters, the real outlaws can hardly maintain themselves in their positions unless they are supported and defended by those who have sold out to them. But there is as yet no clear and widespread understanding of the need not to collaborate with, and to boycott, insane initiatives."

Over and over, Dolci insists that violence is not needed for a true revolution. First, the public must be told the precise reasons why poverty is not an accidental condition. It is caused by a few who keep the world's wealth to themselves and their backers and who hire either soldiers or lawyers to ward off the people. "It is not enough to know, to document, to denounce. We must not only deflate these monsters by not feeding them and not allowing them to feed on us. We must clearly realize, we must know in every fiber of our being, that we have built these monsters and that we can destroy them."

Through his study and action centers in Sicily, Dolci has brought change to a feudal-minded and lost people. Personal

123

awareness and personal assertion work. The houses and dams are there as proof—not happy-ending proof, perhaps, but enough to face tomorrow. Because he believes that institutions, corporations and party politicians have failed the world, Dolci has been called ingenuous and a dreamer. He answers: "I'd say that he who hasn't yet understood that the discovery of truth is the strongest force of all, he's the ingenuous one, he's the dreamer."

SELECTED BIBLIOGRAPHY OF DANILO DOLCI

Report from Palermo. New York: Viking, 1970.
Harcourt, Melville. *Portraits of Destiny.* New York: Twin Circle, 1966.

George Seldes

THE FIRST DAY he went to work for the *Pittsburgh Leader*—long a deservedly dead newspaper—in 1909, George Seldes wrote a story about a street accident. "Stanislas Schmidt, aged 32, of 1811 Center Avenue, driver of a Silver Top Brewing Company delivery wagon, was slightly injured at 10 o'clock this morning at Penn Avenue and Liberty Street when his wagon was struck by a street car." Hours later, in rookie eagerness, he read through the first edition to find his story in print. There it ran: "Stanislas Schmidt, 32 years old, of 1811 Center Ave., driver of a beer delivery wagon..." Seldes immediately read the sign language of his newsroom. "Silver Top was not mentioned," he wrote years later. "Silver Top was a large advertiser. My education had begun."

Seldes did not spend a long time being tutored. In his day, the lessons of sell-out journalism were not complex, quick movements in the underbrush that the public seldom saw amid the grand foliage of The Latest News. Instead, Seldes, learning fast what the press should not be, stayed in the profession to be its critic, to say what the press should be. Many newsrooms today have reporters like Seldes, restive characters who play their typewriter by ear, pressure groups of one, their high standards for ethical journalism trussed firmly to the back of their conscience. Seldes went beyond this, and produced a large body of literature that is among our most insightful press criticism. A few resourceful newspapers now have internal critics—and print them, not just send them around to seminars—but anyone wanting to examine the art as it ran in the early editions ought to consume Seldes.

After surviving several years in Pittsburgh, Seldes went abroad to cover World War I. Again, the young reporter found his copy being gutted, except now it was not a wary night editor striking out risky words but the military propagandists keeping the facts hidden in the first place. Seldes and other correspondents dined with generals and had tea with princes. "The journals (back home) that printed our stories boasted that their own representatives had been at the fighting front," Seldes wrote in *The Freedom of the Press.* "I now realize that we were told nothing but buncombe, that we were shown nothing of the realities of the war, that we were, in short, merely part of the great Allied propaganda machine whose purpose was to sustain morale at all costs and help drag unwilling America into the slaughter." Seldes described the deceits of the military but his dispiritment concerned the complicity of his own profession, which should have known better. "We all more or less lied about the war," he wrote. "On Armistice Day four of us took an oath on the battlefield that we would tell the truth the rest of our lives, that we would begin telling the truth in time of preparation of war, that we would do what was humanly possible to prevent the recurrence of another such vast and useless horror. Then we all went back to prosaic reporting in America."

For Seldes, it did not stay prosaic long. Too much was happening in American politics and industry during the 1930s and 1940s—in the backrooms and board rooms, the old twins—for him to be idle. But as a reporter, Seldes' deepest fascination was with the unreported news about the newsroom. Timid editors, publishers caring more for public relations than public service, predictable columnists, reporters too friendly with government press agents—all this, in Seldes, mind, caused much of the American press to go to seed and come only part way back. "For myself all I can say is that I have never written a story which I knew to be untrue. Most newspaper men, I am sure, can make the same unqualified statement. But such statements are not enough. To them must be added the sin of omission. . . . In Europe I learned that any story derogatory to liberal and radical elements was sure to be published and all stories favorable to them would be played down or left out. . . . (From Mexico) for some reason or another, it may have been due to lack of space, all stories giving the case against the Mexican government got either front page or prominent place while the charges . . . against American business interests got little or no space. When year after year similar experiences occur to a trained newspaperman he usually quits reporting both sides of a controversy. But he still publishes nothing but the truth."

After twenty years in the trade, Seldes wrote in 1929 *You Can't Print That*, a valuable book republished in 1968 by Scholarly Press, St. Clair Shores, Michigan. *Freedom of the Press* came in 1935 and examined the corrupting influences on American newspapers. It, along with *You Can't Say That,* has been reprinted by Da Capo Press (New York). Other books, out of about a dozen, include *Iron, Blood and Profits, Can These Things Be!* and *Never Tire of Protesting* (Lyle Stuart). Aside from his books, Seldes also wrote for ten years—in the 1940s—a newsletter called "In fact." Many veteran reporters in Washington remember "In fact" and recall with affection its influence on their own careers.

One of the few who has written about Seldes in recent years is Nat Hentoff, whose press criticism in the *Village Voice* is in the tradition of Seldes, with much of the same clarity and bite. Hentoff notes that when Seldes criticized the foreign press for third rate journalism his writing was well received, but "when Seldes began to take on American newspapers, he was to put it mildly, largely shunned." Now living in Vermont, Seldes has written letters to Hentoff telling of the shunning. "In the ten years of its publication, 'In fact' never received a mention anywhere, with the exception of two or three small papers, notably the *Gazette & Daily* of York, Pa." Like the tireless researching of I.F. Stone, Seldes says that "In fact" had "many of its greatest scoops from official government documents."

Seldes, now in his eighties, could not help but be pleased with the reporters and editors who stuck with the Watergate story, bucking both government harassment and public indifference. The battle won this time by a free press is not isolated, though, but is part of the same war that Seldes fought in his generation. "In some of these episodes," Seldes wrote, "nothing but stupidity and ancient nonsense is at stake; but in others a new pattern begins to emerge: it is no longer nonsense and small town arrogance, it is self-evident violation of the civil rights of citizens by the forces elected or appointed to safeguard the Constitution, protect the minority, dispense 'equal justice under the law.' We come now to the forces which represent vested interests rather than the Bill of Rights."

One wishes that George Seldes was still in a newsroom, either climbing the walls with fury or tumbling them down in impatience. Many journalists lucky enough to work on newspapers guided by principled publishers and editors may be unaware of their fortunate and, indeed, minority position. To them, Seldes is owed a debt,

127

payable by not only raking the muck but reseeding the ground after. This is the positive reform Seldes believed journalists capable of, beginning in-house.

It is a sadness that Seldes never received official honor for his press criticism, but much of it was directed at those who confer the honors. Better yet that he received another award, journalism's rarest; it is the prize grateful readers give when they read a piece and say: if this subject wasn't written about, the public would not know it.

SELECTED BIBLIOGRAPHY OF GEORGE SELDES

The Freedom of the Press. New York: Da Capo, 1971 (reprint of 1938 edition).
Great Quotations. ed. Secaucus: Lyle Stuart, 1966.
Never Tire of Protesting. Secaucus: Lyle Stuart, 1968.
You Can't Do That. New York: Da Capo, 1972 (reprint of 1938 edition).
You Can't Print That: The Truth Behind the News. St. Clair Shores, Mich.: Scholarly Press. 1968 (reprint of 1929 edition).

Emma Goldman

AMONG THE MANY BENEFITS of the current revival of women's consciousness are the flashbacks to Emma Goldman. Few scenes in today's worthy push for women's social equality cannot be cut back to an idea or event in Emma Goldman's committed life, from her birth in Russia in 1869 to her burial in Chicago in 1940. She was called Red Emma by males accustomed to putting down women with clever sallies—the way arrogant males today dismiss Gloria Steinem as "Gloria Stardom"—and her followers legendized her as an inspired revolutionary. But Goldman lived in the wide middleground between the outposts of quick labels; she had an awareness that the system dumped on both women and workers, and that only by attacking specific parts of corruption would the whole part ever give. Her ideas of fifty years ago, bouncing back at us in history's echo chamber, are in a language that has had to wait half a century for translation.

Although Goldman wrote about women, marriage, schools, prisons, religion and other subjects women were meant to be mum about, her inflamed thinking was always based on her own fiery battles. The combat usually involved irrational males: her father— "the nightmare of my childhood"—a sadist school teacher, an uncle who made the child a work-servant and kicked her if she balked. It was no surprise, years later, that she wrote an essay, "The Child and Its Enemies" and noted that nothing is more astonishing than parents who "will strip themselves of everything, will sacrifice everything for the physical well-being of their child, will wake nights and stand in fear and agony before some physical ailment of their beloved one; but will remain cold and indifferent, without the slightest understanding, before the soul cravings and yearnings of their child, neither hearing nor wishing to hear the loud knocking of the young spirit that demands recognition."

Following an eked-out education, Goldman had no better luck with the next male in her life, her husband whom she married at seventeen. With "ardent anticipation" of finding at least some tenderness in a relationship, she was bewildered to learn on her wedding night that her new groom was sexually impotent. The marriage lasted briefly; the duration of her wifely employment was long enough, however, for Goldman to work up her own job description of marriage. It is an institution, she wrote, that "makes a parasite of woman, an absolute dependent. It incapacitates her for life's struggle, annihilates her social consciousness, paralyzes her imagination, and then imposes its gracious protection, which is in reality a snare, a travesty on human character." It made no difference to Goldman "whether the husband is a brute or a darling. (Instead), marriage guarantees woman a home only by the grace of her husband. There she moves about in *his* home, year after year, until her aspect of life and human affairs becomes as flat, narrow, and drab as her surrounding."

Audiences gagged on talk like this. Instead of easing up, Goldman increased her vehemence, going through the nation's sacred fibers of belief like a ragpicker. She questioned our patriotism: "We Americans claim to be a peace-loving people. We hate bloodshed; we are opposed to violence. Yet we go into spasms of joy over the possibility of projecting dynamite bombs from flying machines upon helpless citizens. . . . Yet our hearts swell with pride at the thought that America is becoming the most powerful nation on earth, and that it will eventually plant her iron foot on the necks of all other nations. Such is the logic of patriotism." Her essay on prisons could have been written this morning: "With all our boasted reforms, our great social changes and our far-reaching discoveries, human beings continue to be sent to the worst of hells, wherein they are outraged, degraded, and tortured, that society may be 'protected' from the phantoms of its own making." Her suggestion that prisoners be allowed to work while locked away, and receive a fair wage, is still an unfulfilled reform.

Goldman had the unfortunate itch suffered by many agitators, wanting to reform everything at once. Her agenda was enlarged to the size that she even took on Christianity, a mistake because she only repeated in banal ways the cliché criticisms of Nietzsche and Renan. "Heaven must be an awfully dull place," she wrote "if the poor in spirit live there. How can anything creative, anything vital, useful and beautiful come from the poor in spirit?" How regrettable that Goldman had no feeling for this basic Christian text; the poor in spirit are those rare people who voluntarily accumulate no possessions, who are detached from the pleasures of ownership, as the rich in spirit blatantly are not. Emma Goldman herself was a model practitioner of spiritual poverty, and perhaps that she didn't know it indicated its authenticity.

Following work in a New Haven corset factory, Goldman came to New York in 1889. She fell in with a young wildman who, in false sympathy to striking steelworkers, plotted to assassinate a corporate tycoon. This mixing of idealism with brutality did nothing for Goldman, except to give her critics an opening to pass her off as another fanatic. She never cleared her head of slogans about collective revolutionary violence. This was a waste because she saw clearly the suffering caused by militarism or by corporate violence.

As a believer in anarchism—a much maligned creed—Goldman was regularly in and out of jails on sham charges. A soldier was once imprisoned for the crime of shaking hands with her. When William McKinley was killed by a gunman who said he had listened once to a Goldman speech, a woman-hunt resulted and Goldman was jailed. She was released when no evidence of collusion was found. Years later, when she opposed American involvement in World War I, the government could take no more. She was deported. The force behind this snivelling deed was the young head of the Justice Department's intelligence division, J. Edgar Hoover.

Taking exile in Russia—a land she had long fantasized—Goldman was eager to see the results of the revolution. She had a close look; perhaps too close, because in 1923 she produced *My Disillusionment in Russia.* In 1931, Knopf published *Living My Life,* Goldman's 933-page masterful autobiography. Two worthy lives of Goldman are *Rebel in Paradise* by Richard Drinnon and *To the Barricades: The Anarchist Life of Emma Goldman* by Alix Kates Shulman.

The importance of Emma Goldman is not so much in the power of her thoughts but in her resolve to follow those thoughts to wherever they would lead: defying war, corporate violence, sexism, the J. Edgar Hoovers. All of us have rich ideas and noble thoughts, but we are cowardly when they carry us to conclusions that demand the courage of acting.

SELECTED BIBLIOGRAPHY OF EMMA GOLDMAN

Anarchism and Other Essays. New York: Dover, 1970.

Emma Goldman Chronology. Brooklyn, N.Y.: Revisionist Press.

Living My Life: The Autobiography of Emma Goldman. New York: Da Capo.

Rich, Andrea and Smith, Arthur L. *The Rhetoric of Revolution.* Durham, N.C.: Moore Publishing Co.

Drinnon, Richard. *Rebel in Paradise: A Biography of Emma Goldman.* New York: Bantam, 1973.

Schulman, Alix Kates. *To The Barricades: The Anarchist Life of Emma Goldman.* New York: Crowell, 1971.

A. J. Muste

.J. MUSTE CAME ON AS THE BEST kind of pacifist—
hardnosed about his facts, wary of sit-in rhetoric or leaflet logic,
unafraid to probe the complexities of non-violence, and free of any
supremacist pomp that said he, a shepherd of peace, was nobler than
you, a sheep of war. On the latter, Muste cannily knew it could easily
be the other way. He wrote in 1965 that "the man who goes into war
having seriously thought his way to his decision is on a higher moral
level than the smug pacifist who has no notion of the ambiguities and
contradictions the decision involves."

During the years of the antiwar movement, Muste's ideas had
special topicality. Never once did he advocate destruction of property, or storming a police line or even inconveniencing the innocent
citizen. Stunts, capers and fits may hypo the emotions of the pro-
tester and perhaps satisfy a need to reject authority, but as an effective stance against war and cruelty, what does it do? Muste's writing
is full of that hard lesson—to oppose the killing and violence of war
means more than a tantrum spree of weekend outrage or a fluency in
the slogans of fashion. It is a life's vocation, based on the astute (a
favorite Muste word) use of the mind and heart. The test is not how
far you go to stop war, but how deep. How deep into yourself to be
sure one's motives are pure, that everything vulgar is removed from
one's tactics and knowing that the institutions of war are the enemy,
not the warriors. Going deep also means, most importantly to Muste,
always being open to "the world of possibility."

Muste was born in 1885 in the Netherlands, in Zierikzee, a town
he jokingly put on a level with the American Podunk. His parents—a
coachman father and a househearty mother—were devout Dutch Reform churchgoers who combined the Old and New Testaments in

133

naming their son Abraham Johannes. The family took a steamer to America in 1891 and settled in Grand Rapids, Michigan. An early experience in the boyhood of Muste was looking into the grounds of the town's old soldiers' home; he romanticized the veterans as he saw them take walks into town. What glamorous figures they seemed. As an adult, in his autobiography—written as sketches for *Liberation* magazine—Muste recalled the sadder reality: "It was to be quite a few years before I knew that what my heroes went down town for was booze, and that veterans of wars are not always, not nearly always, heroic noblemen who volunteered to lay down their lives that some great cause might not perish from the earth." So began the education of a pacifist.

Muste went to the small Hope College in Michigan; beefed heavy with Latin, Greek and Bible study, he came East after graduation to study for the ministry, ending up, at twenty-four, as pastor of a church in upper Manhattan. When World War I came, Muste had read enough of Tolstoy, Gandhi and Quakers like Rufus Jones to embrace pacifism as a way of life, not merely as a way of thinking. His decision caused trouble; now in Boston, his congregation treated him like a traitor to the cause of America's war. This agreed with Theodore Roosevelt's famous warning that "the clergyman who does not put the flag above the church had better close his church, and keep it closed." Muste, unable to fight that mentality, left his good Boston Christians to their war, and went on to organize workers in the Lawrence, Massachusetts, textile mills. The authorities clubbed and jailed him for telling the forgotten workers they had a right to a fair wage. Struggling to control the strikers, Muste slowly convinced them not to outfight the police and the owners but to outsmart them. The strike succeeded.

By now an active unionist, Muste settled in for the next twelve years to teach at the Brookwood Labor College outside of New York. Gradually, though, he lost faith in pacifism and drifted into what were called "revolutionary politics," but which then and now means the same—reaching for a bomb or a gun in a crunch. He read Marx, savored Lenin and went to Norway to meet Trotsky. They were architects of great goals, and Muste liked that, but in the end they built their dreams of world peace with the tool of world conflict. And what did that do in the end, but pile higher the bodies?

In a Paris church in 1936, much like the experience of Paul Claudel years before, Muste had a reconversion to pacifism and religion. In the style of returned prodigals, he stood even firmer now that he knew how easily one can fall. "My earlier experience," he wrote, "was helpful to me in my attempts to develop nonviolent methods and a more revolutionary pacifist movement in later years. If people tell me there is no clearly defined nonviolent way to deal with a situation, then I answer that we have got to experiment and find one. God knows, we have experimented long enough with other methods."

For the next thirty-one years, until his death in a New York hospital in 1967—a quick, peaceful death after eighty-two years of seeing it all—Muste threw in with almost every legitimate peace group to be formed: the Fellowship of Reconciliation, SANE, Committee for Nonviolent Action, the War Resisters League, American Friends Service Committee and the others. More than a few pain-in-the-necks belong to these groups, and often Muste had full hands stopping the office wars flaring between the peacemakers. The best source of his thought is in the thick collection of lectures and writings gathered by Nat Hentoff in 1967 (*The Essays of A. J. Muste,* Bobbs-Merrill). A few years earlier, Hentoff wrote a low-key but thorough biography of Muste, *Peace Agitator.* Both books help to pin down what is often seen mistakenly as the freest-floating of beliefs, pacifism.

Instead of being a way of ducking the force of violence, Muste's pacifism was a method of meeting it with the more powerful force of non-violent resistance. In nearly all his essays on pacifism, he returns to that. "To be effective, those who work for peace must remember that one major reason previous peace efforts have failed is that military and political leaders know that the overwhelming majority of people who take part in those campaigns will consent to be conscripted again when they are called upon. Politicians are not so dumb as not to realize that such paper votes and resolutions can be largely discounted. What is needed is *active* refusal to support violence under *all* conditions." To members new in the peace movement, who might still believe all you need is a good heart and a catchy picket sign, the fatherly Muste advised his children otherwise: "When you're primarily resisting, you have to be careful not to hate, not to win victories over human beings. You want to change people, but you don't want to defeat them."

Unlike the idealist who strains too much, Muste was never messianic, nor did he feel guilty about being a human being who needed pleasures. A story is told of a young disciple's first awesome meeting with the master. "A. J. Muste walked in. I thought of his past revolutionary activities and his consistent courage in working for peace. I waited eagerly for his first word. A. J. looked around, and asked, 'How did the Dodgers make out yesterday?' I was shocked."

Dissent, civil disobedience, non-violent resistance—Muste never believed these actions were anything but the normal behavior of a calm man who sees the world gone mad. The secret of radicals like Muste is that they have no capacity for adjustment to what is truly radical—the horror of another bombing raid, another lap in the arms race, another militarist calling for more defense money. That is the radicalism worth worrying about, he said; it departs insanely from what the earth and its people need, a chance for peaceful social change. Without it, there is only a wilderness—one from which Muste cried for the better part of history's most violent century, the twentieth.

SELECTED BIBLIOGRAPHY OF A. J. MUSTE

Non-Violence in an Aggressive World. New York: Ozer, 1972.
Not by Might: Christianity, the Way to Human Decency (bound with *Of Holy Disobedience*). New York: Harper, 1947.
Of Holy Disobedience. Wallingford, Pa.: Pendle Hill, 1952.
Hentoff, Nat., ed. *The Essays of A. J. Muste.* New York: Simon and Schuster, 1970 (paperback).

Aldo Leopold

WHO IS AMERICA'S GREATEST NATURALIST? Names like Thoreau, Muir, Audubon, Burroughs, even Edwin Way Teale, are proposed. It is a hard question, but because we have more than one definition of *greatness*—one definition per citizen—many would choose none of the above. Instead, Aldo Leopold receives the highest ranking. It is hard to estimate the influence of Leopold, but in these frightening days of strip mine machines ten stories high and the government cheerleading oil-men to gash holes even in the ocean's floor, his responsiveness to the sanctity of the land continues to be a force among those who realize the rhythms of the earth are our rhythms.

At his death in 1948—while helping a neighbor put out a grass fire—Aldo Leopold had spent most of his career in quiet conservation jobs: nearly twenty years with the U.S. Forestry Service, teaching game management at the University of Wisconsin and serving on the inevitable commissions. The most important event of his life came when he satisfied his personal yearnings for "the wild country" and bought a farm in southern Wisconsin. Out of this experience, a try for salvation that all lost souls can understand, came Leopold's only two books: *A Sand County Almanac* and *Round River*. Neither saw completion during his lifetime; the two have been reissued by Ballantine in one paperback. It is a volume of both power and grace, full of sensibilities that recognize that man is only a recent invitee on the list of the earth's house guests; our rude manners, Leopold says in his hoping moments, are only temporary. "Nothing could be more salutary at this stage than a little healthy contempt for a plethora of material blessings," he wrote. No shelf that gives honored space to *Walden* should not also have *Sand County Almanac*.

The sand-soiled farm that Leopold settled on was previously owned by a bootlegger who let the property run to pot: the trees were diseased, roots were tangled and rocks littered the pastures. Amid this depression, though, Leopold came to understand that Nature works in cycles in which nothing is wasted. The diseases and tangles of his woodlot made it "a mighty fortress, unequaled in the whole county." A family of racoons sought out his woodland because it could hide from hunters under the roots of a half-uprooted maple. Wild bees flocked to his hollowed oaks. Chickadees, grouse and rabbits were attracted. "The real jewel of my disease-ridden woodlot is that prothonotary warbler. He nests in an old woodpecker hole . . . in a dead snag overhanging water. The flash of his gold-and-blue plumage amid the dank decay of the June woods is in itself proof that dead trees are transmuted into living animals, and vice-versa. When you doubt the wisdom of this arrangement, take a look at the prothonotary."

The theme of interdependence is constant. Leopold once went hunting as a boy and had emptied his rifle into a mother wolf. "We reached the old wolf in time to watch a fierce green fire dying in her eyes. I realized then, and have known ever since, that there was something new to me in those eyes—something known only to her and to the mountain. I was young then, and full of trigger-itch; I thought that because fewer wolves meant more deer, that no wolves would mean hunters' paradise. But after seeing the green fire die, I sensed that neither the wolf nor the mountain agreed with such a view."

Had Leopold written only as a chronicler of wolves and other home-body beasts read out of the party, he might be dismissed as another stampeding romantic. But his almanac shows him to be more than that. He speaks of "the biotic community," one in which man is a member not a master. "Conservation is a state of harmony between men and land. By land is meant all of the things on, over, or in the earth. Harmony with land is like harmony with a friend; you cannot cherish his right hand and chop off his left. That is to say, you cannot love game and hate predators; you cannot conserve the waters and waste the ranges; you cannot build the forest and mine the farm. The land is one organism. Its parts, like our own parts, compete with each other and co-operate with each other. The competitions are as much a part of the inner workings as the co-operations. You can regulate them—cautiously—but not abolish them."

Leopold never reduced his argument to the mere crankiness that

138

man is a natural destroyer. We don't do it naturally, we do it un-thinkingly. "To build a road," he said, "is so much simpler than to think of what the country really needs." And then, in a reference written twenty-five years ago but applicable to such memorable items as Richard Nixon's habit of seeking relaxation by cruising California's freeways, he notes: "Everywhere is the unspecialized motorist whose recreation is mileage." The reign of the automobile was only beginning in the 1930s and 1940s when Leopold wrote, but even then he saw its threat to the land: "The retreat of the wilderness under the barrage of tourists is no local thing. . . . Take a look, first, at any duck marsh. A cordon of parked cars surrounded it. Crouched on each point of its reedy margin is some pillar of society, automatic ready, trigger finger itching to break, if need be, every law of commonwealth or commonweal to kill a duck. That he is already overfed in no way dampens his avidity for gathering his meat from God."

Without doubt, Leopold would be put in good spirits by the many wildlife and conservation groups now on watch against the land exploiters. "The case for a land ethic would appear hopeless but for the minority which is in obvious revolt against these 'modern' trends," he writes. To be effective, though, a land ethic must be seen not as something written up by a committee [as a humanist society tried to do recently, in offering the world its ponderous manifesto for "new directions"] but a process of social approval for right actions and social disapproval for wrong ones. Leopold believed that nothing as important as a land ethic is ever written; instead, it is an intellectual and emotional development, one that will happen in this country only when we experience an "internal change in our intellectual emphases, loyalties, affections and convictions."

Is such a change possible? Perhaps, but negative evidence pours in. The Interior Department reports that the nation's fuel supply would be vastly increased by extracting oil from the shale deposits in such states as Colorado, Utah and Wyoming. But, the report said, vegetation and wildlife would be destroyed and the water supplies lowered. Thus, a bizarre equation is created: we will ruin the land of the West to get gasoline for the cars of the East, the air of which—we are told daily now—is already hazardous with auto fumes. So it is not true that the twain of East and West will not meet: destruction is joining them.

A number of laws already exist that are meant to "preserve and protect" the land, but the despoiling goes on. Under the National

Seashore Act passed by Congress in 1964, for example, Fire Island in New York was to have its fragile barrier beach kept from exploitation. But a citizens group has been forced to file suit—for the second time—asking the Interior Department to take action.

If we can't get the old laws enforced, what is the sense in passing new ones? Interior Department officials complain that they can't protect Fire Island because they lack money and manpower, but the money for such needs comes from Congress, the same one now promising to save the republic with a land-use bill. To the citizen on the beach, though, it is a case of more laws but less land.

No changes—the meaningful kind Leopold spoke of—are likely to happen until land use is seen more as a matter of ethics than economics. This is difficult because it offers the lone citizen few emotional satisfactions. How can he damn the promoters and developers who tear up the land for profit while he himself keeps using gadgets run on electricity powered by strip-mined coal? What's the difference? In both cases, a wasteland is created, with no ethics to irrigate it. Until a large enough number of citizens assume responsibility personally, one fact remains: we have not only left the land for the cities but, worse, we have left behind also any kind of feelings for that land.

Were Leopold living today, it is easy to imagine the message we would send him: be reasonable, Congress is passing environmental bills, but we still need oil, coal and lumber to remain Number One in the world. Number One? Leopold would ask in shock. "The shallow-minded modern who has lost his rootage in the land assumes that he has already discovered what is important; it is such who prates of empires, political or economic, that will last a thousand years. It is only the scholar who appreciates that all history consists of successive excursions from a single-starting point, to which man returns again and again to organize yet another search for a durable scale of values. It is only the scholar who understands why the raw wilderness gives definition and meaning to the human enterprise."

SELECTED BIBLIOGRAPHY OF ALDO LEOPOLD

Game Management. New York: Scribner's, 1949.
A Sand County Almanac and Sketches Here and There. New York: Oxford University Press, 1949.
Sand County Almanac: With Other Essays on Conservation from Round River. New York: Oxford University Press, 1966.

T. Thomas Fortune

THANKS TO DIGGING BIOGRAPHERS who know an eager audience awaits the buried treasures of history, we have been learning much recently about William E. DuBois, Marcus Garvey, Frederick Douglass and other Negroes of bravery who have influenced American life. We need to know about their thoughts and their past times—the mid-nineteenth and early twentieth centuries—because we are still confused about the American Negro in present times. Many are confused not only about the feelings, rights and responsibilities of these twenty-two million citizens but even about their correct name. Linguistic fashion, as fickle as clothes designer fashions, prefers "the blacks" right now rather than "Negro." Yet, as Professor J. Mitchell Morse of Temple University said in a recent essay, when British colonialists and white trash wanted to insult their slaves, the term black was used. Black was ugly, Negro was beautiful.

Along with DuBois, Garvey and Douglass, the historical richness of American life one hundred years ago runs deep with men and women whose genius went unrecognized because they were the wrong color, and that made all else about them wrong, too. Few illustrate this better than T. Thomas Fortune, an ex-slave who from 1885 to his death in 1928 was a journalist of power and nerve. Fortune is an unknown name today, perhaps because he left behind no important books or followers, perhaps because so much of his energy was used surviving mental illness, destitution, a flawed marriage. Then also, he refused to adopt the role that whites love to assign blacks—"spokesman for his race." Better to deal with a spokesman than the social sufferings of the millions he speaks for. Most of what we know of Thomas Fortune, whose hard journalism spoke only for himself, can be found in the recent and excellent work of

141

scholarship by Professor Emma Lou Thornbrough of Butler University in her biography *T. Thomas Fortune.* The University of Chicago Press published the work as part of its series on Negro American biographies and autobiographies.

No profession was more closed to blacks during the Reconstruction than newspapering. A white press flourished, but Fortune had no way of entering it. His first job, after leaving the Deep South at eighteen and a youth of devouring books, was in the printshop of *The People's Advocate,* a Washington D.C., weekly. Fortune was a Howard University student—three years of formal schooling had qualified him—and began a column. The paper paid little and he left soon for New York and another paper. In the 1880s, Negro weeklies—always four pages—had small circulations, small staffs and small chances for survival. One exception, if only on the last count, was the *Globe,* and Fortune wrote for it. Opinions interested him more than events, so he became an editorial writer. The reasons for a Negro press, he wrote, were "that white men have newspapers; that they are published by white men for white men; give, in the main, news about white men; and pitch their editorial opinions entirely in the interest of white men. . . . Can we reasonably expect other men to use their lungs to cry out for us when we are wronged and outraged and murdered? If we do, let us look at the white papers of the South and learn from them the necessary lesson, that the only way we can hope ever to win our fight is to arm ourselves as our opponents do, support those newspapers alone that support us, and support those men that support us." The Globe's prestige came from its editorial page. Professor Thornbrough noted that throughout Fortune's "life he held the view that the editorial page was the most vital of any newspaper. When at one point it was necessary as an economy measure to reduce the size of the *Globe,* he announced that other matters would be decreased, but the editorial page would remain intact."

Like any editorial writer worthy of his deplorings, Fortune could rankle people not only on one side of an issue but on both sides. When Frederick Douglass married a white woman, Fortune criticized those Negroes who opposed intermarriage. Negroes, he wrote, "are always prating about the unreasonable prejudices of other people and yet show, when occasion presents itself, prejudices just as narrow and unreasonable." As for whites, "we are surprised at the amount of gush which intermarriage inspires in this country. It is in strict keeping with all the sophistries kept alive by the papers and the people about the colored people."

Fortune again took them on two at a time when he denounced the Democrats as "the party of stupidity" which "learns nothing and forgets nothing" and denounced the Republicans as "a mean, cunning, treacherous organization." Fortune correctly saw what men like Jesse Jackson and Geno Baroni are talking about now: "The hour is approaching when the laboring classes of our country, North, East, West and South, will recognize that they have a common cause, a common humanity and a common enemy. . . . When the issue is properly joined, the rich, be they black or be they white will be found on the same side; and the poor, be they black or be they white, will be found on the same side."

Fortune was a close friend of Booker T. Washington, a strange alliance in view of Fortune's total rejection of Washington's "get along" philosophy. As a way of scorning accommodationism, pushed from Tuskegee, Fortune founded the Afro-American League. The term *Afro* is now common, but in 1890 he wrote: "There are some laws which no self-respecting person should be expected to obey. No man is compelled to obey a law which degrades his manhood and defrauds him of what he has paid for. When I willingly consent to ride in a 'Jim Crow Car' it will be when I am a dead Afro-American." Independent from Washington's "get along" view, Fortune never joined with Marcus Garvey's "get out" belief, the back-to-Africa movement, either.

The *Globe* went bankrupt and Fortune started, as sole owner, *The Freeman,* and still later went to *The Age.* He continued to write thundering editorials, as was the style then, but he also learned the art of understatement in which the reader is served more by explaining subtleties and shading than by denouncing evils, which any fool can do. Inevitably, Fortune was seen as an agitator. In 1900, following a speech, in which he said that for every Negro killed in a riot at Wilmington, Delaware, a white should have been killed, the white press took that one loose remark as an excuse to devastate all of Fortune's thinking. A *Washington Evening Star* editorial said Fortune was an enemy of his own people, that he should be suppressed. *The Washington Post*, also hostile to Fortune, joined in. When someone suggested that Fortune and the editor of the *Post* should reconcile their differences, Fortune replied: "Get together? Not much. There is no man or combination of men who can construct a platform on which the editors of the *Age* and *Post* could stand two minutes without a hand to hand fight."

143

Throughout his life, Fortune had no money and little job security, and lived with constant mental and physical pain; all that, plus racism. Toward the end of his life, in 1927, he was called "the beloved dean of Negro journalism" by the National Negro Press Association. But what could the honor have meant, when he was so little honored by a steady income or steady audience? He was worn out and soon to die. To the end, he kept his newspaperman's skepticism, in this case, a suspicion about the good will and cooperation of whites. On his death, the *Amsterdam News* called Fortune "a young old man, a New Negro, who loved America, while recognizing much in it to hate."

SELECTED BIBLIOGRAPHY OF T. THOMAS FORTUNE

Black and White: Land, Labor and Politics in the South. New York: Arno Press, 1968.
Thornbrough, Emma Lou. *T. Thomas Fortune: Militant Journalist.* Chicago: University of Chicago Press, 1972.

Paulo Freire

IN LATIN AMERICA, few areas are deeper sink holes of poverty than northeast Brazil. Hunger, illiteracy and disease have beaten down the defeated poor with daily cruelties, and all the while the military regime talks up the need for industrial development and tighter police security. Few have gone into the backlands of northeast Brazil to work, and fewer still have stayed to succeed. Among the latter, Paulo Freire stands out. Working in the rural villages, Freire mostly taught reading and writing among illiterate adult peasants. He discovered that the conditions of poverty passed from parents to children less because of inherited ignorance or lethargy than because the poor often fear freedom. They "prefer this security of conformity with their state of unfreedom to the creative communion produced by the pursuit of freedom. . . . Self-depreciation is a characteristic of the oppressed, which deprives from their internalization of the opinion the oppressors hold of them. So often do they hear that they are good for nothing and are incapable of learning anything—that they are sick, lazy and unproductive—that in the end they become convinced of their own unfitness."

Freire's work is gaining recognition in the United States, though he runs the risk of being glamorized by the counter-culture hip as another Third World messiah come to save the masses. Freire has pulled in fat lecture fees in New York but he has backed away from having his thought packaged into cocksure slogans like Illich's "de-schooling society." Instead, and perhaps purposely to ward off panhandle followers, Freire's major work, *Pedagogy of the Oppressed* (Herder and Herder), is a difficult, dry and slow book. One reading is not enough. Increasingly, articles on Freire are appearing in North America, but mostly in small circulation journals devoted to what is

145

timeless, not only timely. A few universities are offering courses on Freire's thought, including Michigan State. Professor Brady Tyson of American University believes that Freire's education philosophy may produce an alliance for progress where there really is progress.

At one time in Brazil—the early 1960s—Freire's methods of education were evolving into a successful national movement. It didn't last, though. As if to prove that Freire was on to something, the new bully government of 1964 imprisoned him without charges, labeling his work as—what else?—communistic. Freire was released after seventy days and took exile in Chile. From 1964 to 1969, he worked in the villages and is credited with awakening much of the country's sleeping political potential. Currently, Freire works in Geneva as head of the educational division of the World Council of Churches.

A basic theory of Freire is that education is more a matter of *knowing* than learning. When a person is taught to read and write, "the illiterate is no longer a person living on the fringe of society, a marginal man, but rather a representative of the dominated strata of society, in conscious or unconscious opposition to those who, in the same structure, treat him as a thing. Thus, teaching men to read and write is no longer an inconsequential matter of *ba, be, bi, bo, bu,* of memorizing an alien word, but a difficult apprenticeship in naming the world." As an example of an act of knowing, Freire talks about a group of peasants in the agrarian reform of Chile who took part in a literacy program. They wrote words with their tools on the dirt roads where they worked. When asked why he hadn't learned to read and write, a peasant answered, "Before the agrarian reform, I didn't even think. Neither did my friends. It wasn't possible. We lived under orders. We had only to carry out orders. We had nothing to say." This is the culture of silence, a recurring phrase in *Pedagogy of the Oppressed.*

As Montessori and Jacques Ellul before him, Freire does not believe that education can be neutral. Either it leads to social change or social control. Too often—in some areas of Latin America it is always—control is the result. Traditional education presumes that the student sits before the teacher like an empty bowl, ready to have facts poured in; when full, the student is graduated and sets out to occupy the shelf-space of society's orderliness. Not only has the student filed away bits of information but he himself is soon part of society's filing cabinet. Freire scorns such stifling styles of education as mere transferrals of information. "The students are not called upon to know, but to memorize the contents narrated by the teacher. Nor do the students practice any act of cognition, since the object towards which that act should be directed is the property of the teacher rather than a medium evoking the critical reflection of both teacher and students. Hence in the name of 'preservation of culture and knowledge' we have a system which achieves neither true knowledge nor true culture." What is needed is critical consciousness, what Freire calls *conscientization:* an awareness of one's dignity and choosing forms of political participation to protect and bolster that dignity.

Freire's thought has much of Whitehead and Teilhard in it, especially in his idea that the creation of the world is not finished but still goes on. "As a child in northeast Brazil, I knew many priests who went out to the peasants saying, 'Be patient. This is God's will. And anyway, it will earn heaven for you.' Yet the truth of the matter is that we have to earn our heaven here and now, we ourselves. We have to build our heaven, to fashion it during our lifetime, right now. Salvation is something to achieve, not just hope for."

Liberation is seldom authentic, because often the once-oppressed merely end up in puppet mimicry of the oppressor. The latter may have been joined or replaced but he is still the only model; Lenin replaces the czar, Castro ousts Batista, but what is really the difference between them? The tables may be turned but the poor are still kept from eating at them, "If the goal of the oppressed is to become fully human," writes Freire, "they will not achieve their goal by merely reversing the terms of the contradiction, by changing roles. . . . The moment the new regime hardens into a dominating bureaucracy, the humanist dimension is lost and it is no longer possible to speak of liberation." With notable sameness to Martin Luther King's philosophy Freire insists that "it is only the oppressed who, by freeing themselves can free their oppressors." In a meeting with some Chilean peasants, Freire summarized the complexity of the oppressor-oppressed relationship: *Yo no soy si tu no eres: yo no voy si to no vas*—I am not unless you are, I can not go forward unless you go forth.

Much of the news from Latin America tells about citizen uprisings—in Colombia, Guatemala, Brazil—and always the oppressed are driven back. Freire's method of education—based on the raw experience of the student and his willingness of heart to free both himself and his enslaver—has produced no striking results. He was asked recently if he could point to any instance where peasants have overthrown local oppression, and he could show none. Yet many are convinced that Freire is neither another con-man nor even limited to Latin America. In 1972 the office of HEW Secretary Elliot Richardson had an education specialist who was using the Freire method to sensitize HEW to minority problems.

It is fitting that Freire is becoming known in the United States. Little oppression is found here in comparison with the severity of northeast Brazil, but we share a common culture of silence. Wealth, not poverty, is making objects out of most of us: who can keep count of, let alone actively resist, all the outrages? Freire speaks of an "invisible war" against the common citizens. He referred to Brazil but the front lines are here too.

SELECTED BIBLIOGRAPHY OF PAULO FREIRE

Education for Critical Consciousness. New York: Seabury, 1973.
Pedagogy of the Oppressed. New York: Herder and Herder, 1972.

Harry Caudill

WHEN TALK TURNS TO AMERICA'S best crime writers, names like Raymond Chandler or Rex Stout are spoken. Another crime writer is at work, though, except the murders and thieving he describes are not committed against fictional people but against the defenseless and silent hills of Appalachia. Harry Caudill, a lawyer from the timber slopes of eastern Kentucky, a gentle and modest man, has been a crime writer for the past twenty years, ever since ruthless coal companies began strip mining the region for the black treasure. If there is any difference in the crime writing of Harry Caudill and the others, it is the lack of mystery in knowing who are the killers on the prowl. The strippers do it openly, protected by state laws and civil laws but not the one that counts—the law of Nature. Yet, the horror that killers of the land are on the loose is less tragic than realizing that only a few citizens like Harry Caudill are trying to stop them.

Caudill is a regional worker, a plodder who prefers to pry open the vents of one small hell rather than attack, with melodramatics, entire legions of devils. He is known outside of the mountains in the surface way that people understand Dorothy Day in the Bowery, or the late Hodding Carter in Mississippi, or Robert Roessel among the Navajos; we aren't sure precisely what these restless souls are up to, but the last time we looked—a sideward glance at most—it seemed to be vaguely productive.

"I was born in the Cumberland region of Kentucky," he writes in *My Land Is Dying* (Dutton), a small but powerful volume. "Its expiring loveliness is a part of me. But the same forces that are bringing ruin to Appalachia are now a threat wherever technological competence is yoked with human avarice and folly. Whenever the profit motive is still exalted as a virtue, the urge to acquire and to consume becomes a frenzy. In our own nation, industry, the banks, farm organizations and labor unions, the churches and foundations, and every aspect of government continually whip up and urge on this almost mindless drive. Our institutions stand guard over the status quo in a time when only sweeping changes in attitude and practice can save us from our own human folly. This generation may be the last one granted the opportunity to act before it is too late."

Doomsday talk is an easy commodity, but with Harry Caudill it is no vacuous prattling: he speaks from scenes of doomsday landscapes left barren and scarred by the strip mine companies. Descriptions of the devastation are common, though it is hard to imagine twenty-two story scooping machines with multi-ton blades gulping into hillsides as casually as diners munching on rolls. Mountains have no feelings but mountain people do. Caudill's writing is filled with accounts of what strip mining is doing to the land, but more important, what it does to the victims. He tells about a neighbor in Knott County, Kentucky, standing on the porch of her home one afternoon. Up the hollow came the bulldozers, heading for land that included the family cemetery. The woman, eighty years old, tried shouting that the graves of her children lay in front of them, but the helpless old woman was ignored. Shortly after, the greedy machines puffing at the earth, the children's coffins were flung out of the ground and tumbled over the hill. Saying that the coal was being dug for the Tennessee Valley Authority, Caudill remarked "that all this happened in America and under the protection of the American flag. The Congress, swathed in the bland unconcern that has caused millions of citizens to despise their own government, took no note of these events. There were, instead, murmurs that the lights must not be allowed to go out."

This reference to the lights concerns the frequent and preachy warnings of the coal lobby: if strip mining is banned then an "electric power crisis" may result, because of a coal shortage, and then all you reformers and other pests will be sorry. Caudill, who has long been water proofed to the leaky logic of the coal companies, has a different view. "If you're worried about our lights going out," he wrote, then "consider slowing coal exports to Japan. It is ironic that during World War II we ravaged our land for fuel to put out the lights in the Japanese empire; now we tear up our land for coal to keep those same lights burning."

150

Caudill lives in Whitesburg, part of the Cumberland Plateau, where he practices law in mountain courthouses. The young and unattached no longer flock in large numbers to Appalachia in the summer—the pulley of more fashionable causes tugs at them—but among the small numbers who do come, Caudill's 1962 book, *Night Comes to the Cumberlands*, is carried like a sacred text. He was inspired to write it when on visiting a coal camp school to be the commencement speaker for seven eighth graders the children sang "America The Beautiful," but their community was America the ugly; the land was ravaged by coal operators and the children's fathers were either killed by mining accidents or wheezing with silicosis. "These broken men," Caudill wrote, "are part of the price America has paid for her industrial pre-eminence, though the Madison Avenue firms never mention them in the expensive ads they devise for their coal-mining clients. Their pain and poverty are a hidden part of the highly touted 'American standard of living'."

Caudill often comes to Washington to give testimony before one committee or another. Sleeping Congress has an immense storage bin of yawns for citizens who come begging and pleading action, and it was only slightly different for Caudill. He asked that the politicians come to eastern Kentucky to see the ruination themselves. Surprisingly, a few months later two senators did visit the area—by "official tour" helicopter, not cars—but the grisly scenes were lost on them. They returned to Washington saying that strip mine laws were needed all right, but they should be moderate and reasonable. These are the honored code words, as old as the hills themselves, that flash the signal once again that the powerful few should keep on dominating the powerless many. Only one senator—Fred Harris—came on his own time, to get his shoes muddied and his eyes opened the way Caudill expected. Ban the stripping in six months, Harris concluded.

Harry Caudill's blood and name go back for dozens of decades in the rich culture of Kentucky life, to his grandfather's grandfather who settled in Letcher County in 1792. Few Americans have a deeper sensitivity to roots than the mountain people. Precisely because these roots are being torn out, Caudill speculates that "perhaps the years ahead of us will produce what we most need: advocates for those yet unborn. The present has many voices clamoring on their own behalf: big and little business, farmers, workers, professional groups, the black, red and Chicano minorities—even welfare recipients—are becoming organized, and all are demanding more for themselves. Few and muted are those who speak for the millions waiting

151

to be born, to urge that something of the earth's goods be preserved in trust for them."

Though Caudill may not take comfort from it, citizen groups in the mountains have been organizing their power—not by sitting down before bulldozers but by standing up to the courthouse gangs and the statehouse lobbies. In West Virginia in 1972 the voters ousted Representative James Kee, a coal man who went down hard. Ohio has voted itself a strong strip mine law. So perhaps Harry Caudill's thinking has made a difference, that the bundle of beginnings he tied together twenty years ago has held well. Not only has he been right all these years about the sacredness of a land and a culture, but he remains present among us to say when we go wrong.

SELECTED BIBLIOGRAPHY OF HARRY CAUDILL

My Land Is Dying. New York: Dutton, 1973 (paperback).
Night Comes to the Cumberlands: Biography of a Depressed Area. Boston: Little, Brown, 1963.
The Senator from Slaughter County. Boston: Little, Brown, 1974.
The Mountain Call. Kermit, W. Va. April 1975. An interview with Harry Caudill, p. 3–8.

W. E. B. DuBois

ASMALL ART SHOP in Washington—an operation run by blacks—used to put out a large wall calendar every year. Along with vivid art work and the customary set-out of dates, the calendar noted the patriotically important days of each month. In January, Martin Luther King's birthday was noted. One turned to February expecting to find Lincoln and Washington highlighted; no, the only patriot to make it was W. E. B. DuBois. The artists made their point: to blacks conscious of their past and pressing for a future, DuBois was too sacred a figure to share a calendar page with any great white fathers, particularly a pair whose greatness is being questioned by many blacks and whites—Washington a slave-owner, Lincoln a freer of slaves only after it was politically safe.

DuBois, dead in 1963 after living almost forever to age ninety-five, rarely used the term revolution—a catchword now—but his career of writing, thinking and whipping up entailed exactly that: urging Negroes to revolt against white domination. More and more, DuBois is being seen as the mastermind of current black protest and resistance, an early muscle of black strength whose ideas still flex with increasing power. His Niagara statement of 1905 demanded "manhood rights" for black people. "How shall we get them?" he asked at the end of that remarkable document. "By voting where we may vote; by persistent, unceasing agitation; by hammering at the truth; by sacrifice and work. We do not believe in violence, neither in the despised violence of the raid nor the lauded violence of the soldier . . . we believe in John Brown, in willingness to sacrifice money, reputation and life itself. . . ."

By the end of his life, DuBois held firm to those words, though he had little to grip of black progress. In his personal life, many of

153

his once-close allies rejected him—even "the colored children ceased to hear my name"—and the white American government harassed him. He died in Ghana, not broken but certainly bitter.

"I was born by a golden river and in the shadow of two great hills," writes DuBois in his autobiography about his boyhood in Great Barrington, a Protestant Republican town in western Massachusetts. His mother, a maid, raised him; even then black fathers often could not make it with their families. DuBois became the first of what he called his "clan" to finish high school; the citizens of Great Barrington delighted in the young Negro's intelligence and pluck, their pride seeing him as living proof that the wicked people of the South did not appreciate its colored folks the way the enlightened North did. DuBois did not object to being promoted in this way, though he later saw that it made him withdrawn. "The Negroes in the South," he wrote, "when I came to know them, could never understand why I did not naturally greet everyone I passed on the street or slap my friends on the back."

DuBois made his delicate way to Fisk University in Nashville. Here he saw the reality of racism. "Murder, killing and maiming Negroes, raping Negro women—in the 1880s and in the southern South, this was not even news; it got no publicity; it caused no arrests; and punishment for such transgression was so unusual that the fact was telegraphed North."

After graduating from Fisk with an A.B., DuBois entered Harvard—as a junior. He thrived on the teaching and friendship of the university's great men, such as William James, Santayana, Josiah Royce. With further studies in Berlin—"I was the most conspicuously trained young Negro of my day"—DuBois chose sociology as a way of best resisting and converting white brutality. "I was going to study the facts, any and all the facts, concerning the American Negro and his plight. . . . My long term remedy was Truth: carefully gathered scientific proof that neither color nor race determined the limits of a man's capacity or desert."

In setting out to establish truth, DuBois joined all incurable idealists in history—he believed that once the truth surfaced men would believe it. That, of course, is why idealists generally burn out so early. Society's veins can take only the smallest injections of truth, and definitely not in the huge doses administered by the likes of DuBois. He writes in his autobiography of his surprise at the Supreme Court decision of 1954; he didn't think it could come that soon. Accordingly, he predicted—rightly, it now appears—it would take twenty-five to fifty years before the decision would be accepted in the towns and villages where blacks and whites live, not just on paper. Meanwhile, Negroes, through an "inner cooperative effort" must be smart and not be lulled by the German Jews who "assumed that if the German nation received some of them as intellectual and social equals, the whole group would be safe. It took only a psychopathic criminal like Hitler to show them their tragic mistake. American Negroes may yet face a similar tragedy. They should prepare for such an eventuality." Minus the slogans and the clenched fists—which symbolized a violence DuBois scorned—what is the recent black power movement if not a projection of that thought?

DuBois, by now a well-published and infighting writer with a base at Atlanta University, discovered the crucial irony of turn-of-the-century racism: blacks were worthless humanly but priceless economically. "This was the age of triumph for big business, for industry . . . run by white capital with colored labor." Blessed with this luck, the white politicians and businessmen pushed further and created fear and hatred among the lower classes of blacks and whites; too busy fighting each other, they would never realize their true exploiters were the powers in the legislatures and the board rooms. This was another seed, though, that flowers only now.

In 1910, DuBois joined the NAACP. As editor of the *Crisis* magazine, he goaded, egged on and whipped up his black readers to protest and resist. After twenty-four years, he left the organization; he came back again, then left again.

This shifting and turning symbolizes much of DuBois's later life, a sense of what he called "two-ness." His autobiography—published in 1968—runs with moving prose, though with occasional stumbles too (he swallowed whole the tour guides through Marxist and Maoist countries).

A few years ago, the editors of the *Berkshire Eagle* called for a memorial park in honor of DuBois in Great Barrington. Nothing doing, said the local American Legion, VFW and Knights of Columbus; we'll have no park in our town for some wild revolutionary who renounced his citizenship and became a Communist, which DuBois did at age ninety-three. The joke is on the town fathers, though. Not only was the park built, but Great Barrington is the same village where in August 1774, rampaging citizens chased out of town the red-gowned royal judges of King George. As the first act of revolutionary resistance, it led to the overthrow of an unresponsive government.

SELECTED BIBLIOGRAPHY OF W. E. B. DuBOIS

Dusk of Dawn: An Essay Toward an Autobiography of a Race Concept. New York: Schocken, 1968.

Souls of Black Folk. New York: New American Library, 1969.

Aptheker, Herbert, ed. *The Autobiography of W.E.B. DuBois: A Soliloquy on Viewing My Life from the Last Decade of Its First Century.* New York: International Publishers, 1968.

Logan, Rayford W., ed. *W.E.B. DuBois: A Profile.* New York: Hill and Wang, 1971.

156

John Muir

IN MARCH 1868, A YOUNG MAN with a strong survival instinct left the crowded East and arrived in the open city of San Francisco. One of the many newcomers who was lighting out for the territories, he could put up with San Francisco for only a day; even then, urbanity crushed in. He asked a native for the quickest route out of the din. "Where do you want to go?" inquired the townsman, to which the wanderer replied, "To any place that is wild." The directions must have been adequate; until his death in 1914, John Muir endlessly roamed the valleys, foothills, mountains and icelands of the West, a vacuum spirit that sucked in the nourishing loose ends of nature and fed on them as if no other riches existed.

Many consider John Muir to be America's most profound and most easily read naturalist. Although popular tastes often give that honor to Thoreau, next to Muir the nonconformist of Concord seems like a mere vacationer to wildness. The Sierra of California, the Yosemite and the coast of Alaska were to Muir as Walden was to Thoreau, not visited for a season but embraced for nearly the whole cycle of adulthood. As with many men of action, Muir had little time for book writing, his first one being published at age fifty-six. Yet he rarely let a day pass that some word or thought was not jotted on an odd piece of pocket-crammed paper, stowaway thoughts traveling secretly between his soul and heart. They eventually filled sixty volumes, much of it in the fluent style of the Transcendentalism then popular and all of it in the wisdom of a man who couldn't be bribed by civilization. Muir, in a third-person passage, said his writings gathered themselves as a result of "scribbling by flickering campfires when his body was numb with fatigue; or in the dark lee of some boulder or tree while the storm raged without; or tramping over a vast glacier, his fingers stiff with cold and his eyes blinded by the snow glare."

When he left the lowlands of San Francisco that day, Muir headed for the mountain pastures of the Sierra. Early the next spring, he jotted—almost pantingly—in his diary: "The night wind is telling the wonders of the upper mountains, their snow fountains and gardens, forests and groves; even their topography is in its tones. . . . Would I could understand them! The stream flowing past the camp through ferns and lilies and alders makes sweet music to the ear, but the pines marshalled around the edge of the sky makes a sweeter music to the eye. Divine beauty all. Here I could stay tethered forever with just bread and water, nor would I be lonely; loved friends and neighbors, as love for everything increased, would seem all the nearer however many the miles and mountains between us."

How does a man get to talk like that, without being put away? In Muir's case, the conversion bucked many odds, most of them imposed by his Scotch Calvinist father. At the Wisconsin family farm, Hickory Hill, Daniel Muir couldn't believe a son of his could relish the woodland or delight in animals. The father, a doleful tartar who needed to prove his virility, believed in fighting the harshness of Nature, not seeking out its softer serenity. One approached the forests and beasts with ax and gun, and the good Bible-carrier who used them best prospered most.

This is still largely the ethic of America in its conversation with the wild, filled with big talk of success and loud shouts that more-is-better. The whole environmental struggle today is basically that: exhaling from our national lungs the foul air of progress-at-any-cost that we now breathe unthinkingly.

Many believe that ecology is a new term. Actually, battles to save the land raged one hundred years ago and, unsurprisingly, John Muir, let them. Setting aside Yosemite as a national park captured his interest early. The merchants and speculators asked about Yosemite, "What are a few acres of trees and some herds of elk compared to the development of mining and lumber that will yield millions of dollars?" The axle of this logic has turned a thousand times since, whether the wheels of "progress" carry us to Adirondack timberlands or the oilfields of the North Slope. No one says anymore that "millions can be made"; that is too blunt. We now exploit Nature because of "national security," or "the energy crisis." And besides, a government report says it's safe.

Thanks to his articles in the old *Century* magazine, Yosemite became a national park in 1890. The victory put Muir even more on the watch for industrial cormorants busy against innocence. He had no doubts whose side he would choose in a conflict between nature and man: "Let a Christian hunter go to the Lord's woods and kill His well-kept beasts, or wild Indians, and it is well; but let an enterprising specimen of these proper, predestined victims go to houses and fields and kill the most worthless person of the vertical godlike killers—oh! that is horribly unorthodox, and on the part of the Indians atrocious murder. Well, I have precious little sympathy for the selfish propriety of civilized man, and if a war of races should occur between the wild beasts and Lord Man I would be tempted to sympathize with the bears."

Hard talk? Muir went further. "The world, we are told, was made especially for man—a presumption not supported by all the facts. A numerous class of men are painfully astonished whenever they find anything living or dead . . . which they cannot eat or render in some way what they call useful to themselves."

Libraries are beginning to carry some of the vast Muir literature in all its richness. Houghton Mifflin has published his works in the Sierra edition, from *A Thousand Mile Walk to the Gulf* to *John of the Mountains.* The essence of Muir's life can be had in the anthology selected by naturalist Edwin Way Teale; the Twayne series published an excellent critical guide to Muir's thought in a volume by Herbert F. Smith. *Not Man Apart* is the invaluable John Muir monthly newspaper sent to members of the Friends of the Earth. An application of his philosophy to the wilderness issues of today, the newspaper is available to nonmembers also.

Muir liked to say, echoing Thoreau, that his "profession was living." This put him in genuine communion with nature, that term being only a grand synonym for life itself. Long before Teilhard hinted that rocks and plants are not mere slugs of deadness, Muir understood that they also had claims to livingness. "Plants," he wrote, "are credited with but dim and uncertain sensation, and minerals with positively none at all. But why may not even a mineral arrangement of matter be endowed with sensation of a kind that we in our blind exclusive perfection can have no manner of communication with?"

It is foolish to go to Muir in hopes of "feeling good" about nature. Visit the garden club greenhouse for that. Muir is saying, come be a part of wilderness, if even for an afternoon or weekend. In Cuba once, he wrote about the growth of the agave plant: "It is said to make a mighty effort to flower and mature its seeds and then to die of exhaustion. Now there is not, so far as I have seen, a mighty effort or the need of one, in wild nature. She accomplishes her ends without unquiet effort." That is what Muir wants men to be a part of. It won't hurt, and most likely nature won't mind. It is tolerant of earthquakes, blizzards, storms and all manner of destruction. So it can tolerate human beings, too. Up to a point and provided we come with neither ax nor gun.

SELECTED BIBLIOGRAPHY OF JOHN MUIR

Gentle Wilderness: the Sierra Nevada. New York: Sierra Club Books, 1964 (distributed by Scribner's).
Letters to a Friend. Dunwoody, Ga.: Berg, 1973.
Story of My Boyhood and Youth. Madison: University of Wisconsin Press, 1965 (paperback).
A Thousand Mile Walk to the Gulf. Dunwoody, Ga.: Berg, 1969.
Gunsky, Frederic R., ed. *South of Yosemite: Selected Writings of John Muir.* Garden City, N.Y.: Natural History Press, 1968.

George Orwell

LIKE KAFKA AND *THE TRIAL* or Melville and *Moby Dick* or Joyce and *Ulysses,* George Orwell now sits on many shelves with a one-book identity: *1984,* the masterful anti-utopian novel he wrote as a dying man, has become not only a reference book for modern politics but is also in our daily speech. It is more than startled nervousness—fatalism pushing out optimism—that has many Americans convinced that much of the prophecy of *1984* is being fulfilled before us. We say 1984 has arrived when a politician talks to us in what Orwell called double-think: win peace by killing people, free men by controlling them. Does the following, written in an essay by Orwell in 1946, ring a familiar bell, pealing only lately in Southeast Asia? "Defenseless villages are bombarded from the air, the inhabitants driven out into the countryside, the cattle machine-gunned, the huts set afire with incendiary bullets: this is called *pacification.*" Little wonder we read *1984* and go no further into Orwell. After such calls as this, what truth could be left?

In Orwell's case, plenty. Any number of his other works—novels, essays, collections of columns—contain rhythms of clarity and style that reached their loudest beat in *1984.* "So long as I remain alive and well," he said in "Why I Write," "I shall continue to feel strongly about prose style, to love the surface of the earth, and to take pleasure in solid objects and scraps of useless information." Orwell was the rare liberal who believed that a thinking man should also be a thoughtful man—why bother to Save Mankind unless you also save the poor widow next door from eviction or starvation?; but he also had a windowpane curiosity through which everything alive was given entry. Hardly anything was missed, from his first book, *Down and Out in Paris and London,* to the burlesque novel *Keep the*

Aspidistra Flying, to *Animal Farm*, to the essays "Politics and the English Language" and "Freedom and Happiness." Any one of these is worthy of long study.

Like Whitman and Tolstoy, Orwell knew that two men fought within. "If you look into your own mind," he asked himself and the reader, "which are you, Don Quixote or Sancho Panza?" He answered: "Almost certainly you are both. There is one part of you that wishes to be a hero or a saint, but another part of you is a little fat man who sees clearly the advantages of staying alive with a whole skin. He is your unofficial self, the voice of the belly protesting against the soul. His tastes lie towards safety, soft beds, no work, pots of beer and women with 'voluptuous' figures. He it is who punctures your fine attitudes and urges you to look after Number One, to be unfaithful to your wife, to bilk your debts. Whether you allow yourself to be influenced by him is a different question."

Orwell's fat man generally stayed leashed, with only occasional breakaways to foolishness. Born in 1903 and dead in 1950, he went to preparatory school and on to Eton. He traveled to Burma at nineteen and, as a gangly, unshowy young man, worked five years as a policeman. On seeing British rule as a tyranny, he soon saw himself a part of it—the grimmest part since he was asked to club the luckless criminals and keep order on the streets for the queen's servants. "I never went into a jail" he said revealingly, "without feeling that my place was really on the other side of the bars."

Orwell came back to England dazed by a bad conscience and stirred by a haunting remembrance of the faces of docked prisoners, of begging peasants he turned away, of servants he physically beat. With no money and nothing to lose but his guilt, he sought out the poor and stepped-on in the slums of Paris and London. "What I profoundly wanted at that time," he later wrote, "was to find some way of getting out of the respectable world altogether." What Orwell saw and felt never left his consciousness, even though he left the low life and returned to his natural middle-class surrounding. In *The Road to Wigan Pier,* a personal report on the poverty of coal miners, he praises the welfare families he met; rather than buckling to the state because they were poor, the fathers and mothers took the dole and raised children on it. "It annoys the old ladies in Brighton," wrote Orwell, "but it is proof of the (poors') essential good sense; they realize that losing your job does not mean that you cease to be a human being . . . Families are impoverished, but the family system has not broken up."

Part of *Wigan Pier* was a hard look at socialism, a cure that Orwell personally believed in. The look was too hard for some of his friends, though. But in exposing the weaknesses of socialists—stop jerking your emotional knees to oppression, he said, and learn instead how to outsmart the oppressors—Orwell revealed a firm sense of fairness: cant was cant whether from the left or right. Even today, one can see the eyebrows of the zero population zealots raise in shock on reading that Orwell denounced birth control and contraception as lunacies, as "just another way they've found of bullying us."

Devoted to political solutions, Orwell nevertheless insisted that writers keep their purity. "Whatever else he does in the service of his party, a person should never write for it. He should make it clear that his writing is a thing apart. . . . He should not mind very much if his unorthodoxy is smelt out, as it probably will be. Perhaps it is even a bad sign in a writer if he is not suspected of reactionary tendencies today, just as it was a bad sign if he was not suspected of Communist sympathies twenty years ago."

A good place to start on Orwell—or start over, because who has not read some of him—is with the early novel, *Keep the Aspidistra Flying*. A broke poet, hounded by a nosey landlady, bedeviled by cut-down clothes, watery soup and empty pockets, Gordon Comstock was committed to a principled fight against the money ethic. The novel, much in the witty, detached style of today's Wilfred Sheed novels, describes how the poet gives up the fight against money not to become an impoverished loser but to be a middle-class winner—happy with a wife and an aspidistra flower in the cottage window.

In his own life, Orwell had struggled against the money god, but he appreciated the virtues and comforts of people who worked and saved. At age forty-two, royalties at last providing some security, his wife died, leaving Orwell with a small adopted child who he cared for with whole tenderness. The image is strange. This genius, restless and alone, scared and worried about the atom bombs, the ascendant power of scientists, the decay of language, but amid all these concerns of choler, including the writing of *1984*, caring for a child. What should be made of that? Perhaps only that Orwell had won out against the fat man within, a victory that is crucial for everyone to try for, even if we are the only ones to celebrate it, in our dying days with a child who knows nothing of our struggle.

SELECTED BIBLIOGRAPHY OF GEORGE ORWELL

Animal Farm. New York: New American Library, 1974 (paperback).

Collected Essays, Journalism and Letters: My Country, Right or Left. New York: Harcourt Brace Jovanovich, 1971 (paperback).

Orwell Reader: Fiction, Essays and Reportage. New York: Harcourt Brace Jovanovich, 1961 (paperback).

Howe, Irving, ed. *Nineteen Eighty-Four: Text, Sources, Criticism.* New York: Harcourt Brace Jovanovich, 1963 (paperback).

Luce, Robert B. *The Faces of Five Decades: Selections from 50 Years of The New Republic 1914-1964.* New York: Simon and Schuster, 1964, pp. 365-373, an essay on Orwell by Richard Rovere.

The Spiritual Life

"RETURN TO THE WORLD," an old monk once told the Greek writer Nikos Kazantzakis, who was attempting sanctity in a Sinai monastery. "In this day and age, the world is the true monastery; that is where you will become a saint."

That was startling advice to unload on a young man intent on seeking God and avoiding temptation. But Kazantzakis was humble enough to take it and hop the first donkey back to town. We cannot be certain if Kazantzakis achieved the kind of holiness that is associated with sanctity, but it is known that he intensely sought and valued the spiritual life. That is enough.

It was enough also for those whom I have included in this section. Some have had their virtue officially recognized by the Church, with days of honor set aside in the calendar of saints, while others will never undergo the politics of canonization. The trouble with the saints, the argument goes, is that they led lives of such perfection that mortals of average weakness see them as far beyond imitation. Halos never fit heads crammed with the thoughts and weaknesses of this supposedly wicked world. Little of this applies, though, to the genuine seeker of the spiritual life, or even to many who never go near a church or synagogue. It is more a question of what John Macquarrie noted: "To go out of oneself to commune with a Reality larger, deeper, purer than one's own being."

This is a kind of perfection that others can live with. It is the difference between the moral person and the moralizer. The latter is quick to see what is wrong with others, whereas the moral man looks for what is wrong with himself. This should not take a long time:

165

discovering our secret little methods of duping or gypping others, or our subtle way of self-puffery, none of this should become a lengthy research project because we know it already. We merely think that others don't know it. What is much harder to face, and act on, is what Albert Schweitzer spoke of: "Whatever you have received more than others in the way of health, in talents, in ability, in success, in a pleasant childhood, in harmonious conditions of home life—all this you must not take to yourself as a matter of course. You must pay a price for it. You must render in return an unusually great sacrifice of your life for other life."

This is what my companions here share in common. How exciting they make the spiritual life appear. And if only we could keep their examples before us. But religion today is often made repulsive by the spectacle of so many professionals of religion. Like an ecumenical trinity, Catholics, Protestants and Jews shuddered at the respectability that their Father Doctor McLaughlin, Reverend Doctor Billy Graham and Rabbi Korff (go become a doc, Rabbi!) conferred upon Richard Nixon. Cleverly, Nixon led the clergymen into the White House, inviting them to breathe in the presidential atmosphere and suck contentedly on the roots of power. In return, they need only bless—in their best Holy Joe voice—Nixon's politics. With all these holy pastors running in and out of the White House who would suspect that Nixon was inside trying to kill the Constitution, ignore the poor and do favors for the rich? As he went about demeaning us, it was not a surprise that Nixon sought to be sanctimonious. That was always the most disgusting part of him—his overbearing piety, of which his palace reverends symbolized. Together, king and jesters, they contrived to pull off the magic trick of passing off religiosity as religion, ignoring the truth that Michael Novak expressed: "The religious sense is a sense that needs effort, practice and exploration, like any other."

If Teresa, William Penn, Daniel and the others here are telling us anything, it is that. Begin some kind of exploration. It would be wise also to keep it to yourself. If talk is cheap, then talk about one's own spiritual life is even cheaper. It is even a form of masked egotism: I've found the truth, come be like me. The authentic person who has truly discovered something knows first that it is only a measure of the truth that has been found, and all it does is make him

166

a little more secure amid the world's absurdities and mysteries. It is this security that will be noticed by others; it is the creativeness of this security that will be cherished by others, as well, because it will enable them to feel a little less battered by life and possibly even cheered. Perhaps that is the best way of determining whether someone we know is quietly concerned with the spiritual life: does their strength overflow into my life?

The revolutions around the world—whether in lands like Chile or even in the eruptions of hate in families down the street ("but they seemed like such a happy couple")—all appear to rise from the sentiment expressed by Churchill when someone was trying to short-change Britain in 1944: "I will not be dealt with as part of a blob." This is what the practitioners of the spiritual life realize, a truth which obliges them to use their spirituality not as a homey psychological exercise—how good it feels to be good—but as means of paying homage to the uniqueness of each person around us, and perhaps in some way working to free the other person to the rich diversities of his life. There are no blobs, either in our immediate reach of family or friends, or in the other nations and cultures of the world.

How will this be realized? Some say we will need a long immersion in the brittleness of materialism to bring us to our senses, to be surrounded by so many tools, pills and technologies that the cataracts of progress will finally be removed from our eyes—we have been going backwards all these decades, with progress our "least" important product. Others publicly proclaim or privately worry that we are becoming another Roman Empire nearing decline, with nothing to save us from perishing. Still others depend on new weapons from the Pentagon, more speeches from politicians, more Valium or Librium. They depend on nations, they support regimes, they die for a leader. For myself, I believe there is an unseen fund of goodness in the world. I persist in feeling that it is nourished by the hidden contributions of millions of solitary persons whose only activity is seeking truth and trying to ease the world's suffering. These are the anonymous spirits who override the crudest insinuations of history— that man is no better, even worse, than the animals—and who every day perform deeds of hidden glory and silent joy. They contribute to the fund of the world's goodness by doing but also by being. They live out the advice a saint once gave: be only who you are but be that perfectly.

167

St. Benedict

NEXT TO OUR OWN CENTURY—the twentieth, that has seen Auschwitz, napalm and nuclear buildups that can kill us all many times over—perhaps the one other century that can offer a match in chaos is the sixth. In the West during this time, the Gothic War ravaged Italy for twenty years, causing more ruin than any earlier invasions of Attila, Genseric or other roving statesmen of that day. The progress of the Roman Empire—the citizens suffering famine and war, the arts being abandoned—was seriously slowed and in some places stopped. In the height of their genius and prosperity, the leaders of the empire equipped themselves with nearly everything except the one essential—a strong desire to survive. As the sun set on the West, a young Italian named Benedict had no thoughts of saving Europe, only a few thoughts about saving his soul; that would be trouble enough. Before his death in 547, however, Benedict had not only pulled off the second feat—with plenty to spare—but he also set the compass by which Europe would again find itself. The style of monasticism he founded did much to keep Christianity alive over the centuries.

As a close match for the biographical obscurity of humble St. Joseph, few facts are known about St. Benedict's life. He came from Nursia in the Apennine Valley, had a sister named Scholastica and was sent to Rome for a traditional liberal education. Precisely how long he stayed or what he did is not known. Apparently, though, the town was too fast for him; thinking it better that Rome should burn than he, Benedict packed up one day and settled in a remote hill town. Here, according to the thorough biography of Justin McCann (Image Books), "the whole trend of Benedict's life was towards self-effacement and the quiet service of God. He had fled from Rome to seek a life wherein his spirit might be free to commune with its Creator without interruption."

A lot of people, godly and otherwise, have tried that at one point in their life—"how I'd like to get away from it all"—but Benedict's flight to solitude was different: once he tasted the peace of it all, he thirsted for more. Instead of a return trip to town—"how I'd like to see the old gang just once more"—Benedict went farther into the hills. He became a hermit.

The word hermit has had a bad press in the last few centuries, including the ever-current cartoons of bearded characters carrying "End of the World" signs on downtown streets. But in the sixth century, hermits were respected—though absent—members of the neighborhood. (Often, respect came easiest as the absence grew longer.) The notion of holing up in the woods or the desert for a lifetime was based on one of the most familiar and least heeded parts of the New Testament: "Go sell what you have and give to the poor, and come follow me." The early Christian settlements in the deserts of Syria, Palestine and Egypt were begun by hermits taking those words literally. Even then, the eremitic and monastic styles of the West were borrowed from the East. As far as scholars can record, the first contemplative movement started during the Indian Enlightenment, a period about two centuries after David and six before Jesus. A few Brahminical Indians looked on the elaborate nonsense of their civilization and decided to scrap it. What kept these fellows from being mere cranks was that they did not scrap their civilization, only its elaborate nonsense. That set the tone for all following generations: to be a genuine contemplative, you first had to be a scrapper of nonsense.

Benedict easily qualified on that. So well, in fact, that he soon had the bother that hounds all successful hermits: followers. He tried to brush them off ("get lost"—what else would a practicing hermit advise?), but in time Benedict was persuaded to establish monasteries where disciples could live under his guidance. For the next forty years, large numbers came to him as children to a father. During this time, Benedict kept jottings which, codified after his death, became the seventy-three chapters of the Holy Rule. It is one of the world's major historical documents, dealing with perhaps the one art that Christians have always found the most agonizing: living with other Christians.

That is essentially the definition of a monastery. Anyone can make good time on the straight and narrow path if he or she travels

169

alone; but Christianity was a religion founded around a table and clearly meant to be communal, beginning with the family. St. Benedict's Rule is a master-plan for a colony of brothers who want to pray and work together. Even if one thinks religion is nonsense and faith a matter of blurred vision, it is hard to discount the historical fact that for fourteen hundred years the Rule has helped the members of thousands of Benedictine communities to live in fraternal peace. Who else has done that? Although modern Benedictines run schools and parishes, and often spin their wheels as fast as some Jesuits in trying to be "relevant," many outsiders of no faith see the Benedictines' most valuable contribution to society as one of witness. "See how they love one another"—this was promised as the one sure sign that would distinguish Christians from the others. Down the centuries, though, the sign has been hard to see; instead of loving one another, Christians have been as busy as anyone in waging wars, leading crusades or encouraging the neighborhood pogrom. Often the only place where Christians could be seen living in quiet kindness with each other was the Benedictine monastery. They carried it on.

This is not to romanticize the Benedictines. In their history, more than one abbot has been thrown into the well or over the wall by malcontents in the community. In the Rule itself, Benedict constantly warns against "murmuring," the sixth century term for griping or bitching. Nor have all the brethren been saints or near-saints, as depicted on the holy cards with fat-kid angels hovering over. Most of the saintliness has gone unrecorded. Even today in Benedictine monasteries—such as the well-known St. John's community in Minnesota where Eugene McCarthy was once a novice or in the lesser-known St. Anselm's Abbey in Washington—inevitably there is a father or brother doing some kind of lowly work who has reached the heights of service and charity.

The exactness of the Rule is perhaps one reason it has lasted. In chapter 48, for example, beginning with the famous words "idleness is the enemy of the soul," Benedict says: "The brethren must be occupied at certain hours in manual labor, and again at other hours in sacred reading." This anti-loafing advice was offered not only because manual labor was good for the soul and body but because economically the brothers would be independent. What good is a monastery that is not self-supporting, or one that is so rich that the members need not work? Down the centuries, Benedict's work-requirement rule has been justified: wealth has done in more monasteries than poverty. In fact, one of the troubles faced by some modern Benedictine communities is comfort and ease. How much have we truly sold and given to the poor, ask some brothers who see their own lives of material security contrasted with families down the road with no heat or bread.

Benedict believed mightily in authority and obedience—the modern parent could learn something from the Rule—but he also allowed room for human weakness. In Chapter 40, "Of the Measure of Drink," he hesitates to "appoint the measure of other men's living." Thus the brothers are allowed one pint of wine a day, but not without a sigh from Benedict: "Although we read that wine ought by no means to be the drink of monks, yet since in our times monks cannot be persuaded of this, let us at least agree not to drink to satiety."

Foreseeing that close living produces terrors that not even Satan could dream up, many chapters of the Rule are basic sociology—on receiving guests, on serving at table, on caring for the old, on sleeping (take off your knives, you wild ones, lest you be wounded while tossing), on handling the tools with reverence. Scholars have pored over the Latin text of the Rule as though it were a miniature Talmud. But unlike the latter—which often starts more arguments than it ends—the Rule offers a precise spirituality concerned with the daily and often dull mechanics of worshipping the Lord and serving the brothers. In case anyone in the community might forget, Benedict gives a final reminder in the next-to-last chapter: "Let (the fathers and brothers) bear with the greatest patience one another's infirmities, whether of body or character. Let them vie in paying obedience one to another. Let none follow what seems good for himself, but rather what is good for one another. Let them practice fraternal charity with a pure love. Let them fear God. . . ."

It is odd that in many of the American communes of today, the last thing the gathered free-spirits talk about is a rule. They say that good feeling and good vibes are enough, a statement that proves true until someone has to chop the wood or fix the frozen pipes. Authority, obedience and respect—these are also needed if a community is to survive the weather and its members. Yet interior freedom was much on the mind of strict St. Benedict as on that of any commune "leader" today. The difference is that the present commune assumes interior freedom is an automatic right, whereas Benedict says you earn it after years of work and patience. It is the last luxury to be won because personal interiority is the last mystery to·be faced.

SELECTED BIBLIOGRAPHY OF ST. BENEDICT

St. Benedict's Rule for Monasteries. Collegeville, Minn.: Liturgical Press, 1948.

Chapman, John. *St. Benedict and the Sixth Century.* Westport, Conn.: Greenwood, 1972 (reprint of 1929 edition).

McCann, Justin. *Saint Benedict.* New York: Sheed & Ward, 1937.

Wivdearr, Mary F. *St. Benedict: Hero of the Hills.* New York: Hill and Wang.

Rabbi Abraham Heschel

ABBI ABRAHAM HESCHEL, a survivor of the Holocaust and whose Jewish roots were deep into the Hasidism of his fathers, often told a story about the predicament of twentieth century man. Once upon a time in a kingdom long ago and far away, it happened that after the grain crop had been harvested and stored, it was discovered to be poison. Anyone who ate it went insane. The king and his advisers immediately took counsel as to what should be done. Clearly, not enough food was available from other sources to sustain the population. No choice existed but to eat the grain. All right, the king decided, let us eat it. But at the same time we must feed a few people on a different diet so that there will be among us some who remember that we are insane.

As one whose soul and intellect fed on a different diet, Abraham Heschel sustained a rare sanity in a career that saw him revered as both a wise teacher and a committed theologian. At his death in December 1972, Heschel was a stark rebuttal to the marketing of cheap religion—from the prayer breakfast Peales to the East Wing reverends—and his own life of sixty-five years affirmed his basic Judaic creed that "just to be is a blessing. Just to live is holy." What set Rabbi Heschel apart from those whose piety is easily mouthed, was the insistence that authentic religion is only for those whose moral sensitivity seeks abrasive struggle with ethical questions, because surviving the test of abrasiveness produces a fitness to wrestle with even more questions and issues. Kierkegaard spoke of the "leap of faith" but Heschel, in the tradition of prophets, called for the "leap of action." In the "deep sense," he wrote, "religion is two things. It is an answer to the ultimate problems of human existence, and it is a challenge to all answers. This is a deep ingredient of

173

existence—problems. And the tragedy of our education today is that we are giving easy solutions: be complacent, have peace of mind, everything is fine. No! Wrestling is the issue. Facing the challenge is the issue."

Although he came from a line of Hasidic rabbis and could discourse on the Talmud in four languages, Heschel's writing style in a row of books suggests that communicating truth was as crucial to him as seeking it. He risked being labeled a popularizer by giving his books such titles as *God in Search of Man* or *Man Is Not Alone,* but the theme of these works was the unpopular belief that "God is of no importance unless he is of supreme importance." He wrote about "radical amazement," which was a quality of wonder that tried to see life and the world freshly regardless of the repetition or single tones of it all. "To the prophets, wonder is a *form of thinking.* It is not the beginning of knowledge but an act that goes beyond knowledge; it does not come to an end when knowledge is acquired; it is an attitude that never ceases. There is no answer in the world to man's radical amazement."

Heschel was not accepted universally by American Jews, many of them either too busy building emotional gates to walk out of the Diaspora or lazily content to be mere Yom Kippur Jews and rational blend-ins the rest of the time. In 1965, the conservative community disapproved of Heschel visiting the Vatican; he paid no attention, holding that unless there is interfaith exchange, there is only inter-nihilism. Often the strongest appreciation of Heschel came from non-Jews. Thomas Merton, who received a visit from Heschel, called him "the greatest religion writer in America." Once when a group of Catholic nuns were stuck on the question of changing from their traditional dress to a more modern cut, they went to Heschel for advice. Anne Perkins, a worker at New York's Union Settlement and a friend of the rabbi, reports that she visited him once in his small book-cramped office at the Jewish Theological Seminary and talked of Christianity. "Would you want me to give up my religion?" he asked. Ms. Perkins said no. "I'm glad," Heschel answered, "we agree then."

The rabbi—a short man with a full Old Testament beard—was a professor of Jewish Ethics and Mysticism but he did not use his scholarship as a bunker to hide from the messiness of his time. He was issuing moral warnings about Vietnam as early as 1966, and was a major influence—*the* supreme Jewish voice, one observer said—in the peace movement in the hard years after. He sought peace in other wars, too, especially in the battles between parents and children. "In the past, it was the role of the father to lead the children through moments of exaltation. Whatever stood out as venerable and lofty was associated with the father. Now we are entering a social structure in which the father is becoming obsolete, and in which there are only three ages: childhood, adolescence and old age. The husband of the mother is not a father, he is a regular guy, a playmate for the boys, engaged in the same foibles and subject to similar impulses. Since he neither represents the legacy of the past nor is he capable of keeping pace with the boys in the pursuit of the future, his status is rather precarious. Children today experience their highest moments of exaltation in a children's world, in which there is no room for parents. But unless a fellowship of spiritual experience is reestablished, the parent will remain an outsider to the child's soul. This is one of the beauties of the human spirit. We appreciate *what we share*, we do not appreciate *what we receive*. Friendship, affection is not acquired by giving presents. Friendship, affection comes about by two people sharing a significant moment, by having an experience in common. You do not attain the affection of your teenage son by giving him an expensive car."

In parts of the Jewish community today, especially among families with young children, a renewal is occurring that seeks both a return to Judaic traditions and a rejection of cultural assimilation. One of the means to this renewal is through observing the dietary laws. Rabbi Heschel himself remained faithful to them throughout his life. Reinhold Niebuhr once asked him about it. "My friend," Heschel answered, "I will give you a strange answer. I observe the dietary laws because I do not understand them."

Robert McAfee Brown, the Protestant theologian, called this "vintage Heschel. We do not make up the rules. We do not impose ourselves on the universe and demand that it conform to us. The rules are provided. They impose themselves on us and demand that we conform to them. We do not understand them? Then let us accept mystery even at the mundane level of eating and drinking. Let us bow before that which we do not understand, so that we may be more fully conformed to a pattern that is not of our design. Heschel did not insist that others must obey the dietary laws but only that he must."

The last book of this luminous Hasid was *A Passion for Truth*, delivered to the publishers a few days before his death. Unlike scientific truth, which can be discovered once and serve for all generations

175

everywhere, religious truth must be discovered again and again, perhaps not finding it for long periods, and learning only, as Heschel did, that the passion for truth can be as rewarding as its discovery.

SELECTED BIBLIOGRAPHY OF ABRAHAM HESCHEL

God in Search of Man: A Philosophy of Judaism. New York: Farrar, Straus and Giroux, 1955.

Insecurity of Freedom: Essays on Human Existence. New York: Schocken, 1966.

Israel: An Echo of Eternity. New York: Farrar, Straus and Giroux, 1969.

Man Is Not Alone. New York: Harper and Row, 1967.

A Passion for Truth. New York: Farrar, Straus and Giroux, 1973.

Theology of Ancient Judaism. New York: Bloch, 1973.

"To Grow in Wisdom," the text of Rabbi Heschel's address at the 1961 White House Conference on Aging was published by the Synagogue Council of America, 110 W. 42nd St. New York, N.Y., 10036.

Christianity and Crisis. Dec. 1973, pp. 256-259, an essay on Rabbi Heschel by Robert McAfee Brown.

Intellectual Digest. June 1973, carries an interview with Rabbi Heschel by Carl Stern of NBC News.

Newsweek. Jan. 8, 1973, on the death of Rabbi Heschel by Kenneth L. Woodward.

William Penn

MONG THE GRASSLANDS AND FORESTS of the Valley Forge State Park, a few miles west of Philadelphia, a large multi-acre hump in the earth is known at Mt. Joy. Legend has it that William Penn gave the groundswell its name, from the joy he felt when looking out from its vantage point to a virid sanctuary settled by his peaceful Quakers. It is open to question whether William Penn had those thoughts on that particular site, but no doubt exists that 300 years ago his "Holy Experiment" was beginning in that area. In the nation's bicentennial fever, which history may call a *buy-centennial* from intense commercialism now seen, a few citizens are looking back another century to the 1670s and 1680s when a pacifist community took up plows, not guns, to create independence from England. William Penn has come down from that time with little of the glamour that posterity confers on warlords and generals, but if modern America bloomed with only a few of the seeds he planted in early Pennsylvania, we would surely be less surly to others abroad and more humane to each other at home.

Much the way that Quakers are often misunderstood by outsiders, confusions persist about Penn. He is seen today as a social philosopher who should have confined his dreams to pamphlets, rather than acting on them in the rough world of seventeenth century London and America. He was a spiritual leader who couldn't keep his people from drifting into materialism; even in Penn's day, his "City of Brotherly Love" became the butt of colonial jokes because of the unbrotherliness between one murderous citizen and another. As a pacifist, he allowed a militarist to be Pennsylvania's governor in his absence.

Those are contradictions, to be sure, but they amount to little more than splotches on a drop cloth beneath the grand brushwork that Penn painted on the early American scene. For an innocent moment in its history, America had one politician who did not believe in force or guile to achieve his ends and who knew that personal ethics and public postures had to be one. Penn's "Holy Experiment" came during the era when the Cromwell protectorate and the Stuart restoration were benumbing the citizens, but he did not fear going to his people with this plea: "Be most just, as in the sight of the all-seeing, all-searching God; and before you let your spirits into an affair, retire to him (who is not far away from every one of you; by whom Kings reign, and princes decree justice) that he may give you a good understanding, and government of your selves, in the management thereof; which is that which truly crowns public actions, and dignifies those, that perform them . . . Love, forgive, help and serve one another; and let the people learn by your example, as well as by your power, the happy life of concord."

Penn's own measures of concord were often small. The son of a bold admiral who cherished shipboard battles more than homelife, he was quiet and bookish. Loud fathers often get stuck with sons like that, but for a time, in young Penn's adolescence, it appeared he might snap out of it. He went to Oxford, traveled in France and had learned Cavalier ways. At twenty-three, though, he experienced "convincement," the Quaker phrase for religious conversion. A sermon at a meeting of Friends put him on a path of devoutness on which he would stay until his death fifty years later.

Predictably, Penn's first fervor opened not only his mind but also his mouth. He preached loudly about "Jehovah, the Everlasting Power" and "the rule of Scriptures," but soon he was hauled off to prison for blaspheming against the Church of England. He stayed in the Tower of London for seven months. During his stretch he wrote "No Cross, No Crown," a testament that was to be as famous as his later "Fruits of Solitude." Although Penn had little of the mysticism of a Ruysbroeck, a Kempis or Meister Eckhart, his writing was an expression of a spiritual sentiment that stood for both an earnest crusade against personal failings—pride, avarice, the usual—and a form of religious liberty totally denied by the established church. The Friends were a grubby mix of dissenters without contacts in court and could easily be abused. But with Penn now among them— an admiral's son, a man of education—they could no longer be entirely dismissed, however much they could be jailed or bothered. It was still rankling that the Quakers would not go to war for the crown, nor take oaths of allegiance or doff their hats to the wellborn.

As he presevered in Quakerism, Penn became less the evangelist and more the organizer. He asked the crown for a grant of American land in the mid-Atlantic region. At the time of this request, King Charles II owed Penn's father some 16,000 pounds. That fact, plus his desire to appear a tolerant ruler who understood such dissenters as the Quakers, induced the King to give over 45,000 square miles of unsurveyed territory in the new world. A further bonus for the King was that the nuisance Quakers would be gone. Penn wanted his new expanse to be called Sylvania, from its vast woodlands. Modestly, he argued, the prefix Penn wasn't needed. The King insisted on Pennsylvania, suggesting that the land be named after Penn's father, the admiral. So it was, though only a few historians and other remembering minds know that Pennsylvania was not named after William Penn.

The people enlisted for the new Quaker plantation, Penn demanded, must be 'of universal spirits, that have an eye to the good of posterity." Penn said his own eye "is to a blessed government, and a virtuous, ingenuous and industrious society." When he came to his colony in 1682, Penn acted in a way that was politically unheard of then and which is rare today: he established a frame of government that took power out of his own hand and distributed it among less powerful politicians. Among other innovations, he insisted that the native Indians not be treated with the cruelty they suffered in other colonies. One biographer has suggested that Penn related easily to the Indians because the latter "were natural-born mystics, and Quaker and Indian concepts of the divine being were similar." The economy in the planned community of Philadelphia did well, political harmony prevailed and no guns or soldiers could be found in the peaceable villages.

When Penn returned to a Tory England after but two years in America, he foresaw only a brief stay. He was to remain fifteen years. He lobbied in court for imprisoned Quakers, played politics with James II, fought off personal attacks and sought immigrants for America. In Pennsylvania meanwhile, factions developed and deteriorations grew. In "William Penn," the most thorough of the many Penn biographers, Harry Emerson Wildes wrote that the breakdown was evident. "Quaker youth were no longer using the appropriate plain language, no longer wearing plain apparel. Quaker tailors, in fact, corrupted youth by making fashionable clothing for them. Youth was misbehaving, taking dancing and fencing lessons, playing noisily in the galleries during meeting, wandering about town on

First Day evenings."

It wasn't as bleak as all that. The Society of Friends was persisting in the purity of the original Penn vision; problems existed because they were becoming a minority as the colony was settled from New England. On returning to England again, in 1699, Penn knew that his "Holy Experiment" was no longer holy, nor did it retain its original simplicity. Penn's own son had become a drillmaster for the new state militia; pacifist fathers often raise war-loving sons, no less a mystery when it happens the other way, as it did decades earlier with Penn and his admiral father.

Penn died in 1718 in England. Today in Pennsylvania, small Quaker meeting houses can be found in which "the convinced" worship in much the manner of the original Friends 300 years ago. As then, their pacifism and simplicity are much needed by the larger community.

SELECTED BIBLIOGRAPHY OF WILLIAM PENN

Fruits of Solitude. New York: P.F. Collier (The Harvard Classics) 1909.

Bronner, Edwin B. *William Penn's "Holy Experiment."* Philadelphia: Temple University Publications, 1962.

Dunn, Mary Maples. *William Penn—Politics and Conscience.* Princeton, N.J.: Princeton University Press, 1967.

Peare, Catherine Owens. *William Penn: A Biography.* New York: Lippincott, 1957.

Wildes, Harry Emerson. *William Penn.* New York: Macmillan, 1974.

St. Teresa

SAINT-WATCHERS, SPANIARDS and the occasional odd person who still believes that modern man has much to learn from the past, received happy news in early 1970. St. Teresa of Avila, mystic, reformer, writer but above all a common-sense Christian, was proclaimed a Doctor of the Church. The event probably would have passed unnoticed in the secular press were not women's liberation a growth industry. In the case of St. Teresa, the liberation means that she is the first woman to get on the Church's list of doctors, now in the club with twenty-nine male giants of theology that includes Augustine, Aquinas and Francis de Sales. Of all the so-called babies who have come a long way, Teresa has perhaps come the longest; at the height of her career, which then seemed like the depth, she was written off by an angry papal nuncio as a restless gadabout—or in the Latin, *femina inquieta*. The Vatican's man sneered that she was proud and disobedient and "teaches theology as though she were a doctor of the Church." In making Teresa exactly that, the Vatican admits the laugh is on them.

The importance of this Spanish nun in the sixteenth century is much the same reason for her importance in the twentieth: as then, the Church is now in disarray and in need of direction; as then, holiness is still mistakenly seen as a goal meant only for a few gymnasts of piety, not the many mortals of ordinary muscle; as then, the times now need nothing so much as a reformer with a sense of delight and a gift for humor. On this last point, Teresa said it best in her famous one-liner, "God deliver us from sullen saints." Today, she would beg relief also from sullen politicians, sullen pundits, sullen everybodies.

Teresa was born to middle-class parents in 1515 in the walled city of Avila, fifty miles west of Madrid. The times were stormy. During her life of sixty-seven years, Henry VIII ran England on the whim of his lust, Pizarro killed and plundered in Peru, Luther nailed his gripes on a church door, El Greco brooded over Toledo and Calvin concocted his theory of total depravity. As if this weren't enough, Spain hosted the Inquisition, a period of death and torture that Catholicism has never lived down.

At twenty, Teresa entered the Carmelites, a contemplative order named after Mt. Carmel in Palestine where the prophet Elijah disappeared into heaven. That Teresa enjoyed a youth of gaiety and romance is shown in her remark to a young man at a banquet who couldn't take his eyes off her pretty feet in dancing slippers: "Have a good look, caballero," said Teresa, leaving shortly for the convent, "you won't be getting another chance."

Once in the cloister, the young woman saw the need for reform: the Carmelite convents, like all of Spain, were no more centers of Christian living than the country estates of the Castillian rich. Nuns wore jewelry, threw parties, nibbled on sweetmeats and settled in for the good life, not the spiritual life. Since Teresa had a natural and searching honesty, it was all too much for her. "Serving God in justice, fortitude of soul and humility" should be the only adventure for the contemplative sister.

Before beginning her reform of the Carmelites and shakeup of the Spanish church, Teresa lived as a simple convent nun. She suffered what her friend St. John of the Cross called "the dark night of the soul," a state of spiritual pain in which all feeling of God is lost, but which, once passed through, teases the soul into a new and higher level of consciousness. Yet, Teresa was anything but long-faced about the trial. "No wonder You have so few friends," she said familiarly to God, "when You treat the ones You have so badly."

After thirty years as a nun in the ranks—"even in the kitchen, our Lord moves among the pots and pans"—Teresa was ready to take on the Spanish hierarchy and empurpled errand boys from the Vatican. With a wily knowledge of church intrigue, she not only reformed her order by founding seventeen new convents in Spain in which obedience, poverty and charity were restored; Teresa also, says British biographer Victoria Sackville-West, "was attacking by implication the whole rot and demoralization of the Spanish church, and the clergy knew it." But always the light touch was present. To a young nun, who like so many then and today, exaggeratingly pictured herself as the worst of sinners, Teresa quipped: "Now, Sister, remember

182

none of us are perfect. Just make sure those sins of yours don't turn into bad habits." The two classic works of the saint are *The Way of Perfection* and *The Interior Castle,* both of which are still widely read.

The modern church needs a St. Teresa as badly as the church in the sixteenth century. One, perhaps two or three are probably working for reform today, but it is hard to recognize them. The papal nuncio mentality is still around, ready to tell the nuns how to live their lives and keep their halos shiny. In the summer of 1970, a historic meeting of contemplative sisters—as opposed to ones in the active ministry—was held in Woodstock, Maryland. Resolutely, they decided to go ahead with renewing their orders, including the Carmelites, whether Rome smiled or not. Reports from the week-long meeting say that never was there a group of women so full of enthusiasm, hope, common sense and laughter. If a Teresa was there, the Church is lucky again.

SELECTED BIBLIOGRAPHY OF ST. TERESA

Hatzfeld, Helmut A. *Santa Teresa de Avila.* New York: Twayne, 1969.

McGinley, Phyllis. *Saint Watching.* New York: Doubleday, 1974.

Peers, E. Allison. *Teresa of Avila, The Life of Teresa of Jesus: the Autobiography of St. Teresa of Avila.* New York: Doubleday, 1973.

Peterson, Robert T. *The Art of Ecstasy: Teresa, Bernini and Crashaw.* New York: Atheneum, 1970.

Paul Hanly Furfey

NOT LONG AGO, at the end of a corridor on the dark end of an isolated building on the campus of Catholic University in Washington, Paul Hanly Furfey had just sent off another manuscript. This one was a book review to the *New Republic,* an essay of lucid scholarship. Readers of the Furfey article were delighted to have word again from this scholar and author, ever a voice of independence and ever suspicious of the easy solution. Paul Hanly Furfey is a Catholic priest who has been a sociologist in Washington since 1922. He began as an instructor of sociology at Catholic University, and in a rare example of academic stability—how many professors stay in one department in one school for even ten years, not mentioning fifty?—he has tried to train thousands of students to be "specialists in social ethics."

It is not known how many lives or minds Paul Hanly Furfey has influenced over the years—both Dorothy Day and Thomas Merton paid him homage in their autobiographies—but no doubt exists what has influenced his own genius: the social teachings of Christianity. In his books, he has always been careful to insist on the difference between religion and religiosity, the latter being an exercise in feel-good piety, such as we may have seen lately in Washington in some well-publicized "conversions to Jesus." Hanly disdains the pretenses of prayer-meeting fervor uncoupled with fervor to go into the ditch to retrieve the victims of injustice and cruelty. The goal, he said, "is simply a society controlled by the law of charity, the ethic of Christian love. . . . If charity is beautiful, then lack of charity is correspondingly abominable. Not only hatred, but even a careless disregard of one's neighbor and his necessities is enough to deserve

184

damnation. Those condemned to hell in that terrible twenty-fifth chapter of St. Matthew did not, apparently, really hate their needy neighbors. They were simply too busy with their own selfish lives to care about them. Obviously, then, a mere lack of concern for human suffering is itself damnable."

The strength of Monsignor Furfey's moral imagination can be examined in *The Respectable Murderers* (Herder & Herder), a memorable study on social evil and the individual conscience. "It is an infinitely tragic fact that the greatest crimes of history are committed with the cooperation or at least with the passive consent of the solid citizens who constitute the stable backbone of the community. The sporadic crimes that soil the front pages, the daily robberies, assaults, rapes and murders are the work of individuals and small gangs. But the great evils, the persecutions, the unjust wars of conquest, the mass slaughters of the innocent, the exploitations of whole social classes—these crimes are committed by the organized community under the leadership of respectable citizens." His writing is filled with examples of respectable crimes. "Among all frauds perhaps the most despicable are those that injure the health of the buying public. A manufacturer of a patent medicine persuades a cancer patient to use his nostrum instead of seeking prompt medical treatment. The patient dies and the manufacturer is richer."

Sociologists can be masters at keeping themselves remote— sociologists moonlighting as masons and bricklayers build the securest ivory towers—but Monsignor Furfey's style of sociology has been the opposite. He has lived among the poor he studied, and even today he chooses to live in a commune near the CU campus rather than the comfort of a rectory. As a sociologist, he has the rare combination of passion and persistence. At a celebration of his fifty years as a priest, he spoke of his studies in slum housing, juvenile delinquency, unemployment and the injustices of the ghetto. "Slow, toilsome research is very necessary for social planning. There is a constant temptation to oversimplify. The result is the widespread acceptance of opinions that simply are not true. 'Slum people are poor because they are lazy and refuse to work.' Or, 'ghetto dwellers have no moral principles; that is why crime rates are so high there.' Actually, inner-city slums are a world of their own with a distinctive lifestyle. It is extremely difficult for a middle-class person to put himself imaginatively into the person of a ghetto dweller, and to see the world through the eyes of the latter. Yet without this deep and laboriously acquired insight, no one can plan intelligently about ghetto problems. Simplistic planning is worse than useless. Intelligent planning presupposes long and wearying preliminary research."

An example of this kind of meticulous research can be found in a 1972 Furfey study called "The Subculture of the Washington Ghetto" (available from the Sociology Department at Catholic University). Among the discovered falsities, the study noted that "again and again one hears that ghetto people are too lazy to work. The facts show that they have to work exceptionally hard in order to survive. Generally speaking, they are unskilled. To survive, they must substitute *hard* work for *unskilled* work."

Monsignor Furfey has labored doggedly and long in social ethics but he has gentle tolerance of the upstart activists forever popping up for a new cause. Biafra last year, lettuce this year. He has seen demonstrators come and go, and often it is mostly go. "I've noticed the fervor some of them show when they picket Safeway for Cesar Chavez, who is 3,000 miles away. But meanwhile, what about the poor who live three blocks away? It's exciting to picket and make speeches, but what does it do about getting heat in the homes in the ghetto down the street?"

Somberness is the crippling disease of sociologists, but Monsignor Furfey, a cheerful man, has no limp. In conversation, he smiles easily and tells wry anecdotes on himself. His personal life is one of simplicity; he rises at 4:00 A.M. and retires at 8:00 P.M. He reads and writes most of the day, sharing much of his thought with Dr. Mary Elizabeth Walsh, a respected sociologist at the university. Followers call Monsignor Furfey a radical, and perhaps he is. But he has shown that radicalism has nothing to do with boisterous rhetoric or storming forts. It involves plodding and painful struggles to guarantee justice and mercy to those who most need it. This is radical only because it opposes the excessive neglect suffered by so many. If the neglect wasn't excessive, normal cures, not radical ones, would be sufficient.

SELECTED BIBLIOGRAPHY OF PAUL HANLY FURFEY

The Morality Gap. New York: Macmillan, 1968.
The Respectable Murderers. New York: Herder and Herder, 1966.
Scope and Method of Sociology. New York: Harper, 1953.

Daniel

(For Daniel Mintz, son of a noble father and a gentle mother)

NEWS STORIES REGULARLY tell of a quiet turmoil within the Jewish community. A rabbi who heads the American Jewish Congress notes that among American Jews "there is an alarming ignorance of the content of Judaism, a profound crisis of faith—particularly among the young generation." A rabbi with the American Jewish Committee warns of the "erosion of Jewish family life." Still another rabbi, chairman of the World Jewish Council, worries that "if we continue an uncharted course toward the end of the twentieth century, we might find ourselves not merely decimated in numbers, but utterly bereft of a spiritual existence which makes possible the unique contribution of Judaism to civilization."

In their personal lives, many American Jews do what they can to keep a candle lit—teaching the children Hebrew, running a kosher kitchen, wearing yarmulkes on the Sabbath. But even here, are these practices expressions of culture because they produce sobersided feelings, or are they ways of bending from the harder questions of whether prayer to a personal God means anything, or whether there is still belief in the ancient religion of "mitzvoth," holy acts?

The issue is hard to avoid, whether it involves Conservative, Orthodox or Reform Judaism, but unfortunately it is one modern problem that may be solvable without a roll call vote or a task force. There is the Book of Daniel, with its reasonable approximation of being a Jew amid the hazards of secularism. It is the classic story of the alienated man, without the modern faucet dripping or pouring over him excuses for self-pity. The uncommon beauty of the Book of Daniel is that its story does not come packaged in stylized

187

antics—one more hero flashing the sword of faith—but reveals itself as a living narrative of interior adventures, an account of a man plunging into mysteries and swimming less to safety than to self-assurance. It is the Old Testament theme that obeying the law means more than trying to understand it. God is God, and that is enough. For the religious Jew, whether in this century or in Daniel's, obedience becomes not only the substance of his interior belief but also his outward strength.

Daniel has indeed come down to us as a strong citizen. Everyone knows of his trial in the lions' den, when he went one on one against the mean beasts. But Daniel had strength long before this, as shown in the opening lines of the book. Nebuchadnezzar, the king of Babylon, went with his army and conquered Jerusalem. He took the usual booty of temple treasures but he ordered also that some Jewish boys—"of good appearance, trained in every kind of wisdom"—be brought back to Babylon to become the king's special assistants. Included was Daniel, as well as Shadrach, Meshach and Abednego. Lavishly, Nebuchadnezzar insisted they eat the rich foods and wines from the royal table. Daniel declined. The Jewish dietary laws were based on health foods, not the king's junk food, so he asked only for simple garden-fresh foods. As with many politicians, the king was a nutritional illiterate, so Daniel requested "a ten day trial, during which we are given only vegetables to eat and water to drink. You can then compare our looks with those of the boys who eat the king's food; go by what you see." Not surprisingly, the health food diet paid off. In ten days, Daniel and his companions looked and were in better health than any of the boys who had "eaten their allowance from the royal table."

Accepted now into the court—Daniel was "ten times better than all the magicians and enchanters that were in (the) kingdom"—he became a dream analyst for the king. The job had risk. The previous analysts were slain, not because they came up with unfavorable interpretations but because they could not tell the forgetful king what he dreamed in the first place. Daniel could. The dream he described contained a "statue of extreme brightness." The empire of Babylon has been long forgotten but history remembers this statue because it had "feet of clay," a phrase that is among the most common metaphors of the English language. Daniel received a promotion for his skill with dreams, and the king, impressed by the interpretation—that earthly kingdoms do not last—said the Jewish Lord was the "God of gods."

As often happens among the mighty and the noisy, the king's publicized conversion didn't last. He was soon building a statue and ordering the people to worship it. When Daniel's companions refused, they were thrown into a "burning fiery furnace." But instead of these three believers burning, the flames licked out and killed some of the king's men. Before going into the holocaust, Shadrach, Meshach and Abednego addressed Nebuchadnezzar and offered what has been called the Old Testament's most eloquent statement of faith: "If our God, the one we serve, is able to save us from the burning fiery furnace and from your power, O king, he will save us; and even if he does not, then you must know, O king, that we will not serve your god or worship the statue you have erected."

The Book of Daniel strongly affirms the value of dreams: they are sources of information about ourselves. Rather than being the mere scenery of sleep, they are communications from the unconscious. Although Nebuchadnezzar had flaws—his talent for the table, for one—he was open enough to know that the symbols in dreams are potent and that a skilled dream analyst is the wisest of counsels. In analyzing a later dream—a tall tree is reduced to stump and roots—Daniel warns the king that he is the tall tree but that he will be cut down because the king's arrogance has made him godlike. A year later—the king did not heed Daniel's advice to "break with your crimes"—Nebuchadnezzar "was driven from human society."

The Book of Daniel offers not only timeless religion but also, amid the shuffling of symbols, timely politics. The powerful are brought low not by their enemies but by their belief that they are above the law—laws of ethics, of justice.

The author of the book of Daniel—he is anonymous, like many editorial writers of the Bible and other publications since—doesn't tell us how his man ended his days. He did befriend a rape victim, Susanna, and brought two elders, the original dirty old men, to justice. When Daniel's story trails off, he is still trying to knock sense into the heads of kings, finding them as dense and defiant as ever. But mostly, he is working on himself. That is how all authentic believers busy themselves, and it is why their religion remains respectable. People don't lose their faith because of doubts, but because they see few Daniels obeying the Law faithfully and continually. As the captured Jews of Babylon knew, a people live by symbols and examples, or they hardly live at all.

SELECTED BIBLIOGRAPHY OF DANIEL

Greenberg, Noah and Auden, W. H. *The Play of Daniel: A Thirteenth Century Musical Drama.* New York: Oxford University Press, 1959.

Luck, G. Coleman. *Daniel.* Chicago: Moody, 1969.

Smith, Uriah. *Daniel and the Revelation.* Nashville, Tenn. and Fort Worth, Tex.: Southern Publishing Association, 1912.

St. James

HIDDEN IN THE BACK PAGES of the New Testament, long after wordy Paul has either put us to sleep or put us off and shortly before the picture-book prose of the Apocalypse, is the letter of James. It is brief, orderly and noble, tending in its one thousand words towards a pure expression of human ethics, as explained by Buddha five hundred years earlier and repeated sixty years before by Jesus. Unlike some other letters written in this period when the new religion of Christianity was still a pilot project, James is not a dumping-ground for doomful threats or brimstone warnings. His letter is largely a sewing machine text that threads and pulls together the essential garments of Christianity, minus the fancy dress of dogmas and doctrines.

The letter of James was written circularly to the twelve tribes in the Dispersion, which means to all Jews scattered throughout the Roman world at that uneasy time. Not much is known about the true authorship of the letter, nor its date. The scriptures do contain two Jameses—called major and minor—but scholars have hard doubts about what each put to paper. Because the letter was written originally in Greek, with billowing metaphors and idioms floating like parachutes to the ground of James' message, it is probable that the author was Hellenistic and a product of the Greek school system where writing and language were important.

Much in the nineteen hundred-year-old work of James is repeated in the thoughts of modern writers, further proof that nothing new about human relations can really be said, only reaffirmed. James remarks that "if a brother or sister is ill-clad and in lack of daily food, and one of you says to them, 'Go in peace, be warmed and filled,' without giving them the things needed for the body, what does it profit?" This thought is not much different from the lament of Albert Camus in *The Plague:* "Kindly, well meaning speakers tried to voice their fellow-feeling and indeed did so (to the victims), but at the same time proved the utter incapacity of every man truly to share in the suffering that he cannot see." Later: " 'Oran, we're with you' they called emotionally. But not, the doctor told himself, to love or to die together—and that's the only way. They're too remote."

Near the end of his letter, thundering a little, James speaks out against the rich, particularly the bigwigs of the time who were—what else?—exploiting the workers. "Come now, you rich . . . behold, the wages of the laborers who mowed your fields, which you kept back by fraud, cry out; and the cries of the harvesters have reached the ears of the Lord." A few years ago, in his non-fiction *Remember to Remember*, Henry Miller—not a likely reading companion to James—wrote about the same exploitation: "Wherever one goes in this civilized world, one always finds the same set-up. The little man, the man who does the dirty work, the producer, is of no importance, receives no consideration, and is always being asked to make the greatest sacrifice. Yet everything depends on this forgotten man. Not a wheel could turn without his support and cooperation."

James was evidently a pacifist, as were nearly all early Christians who were not yet bothered by theologians who devised the illogical "just war" theory. He asks: "What causes wars, that causes wars, what causes fighting among you? . . . You desire and do not have, so you kill. And you covet and cannot obtain, so you fight and wage war."

The thinking of James is seldom profound but it is always clear. He has much to say about the religious impulse of man; at one point, perhaps to light a match against potential darknesses over his precise meaning, he writes: "Religion pure and undefiled before God the Father is this: to give aid to orphans and widows in their tribulation, and to keep unspotted from this world." This is not the kind of holy Joe preaching that can make a joke of any religion it may pretend to serve. Instead, it is a clear statement of ethics that cares nothing about personal belief or individual piety. If two persons—one a believer, the other not—reach out to a widow or an orphan, that is enough, James seems to be saying. In what is now called by many the post-Christian age, the idea can be put another way: organized religion may have the message of salvation, but it is often others who do the saving.

James ends his short letter with a thought borrowed from Peter—about love being able to cover "a multitude of sins." It is not known whether James wrote other letters or had other thoughts. But it doesn't much matter; he said it all in this one.

SELECTED BIBLIOGRAPHY OF ST. JAMES

James: A Critical and Historical Commentary on the Bible. Philadelphia: Fortress Press, 1975.
Fickett, Harold. *James: Faith That Works.* Glendale, Calif.: Regal, 1972.
Gwinn, Ralph. *James.* Grand Rapids, Mich.: Baker Books, 1967.
Howard, Fred. *James: Epistle in Action.* Grand Rapids, Mich.: Baker Books, 1969.

Charles de Foucald

WHENEVER THE DEPTHS OF SUBHUMAN conditions at one of society's dumping grounds is reported—one week it is a story about a prison, the next an orphanage, another at a "home" for the retarded—someone inevitably gets out the hammer of logic and bangs away at the obvious: the employes at those places should be paid more. As indeed they should. But how much can be offered a man or woman to arrange his life around the earth's forgotten and tormented?

Is there a union scale for the corporal works of mercy and rescue? Miles to the contrary, money is the last come-on by which a Damien is lured to the lepers of Molokai, or a Martin de Porres to the slums of Lima or a Dorothy Day to the Bowery. Something else induced them to get away and serve the wounded—a bigness of spirit which insists that wanton man-made cruelty is eased best by getting into the ditch with the victims.

Charles de Foucauld was a French Catholic priest who lived at the beginning of this century among a poor and famished people—the Touaregs—in the Sahara of southern Algeria. Maps today show the area as still a sea of sand, with the dot of Fort Laperrine afloat as the only city. The importance of de Foucauld's thinking is the still current idea that the culture of the natives is as true and deep as the culture of the visiting outsider. De Foucauld rejected the traditional haughtiness of Western missionaries who sought to convert the "infidels" by drying out their tribal loyalties, manners and customs, and then drenching them with the superior culture imported cut-rate from Europe. He wrote that "in countries so poor, where life is simple, the missionaries, if they are not to build a wall between themselves and their flock; if they are not to alienate those whom they hope to attract; if they are not to gain an unpleasant and unevangelical reputation for wealth, will be obliged to live in great poverty."

The idea of de Foucauld seems so obviously fundamental when you look at Africa in the nineteenth century, busily colonized by Europeans, and compare with it the hotly independent African nations now. How stupid, we say, of the Europeans not to realize that their arrogant and superior ways would one day backfire on them. Yet how perceptive is America before this fact? The chorus of "Yankee go home" is not being sung by Third World people because they resent American technology or money; they are glad to get that, if it can feed people, grow houses and change an institution or two. And many of them, sadly, are also glad to get our arms. What is resented is American aloofness to, and even contempt for, the foreign culture, history, language and feelings. After all our years in Vietnam, for example, how many of their poets, artists and philosophers do we know, either living or from Vietnam's long and rich past?

Great attention has been given to the life of Lawrence of Arabia, but in many ways de Foucauld of the Sahara lived far more complexly and passionately. Born an aristocrat in 1858 in Strasbourg, he came into money at an early age and by the time he finished at St. Cyr, the French officers school, de Foucauld had learned well the ways of spending it. He had double talents—for the table and the bedroom, the latter shared by a mistress for whose charm he dropped out of the army. By twenty-four, his traipsing had brought him to North Africa. In one of the better de Foucauld biographies (many drip with syrup), Anne Fremantle said the experiences opened his mind. "The Arabs' extraordinary detachment grew on Charles . . . who realized that these primitive, savage, conquered peoples enjoyed existence with an intensity he had hitherto missed. He began seriously now to study Islam, to read the Koran, appreciating the fact that their faith nourished the Arabs in a way Christianity did not nourish him."

De Foucauld stayed in the Sahara for six years. On returning to France, he was a changed man, the old one thrown off for good. He had explored Morocco with a wise rabbi and wrote a well-received book on his findings. More disturbing to his playboy past, he couldn't forget the religious zeal of the Arabs he met. Still an unbeliever, he began studying Christianity with the same fervor he had studied Islam a few years before.

Making the complete turnaround that is common in the history of conversions—though still shaking to family and neighbors when it happens—de Foucauld entered a Trappist monastery at age thirty-two. He stayed seven years. He left mainly because the monastery, despite its austerities, gave him too much material security, a safety net that would break the fall into the poverty of the truly poor. This, he thought, was an unfair advantage. "You hope I have enough poverty," he wrote to a friend. "No. We are poor as compared with the rich, but not poor as our Lord was poor, not poor as I was in Morocco."

After a stay of three years in Jerusalem, where he lived in a backyard hut and worked as a handyman for a convent of Poor Clare nuns, de Foucauld was ordained a priest. Quickly, he made for the Sahara, like an advance scout riding off to penetrate the frontiers of service and sanctity, hoping to bring back the news that the effort is worth it. His desire, he told a friend, was to be "among the sickest souls, the most abandoned of the sheep." His priesthood was "not to serve the rich, but for the lame, the blind and the poor."

That it was. Father de Foucauld lived in the desert from 1900 to 1916, most of that with the Touaregs. He had a perfect record for converts: none. Although he drew up a rule for a religious order, no one ever joined him in that either. In December 1916, fifty-eight and just picking up speed, the kindly marabout (man of God) was pulled from his hermitage one evening by a band of marauders. They put a bullet through his head and threw him—oblivious of the symbol—into a ditch.

The religious order he could never start during his lifetime now flourishes. In northeast Washington, a community of 12 gentle, poor and hospitable women—called the Little Sisters of Jesus—live in what they call a fraternity. In 50 other countries and 180 fraternities, 1100 Little Sisters, as well as 200 brothers in a male order, work among prisoners, nomads, gypsies, the poor.

How is this vocation explained, except that it is the essence of Christianity, or any religion, to see a beloved brother in every person. De Foucauld and his followers do it one better—seeing a beloved brother in exactly the lowest outcasts in whom there is so little to see of anything.

SELECTED BIBLIOGRAPHY OF CHARLES de FOUCAULD

Fremantle, Anne. *Desert Calling; The Life of Charles de Foucauld*. London: Hollis & Carter, 1950.

Lorit, Sergius C. *Charles De Foucauld,* Jamaica, N.Y.: New City, 1966.

Six, J.F., *Witness in the Desert: The Life of Charles de Foucauld.* Westminster, Md: Christian Classics, 1965.

Swami Bhaktivedanta Prabhupada

SWAMI BHAKTIVEDANTA PRABHUPADA

MANY THINKERS ARE CONTENT to lie in wait—in their private worlds where nothing orbits but pure certainty—and let public discovery come when it may. Sometimes as with Kahlil Gibran or Herman Hesse, the cymbals of discovery clang long after the thinker's death, when his ideas sell in paperback at hardcover prices and he himself has become a priceless legend. Other thinkers, though, take no chances on the motors of posterity reviving up after they are gone, so they put on the gas now. One of these is Swami A.C. Bhaktivedanta Prabhupada, a well-known explainer of the sacred Bhagavad Gita—some say his commentary is among the most facile to date—and founder of the International Society of Krishna Consciousness. In the fall of 1965, in the less than cosmic-conscious neighborhood of New York's lower East Side, the seventy-year-old swami came out of his eastern Hindu isolation to share with a few Americans his spiritual knowledge.

Eager for news that something better than the U.S. version of the twentieth century reality might be available, crowds gathered around Swami Bhaktivedanta as he strolled in Tompkins Square Park speaking on such topics as Krishna (the god narrator of the Gita), maya (illusion) and mukti (liberation from maya). Soon he began chanting the sixteen-word Hare Krishna mantra, with the crowd joining in, smiling and—a New York Miracle—enjoying each other's company.

Americans have trouble with Hinduism. Images of mobs swarming into the Ganges, haggard cows wandering the streets, the apparent formlessness of the Vedas, Upanishads and the Gita: all of this mingles with our already careless ignorance of another culture,

India's, the world's oldest and perhaps richest. On top of that, and little fault of ours, is the tangled problem of separating genuine swamis from the talk show kind. We were burned a few years ago by Maharashi Mahesh Yogi. He seemed like the true article at first, but then, like a pro wrestler, the show biz came through. He tied in with the Beatles, Mia Farrow Sinatra Previn (only Sinatra then) and planned a U.S. tour with the Beach Boys. Nothing is wrong with that selection of mammon's children, except that we soon learned the kind of spiritual dishes the Maharishi was serving their sweet-tooth appetites. "Live 200 per cent of life," he said. sounding much like the famous American maharishi, Norman Vincent Peale, "100 per cent outer, material life, and 100 per cent inner, spiritual life." In other words, have it both ways, just what a Beach Boy or beach girl would like. That message, however, is troubling because it contradicts the lessons of material detachment that all the major religions—Taoist, Buddhism, Judeo-Christian, Hinduism, Mohammedanism—teach. The Gita is firm: for man, a "mind absorbed in sense objects is the cause of bondage, and [a] mind detached from sense objects is the cause of liberation."

Evidence suggests that Swami Bhaktivedanta is not a here's Johnny man. His teachings and work have drawn attention from serious students of eastern thought, Denise Levertov, Allen Ginsberg and Thomas Merton. "Swami Bhaktivedanta," wrote the latter, "brings to the West a salutary reminder that our highly activistic and one-sided culture is faced with a crisis that may end in self-destruction because it lacks the inner depth of an authentic metaphysical consciousness."

The excellence of the Bhaktivedanta commentary is the easy way it builds up pillars of clarity to support the often heavily worded conclusion of the Gita text. For example, the Swami takes a section of the sacred book given over to "irreligion in the family" which can lead to "unwanted progeny." As relevant as this morning's warning on planet overcrowdedness, he writes: "Good population in human society is the basic principle for the peace, prosperity and spiritual progress in life. The Vedic religion's principles were so designed that the good population might prevail in society for the all-around spiritual progress of state and community." On womanhood, the sage is less than sagacious. Women, he claims, being easily misled and lacking in trust, should be kept busy with "religious activities." If not, "naturally the women become free to act and free to mix with men, and thus adultery is indulged in at the risk of unwanted population." Apparently, the Swami wrote this before the Indian government began its extensive birth control program, so perhaps the next edition of the commentary will be revised.

A few years ago, in a talk to followers in Columbus, Ohio, Swami Bhaktivedanta posed, and amply answered, the question, "What is the difference between an ordinary man and a Krishna conscious man? He also is living in this world, in this apartment and using everything that is utilized by others. He also eats and sleeps, but what is the difference? The difference is that he accepts that everything belongs to Krishna. Others do not. That's all. Everything actually belongs to Krishna. Others do not know. They think it belongs to them, or 'This is my nation, this is my country, this that.' So many things they manufacture, but we know the simple truth: everything belongs to Krishna. So let everything be offered to Krishna. That's all."

Among those who have followed his advice literally are the American members of the Swami's Krishna Consciousness society, now with about five hundred full-time members. Neighbors of the Washington temple call its some dozen members "the Hare Krishna people," a reference to the chant the robed group happily sings on Washington street corners. These groups, in this city and twenty-two others, are among the nation's growing street population, and in many ways a bonus addition to it. A California Protestant minister who works with the wandering young recently said he has more respect for the Bhaktivedanta followers than many of the celebrated new crop of Christian fundamentalists. "The Hare Krishnas at least have the monastic tradition of hospitality."

Although the teachings of the Swami are in the classic traditions of asceticism and mysticism as explored by masters from Lao Tzu and Eckhart to St. Teresa, it is hard telling how stable his movement is or how enduring it will be. Members of the Washington group, young people with the right ties to friendliness and charity, speak casually of how they are acquiring consciousness of the divine. Unfortunately, it isn't that easy and assuredly not so quick. The way leading to union with the divine—whether called Krishna, God, Providence, the Prime Mover or the Scorekeeper, as Grantland Rice phrased it—is a life-long venture, a no-looking-back journey through dry spiritual deserts and dark nights growing darker. It is always that way, despite the early-game fervor of novices. In the Gita, Krishna leads Arjuna in three paths of liberation: action, knowledge and devotion. "This is the permanent solution of life," says Swami

Bhaktivedanta. That may be true, but as in all religions, few facts are offered on where one gets the faith to believe that it all makes sense.

SELECTED BIBLIOGRAPHY OF BHAKTIVEDANTA PRABHUPADA

Eternal Companion: Brahmananda, His Life and Teachings, trans. by Christopher Isherwood. Hollywood, Calif.: Vedanta Press, 1972.

The Sermon on the Mount According to Vedanta, trans. by Christopher Isherwood. New York: New American Library.

Spiritual Heritage of India, trans. by Christopher Isherwood. Hollywood, Calif.: Vedanta Press.

Yoga and Mysticism, trans. by Christopher Isherwood. Hollywood, Calif.: Vedanta Press, 1969.

James Pike

AT FIRST, THE REPORTS in August 1969 that the Rt. Rev. James A. Pike was lost in the Judean desert seemed slightly typical. Friends were always coming upon him rushing through airports, lost in a choice of arrows pointing to gates A9 through 9K to the right or 10L through 10R to the left, Pan Am straight ahead, Braniff behind. Then also, Pike believed that the origins of Christianity were one with the spirit of the desert, "the nomadic life of the wilderness: God on the move with his people. . . ." It was easy to imagine Pike showing up a few days after he was lost, fresh from communication with his medium pals, asking, "Why all the fuss, didn't Jesus go into the desert?"

Unlike Pike, Jesus was a young man, with a wineskin of water and plenty of local knowledge. The tragic fact that Pike had fallen to probably an instant death from a steep cliff erased the final coincidence that the area was the same alien wilderness, wrapped in sand and heat, where Christ fasted 40 days and nights.

Among the twentieth century's Protestant theologians, Pike is perhaps the best one for those in high school or college who want to investigate their beliefs rather than merely let them slide away. Pike is like an investigative reporter tracking down the fakes and frauds, in this case not men but myths. In *If This Be Heresy* (Delta), he discusses the sense of security that is felt by many when they affirm a belief in God. Security is fine, Pike wrote, but not as a "basis for belief in God. First, that He actually 'comes through' in times of need—however properly and insistently implored—is far from verifiable; in fact there is a good deal of contrary experience. Second, required is belief in the doctrine of Special Providence. It is unduly anthropomorphic to regard God as making particular decisions in this way. He does not tinker; He plays no favorites. . . . *No atheists in foxholes?* When the phrase was 'a hit,' no statistical surveys were produced as to the belief patterns of men whose military service required them to frequent foxholes. But directly entailed in the statement are two convictions: that men with such stark reasons for fear and terror would for that reason believe in God, and that belief in God would quiet their fear because He would protect those who believed in Him. Attributed to Jesus is the observation that the rain rains on the just and the unjust alike; and this is just as true of a rain of machine gun bullets as it is of an aqueous downpour. We were told of the infantryman (American, of course) preserved because a pocket Testament in his shirt pocket blunted the force of a bullet. Would the presence in the same pocket of a small pornographic paperback of equal thickness have failed to effect this result? If fear and naive trust of this type is the basis of theism, there should have been atheists in foxholes!"

Short, with a boxy figure, wearing a gaudy scarlet dress-shirt and purple tie dotted with peace symbols, Pike greeted me with easy cordiality when I visited him in early 1969 at the Center for the Study of Democratic Institutions. "I've xeroxed a hundred copies of that piece on religion you wrote a couple of months ago for the *New Republic*. I pass it out to people," Pike laughed, "whenever I want them to know I'm not the only heretic running around loose." Humorously, Pike talked about the difficulties of being a maverick bishop more famous for heresy than holiness. "I'd like to get invited to the White House to lead a Sunday prayer service. But I'd never pass the Safe Preacher saliva test. Nixon knows I might get carried away and give him a little subversive Christianity, instead of the smoothy-soothy kind he can safely expect from my brother ministers Graham and Peale."

Beneath the joking, Pike was hurtingly aware of his brother ministers, though ones much different from Graham or Peale. Specifically, ex-Catholic, ex-lawyer, ex-teacher, ex-husband, ex-drunk, James Pike became an ex-bishop chiefly because of the dealing of an Episcopal churchman in California who tried to thwart Pike's third marriage. "As an ecclesiastical issue," Pike wrote, "it was extraordinary to the point of being ridiculous. But it touched me at the deepest levels, since it involved both an attempted denigration of my union with the one I love and a partially successful effort . . . to unfrock me."

Pike, who liked riling and needling the Establishment almost to the point that it seemed a psychological need, made one of his last splashes with an article in *Look*, "Why I'm Leaving the Church." In the style of many *Look* articles on religion, it said nothing new about the church, repeating the cliche that it was out of touch and, unless reform came, would soon be out of sight. But it said much about the turn-around thinking of the restless and hoping Pike. Only a few months before his why-I'm-leaving article, Pike wrote to the contrary in the lively *National Catholic Reporter,* an essay titled "Speak Out Boldly and Stay In." Don't vote with your feet, he told Catholics, over the birth control issue. Disagreement doesn't mean discarding. Protestants have been disagreeing for centuries over official policy and they're surviving. "Were (total agreement) the case, very few thoughtful people could be members of any political party, teach in any university or remain employed by any business. Affiliation is based on being generally *with it*, not on being in accord with every single policy or action."

Pike's life, full of conflict and tragedy, plus a prodigious bouncing-back talent, exemplified Pascal's remark in *Pensees,* "There is internal war in man between reason and the passions." But instead of taking to the tower, like a Tillich or a Barth, to hammer out a strong theology against the basic mystery of life, Pike was a pastor in disarray who had an appetite for man—not Mankind, but man as found in strangers and brothers, the weary, confused and the low who came to him for comfort and light.

Because he enjoyed the hard crust, Pike was always showing up in bizarre places, like the old Joe Pyne Show at midnight where, incredibly, he delighted in parrying with sophomore Joe and the half-boobs in the beef box. In a career of wild statements, Pike was often wildly wrong. He wrote in *Playboy* that the Jesuit Order owned major control of both the Bank of America and Creole Petroleum, and as a result had "a yearly income of $250 million, on which they pay no taxes at all." The accusation was completely false. Challenged on it—though not by a sloppy Playboy research staff—Pike admitted he erred. He was better when he stuck to his own truth. He was not particularly upset, as are many of today's ever-so-intense young ministers, about the country club air of some churches. "I rather like the club aspects," he said. "It can be a very happy kind of thing." But the mockery comes in when the congregation "thinks that's the end of it and are sometimes quite uncomfortable when they find their own church in the fray." Pike knew that country club Christianity in America is now openly retaliating against its social-minded ministers at the collection plate, and it was better to get out and fight real battles. "In February, 1969," he wrote, "the Episcopal Church reported that decreased giving last year forced a cut of nearly 12 per cent in the previously adopted national budget."

Although Pike's theology was often shallow and scattered—only so much mileage could be had by doing in the Virgin Birth or the Trinity—it was possibly because, as Virginia Woolf said of a contemporary, "where so much strength is spent on finding a way of telling the truth, the truth itself is bound to reach us in rather an exhausted and chaotic condition."

At the Center in Santa Barbara, which became his shelter from the ecclesiastical shooting gallery, Pike was a popular and loved member who enjoyed the pleasure of being taken for granted. With a skill at making a long story longer, he fit in easily with the men of discourse gathered by Robert Hutchins.

"As far as I'm concerned," Pike said happily in 1966 when joining, "I'm settled here permanently unless it appears to my colleagues that it would be better if I were to leave." Eventually, the colleagues thought just that, though the 1968 shakeup at the Center was not the cruel purge many believed it to be. Hutchins, a man of tenderness, had difficulty one morning telling Pike he was not chosen to stay on. Instinctively feeling the scene was harder on Hutchins than himself, Pike went over and wordlessly embraced the old scholar. No one in the room was not moved by Pike's noble courtesy of the heart.

In April, 1969, the fifty-six-year-old bishop borrowed a building from his Franciscan friends in Santa Barbara and opened the Foundation for Religious Transition. It was a place for "hangup shedding" for the growing number of ministers and priests leaving the church. Pike planned to be on hand, first, to help in the practical problem of finding jobs for the ex-clergy and, second, to persuade them they were not foolish to follow Jesus in the first place.

Pike knew something about the latter; his life was based on following his Master—not the figurine Jesus who saves but the human Jesus who served. Pike's own service took him away from the highroads and into countless Samarian ditches that only Pike and the rescued themselves knew about. Fittingly, death came when the fifty-six-year-old bishop was literally practicing in the Judean hills what he preached over a lifetime: follow Jesus.

SELECTED BIBLIOGRAPHY OF JAMES PIKE

Doing the Truth. New York: Macmillan, 1965.
The Faith of the Church (with W. Norman Pittenger). New York: Seabury Press, 1966.
If This Be Heresy. New York: Delta Books, 1969.
A Time for Christian Candor. New York: Harper & Row, 1964.
Stringfellow, William and Towne, Anthony. *The Bishop Pike Affair: Scandals of Conscience and Heresy, Relevance and Solemnity in the Contemporary Church.* New York: Harper & Row, 1967.

The Curé of Ars

I N LATE SPRING 1786, IN A SMALL French town near the slightly larger one of Lyon, Jean Baptiste Vianney was born. No one, of course, noticed; the family was poor, its currency being in cattle-wealth, which wasn't much because the cows weren't much. The Bourbons ruled, though in three years the citizens would end the aristocratic fun by a ten-year revolution. John Vianney was to live seventy-three years, most of it as a country curé in a tumbledown, hidden village named Ars; during his lifetime, Marx was devising communism, John Stuart Mill pushed pragmatism and Schopenhauer taught pessimism. None of these modern ideas ever reached Ars, much less infected its priest. He was too busy becoming a saint, on fire with love of God and service of souls, a long and low flame that burned deeply far away from the choking air of instant reformers and their isms.

In the calendar of saints, which many of the faithful and others still observe despite the purging of some of their favorites in 1969 by the Vatican, the sainthood of the Curé is observed in early August.

Although the wire services do not cover the event, two groups most likely note the day with full hearts. First, those thousands of priests and ministers who, despite an age of hang-loose liturgy, "relevant" religion and football stadium preaching, remain in their parishes caring for souls, performing the corporal works of mercy and rescue, and being as sold on the idea of their vocation now as on the day of ordination. Thousands of priests have left the Church in recent years, as the headlines have shouted, some to take a wife, others just to take a powder. But many more priests have stayed, choices that are rarely reported to the public but which may contain a message of ever deeper meaning than the walkouts.

The second group are those ordinary believers lucky enough to have in the local parish a pastor who has the Curé of Ars touch. Perhaps before this, they are even lucky to have a parish at all, one that is more than a building where strangers go once a week to hear Mass because they must or else break a Church law. Many of the more alive parishes are in ethnic communities which have an almost natural insulation from pluralism and secularism, the two erosions that have virtually destroyed the sense of community in non-ethnic neighborhoods.

In his early years, Vianney worked the farm and read the scriptures. He was pious and obedient and at nineteen went to the local pastor and told of a desire to be a priest. Although he had little schooling, could barely read and was hardly more than a country yokel, Vianney was encouraged. But soon he was drafted into Napoleon's army. After getting a taste of it, he deserted, saying he had better things to do than carry out the state's violence. He hid for two years, living in barns and stables. Eventually, the French government had the sense to declare amnesty for deserters and Vianney surfaced.

In the seminary he was a dolt, grasping neither Latin or philosophy, an all-around poor student, like Roosevelt at Harvard. He lasted six months before flunking out. The local pastor, ever faithful, and saintly himself, agreed to tutor him; after a few years of painful struggle, Vianney finally made it. Fittingly, his first assignment was to his mentor. "You got your way with this dullard," said the Bishop's office, "now you keep him."

When his mentor died soon after—from old age, not Vianney—no one knew where to send the inept young priest. Boring and slumbering Ars was chosen by the chancery, a town to which they thought Vianney was ideally suited.

The people of Ars had let their faith slip during the years of religious persecution by the government. They drank, worked on Sunday, swore and cheated each other. Instead of a grand scheme to recapture his flock, which is how some rookie curates use their zeal, Vianney merely settled in. Show them Christianity was his jumping-off point, then preach it. Accordingly, he visited the sick, cared for the old and counseled the troubled. He painted the church and hung a bell in the steeple, so at least the people could see and hear and would know where their parish was, and be proud of it. Catechism was started for the young and confraternities for the adults. Personally, the Curé ate and slept little and preached his sermons simply. In time, the people noticed. "They have sent us a saint," said the mayor one day, glad to have any kind of asset for his town.

In one of the few English biographies of the Curé of Ars—by Henri Gheon (Sheed and Ward), long out of print and carried only in a few libraries—the author says that the style of the simple priest gradually took hold. "From 1830 onwards, Ars was a changed place—The humble ministry, discredited, contradicting in every way the ideas of the age, regained its authority. Men got into the habit of slipping into the church on the way to the fields, leaving their tools outside and their flocks waiting in the road. When the bell sounded for evening prayer, all the women gathered round the pulpit to make the responses to their pastor's prayer. No one would steal a root from the field. Then referring to the business ethic—always the last holdout to a moral reform—the biographer adds: "No one would cheat his neighbor of a sou, still less would anyone dare to dummy a filly or a cow to sell at a better price. A new delicacy came in, and with it new politeness."

Not everything nor every heart was changed. The story is told about a group of seemingly pious ladies who for some fourteen years had the Curé of Ars say the 6:00 A.M. mass "for a special intention." As the years wore on and the same special intention kept being requested, the priest's curiosity grew. Finally, he approached the ladies and asked exactly what impossible favor they were asking from the Lord that it wasn't granted in fourteen years. "We've been praying you get transferred," they replied.

Among the few pleasures the Curé allowed himself in his daily over-work was a mystical devotion to St. Philomena. She was the young third-century Roman girl put to death for resisting the empire and one of its soldiers. In 1969, with sales already bankruptcy-low on holy cards and statues, the Vatican puzzlingly removed St. Philomena from the lists of Saints. It had no proof she ever existed. The latest edition of the *Catholic Encyclopedia* notes cooly that the Curé's "devotion to St. Philomena was more trusting than modern hagiographical research permits."

Little is known about the interior life of St. John Vianney, except that he prayed naturally, simply and often. In the gripping and still widely read novel, *The Diary of a Country Priest*, Georges Bernanos portrays the inside travels of a man who goes to the depth of suffering and the heights of compassion. "I believe, in fact I am certain," wrote Bernanos's fictional priest who was much like the real one of Ars, "that many men never give from the whole of themselves, their deepest truth. They live on the surface, and yet so

209

rich is the soil of humanity that even this thin outer layer is able to yield a kind of meagre harvest which gives the illusion of real living."

By life's end, St. John Vianney was famous in France. Pilgrims came for blessings and counsel. The government from which he once hid awarded him the Legion of Honor; he accepted the prize but sold the insignia to give money to a poor man.

Dying was no problem for the old curé, as it seldom is for anyone who lives fully. After a peaceful death in a hot French August, thousands of the weak and poor came for the funeral, a traditional way for humble constituents to thank a great man. Vianney would like to have insisted that the greatness was in them, that a priest's work is merely to bring it out. Instead of looking down on the poor and weak, he might have said, look up to them.

SELECTED BIBLIOGRAPHY OF THE CURÉ OF ARS

Gheon, Henri. *Secrets of the Saints.* New York: Sheed & Ward, 1974.

St. Francis

ACOMMON ASSUMPTION—WIDELY MISTAKEN—is that we die only once, the final tick of the physical heart that lets the sheet be pulled over our eyes and a call placed to the mortician. The literature of Christian saints, though, runs deep with another kind of mortality: the death of the self. Life does not expire but a *way* of life, and the corpse of wordly ways is buried with unpompous finality.

Few living deaths were more painful or dramatic than John Bernadone's, a young Italian of the early thirteenth century. During a stretch as a prisoner of war—he was unhorsed in the first skirmish of a battle defending his hometown from German invaders—Bernadone suffered a strange ailment of the spirit that neither family or friends could figure. His father, a businessman with an image to protect, said another stint in the army would bring the boy around. On wind of that, the son took for the hills and lived in a cave. When he came out one day, it was not for sunshine but to go to his father's clothing store to steal some scarlet cloth of high value. He would sell it and give the money to the poor, whom he had seen for the first time. Now he was truly crazy, his father believed; in the best traditions of mental health, the boy was locked in the cellar, in chains.

These were the last days of John Bernadone and the first for St. Francis Assisi. He is at once the most Christian of all the saints—like Jesus, he owned everything because he could give it away—and the most accepted by the secular world. He is seen not as a preacher of truth or upholder of virtue, but a practitioner of innocence. There will always be plenty of truth and virtue, but innocence?—its production

211

is in decline, and who is making any more of it.

The beginning days of St. Francis of Assisi, confined to a cellar, saw the old self being slain from within. It is often the other way; St. Paul's conversion was from without, as was Paul Claudel's, in Notre Dame cathedral. If his new life was not in the classic tradition of religious conversion, getting the works from his father was traditional family justice. Pietro Bernadone gave his boy the proverbial "best of everything." For awhile, the investment seemed to be paying off. The son dressed well, sang the newest songs to the prettiest Assisian women and had the usual store of wild Italian oats to be sown. In fact, he earned the nickname "il Francesco"—the Frenchman— because of his fondness for fancy French ways. (If living today, Francis would be similar to our unsaintly Mafia citizens and their flair for nicknames—John (the Frenchman) Bernadone). All this changed suddenly, dapper clothes to rags, prayers in place of songs. History has been harsh on St. Francis's merchant father, but what parent today—a child comes home from college dressed in tatters and chanting mantras—cannot sympathize with old Pietro's shock? If only there was a guarantee the kids would become self-supporting and stay with it, until canonization, as Francis did.

After returning all his money and materials to his father— another custom the budding Nature Children of America usually overlook—Francis wandered the mountains clearing his head. For work, he settled on restoring churches, what Verlaine called "the humble life of tiresome and easy achievements." The townspeople— how often do local people everywhere have to suffer their young clowns who announce a new way of life every other week—were impressed by Francis because he presevered. Living in voluntary poverty was not a whim but was seen as a possible career.

Within a few months, friends came and Francis established a small community—called the Brotherhood—at Portiuncula. Perhaps because the Benedictines already had the market on the contemplative life, Francis decided his band should be travelers. The vocation of the road will not be easy, he warned the brothers on their first trip through the local Lombard region. "Go out, my beloved ones, and announce the gospel of peace and conversion. Be patient in trouble, give to all who insult you an humble answer, bless them who persecute you, thank who do you wrong and slander you, because for all this your reward shall be great in heaven. And fear not because you are unlearned men, for you do not speak by yourselves, but the Spirit of your Heavenly Father will speak through you. You will find some men who are true, good and peaceful—they will receive you and your word with gladness. Others, and these in great number, you will on the other hand find to be revilers of God—they will oppose you and speak against you. Be therefore prepared to endure all things patiently."

As with all the saints, Francis said his only goal was to live according to the Scriptures. But as Nietzsche was to say, there has only been one true Christian and that was Christ. Emulating the whole Scripture is impossible, as Francis knew, so he took one part of the whole and made a wholeness out of that—detachment and voluntary poverty. "We said the Office, those of us who were clerks, like other clerks, but the lay-people said the 'Our Father,' and we liked to be in the churches. And we were simple (idiotae) and subject to all men. And I worked with my hands, and moreover wanted to work, and I desired that all the Brothers should be occupied with honorable work. And those who could do no work must learn it, not for the desire of remuneration, but to give good example and not to be lazy. And if they will not give us pay for our work, we must have recourse to the table which the Lord has spread, as we go from door to door and beg for alms."

Down the centuries, St. Francis has been a tempting figure for biographers. Everyone from St. Bonaventure to G.K. Chesterton to Nikos Kazantzakis has taken a try. Historical distortions abound. One biographer, Thomas of Celano, like a modern cereal manufacturer, added excessive sugar to his product, making Francis sweet to the taste but of no substance. The "Saint Francis" (Simon and Schuster) of Kazantzakis, written as a fictional diary of Brother Leo—the saint's straight man and secretary—is a compelling account of Franciscan spirit. In Kazantzakis's words, Brother Leo tells Francis: "I know things about you that no other person knows. You committed many more sins than people imagine; you performed many more miracles than people believe. In order to mount to heaven, you used the floor to the Inferno to give you your momentum. 'The further down you gain your momentum,' you often used to tell me, 'the higher you shall be able to reach.' The militant Christian's greatest worth is not his virtue, but his struggle to transform into virtue the dishonor and malice within him."

Although he shared some of the Church's aberration for the Crusades—he went on one briefly but on meeting a Saracen began talking to him—Francis was a strict pacifist. As all pacifists eventually learn, often more is to be feared from one's own countrymen than from the "enemy." Kazantzakis describes a scene where Francis and Leo seek refuge with some of the good fathers. "Open the gate, Brother Doorkeeper," said Francis. "We are two humble servants of Christ who are hungry and cold and who seek refuge tonight in this holy monastery." The doorkeeper bellowed: "Go about your business. You—servants of God? And what are you doing roaming about the streets at such an hour? You're brigands and you waylay men and kill them and set monasteries on fire. Off with you." "We are Christians," Francis replied, "take pity on us." Instead, Brother Doorkeeper pounded the pair with a cudgel. "Do not resist," Francis called to Leo. "This is perfect joy." Leo had other ideas.

The most recent book on Francis is by John Holland Smith, in a work of readable scholarship published by Scribners. We learn here that Francis may have had a saintly soul but his head was often clouded with worldly stupidity. A novice who could read came once to the Master for permission to own a psalter. Never, said Francis. Books cause trouble, knowledge leads to pride. "There are too many Christians," Francis told the newcomer, "ready merely to read what the saints had done" and leave it at that. Although he continued to rail about books through the years, Francis eventually had to admit that, like sinners, they were here to stay.

With such a mentality leading what was becoming a growing religious order, the Franciscans soon had organization troubles. Moreover, their founder had a blunt tongue, quick to rebuke bishops for owning too much and his followers for praying too little. The legends of Francis talking with the sparrows and wolves are worthy of fireside repetition, but the saint also had to deal with beings considerably less lovable than animals: popes, bishops and the crowds. He could be gentle and happy, notes historian Smith, "when it suited him. But he could also be ruthless in defending his own vision and pitiless in making either his own brothers or outsiders feel and look like fools, if he thought that would serve his ends."

Had Francis been only a dreamer among the birds, it is unlikely he would have founded the Order of Friars Minor, a congregation that has lasted to the twentieth century. In 1210, Francis walked to Rome, for a meeting with the pope to get a blessing on his work to establish his order officially. Papal assistants, ever cautious about tramps who denounced money—the assistants took it personally— advised against Francis. His rule was too hard, they said, especially the strange notion of living without property (Blessed are the property-holders . . .). For once, a pope rejected his narrow advisers;

Innocent III—a man who lived on lemons and called his clergy dogs—gave a conditional sanction to Francis's order. For the Brothers, this meant little in winning the daily battles, but it was roughly similar to getting a famous name endorsement: the common people would be impressed. We're not just another roving gang of schismatics, Francis could say; the pope backs us.

One of those apparently taken with Francis's new importance was Clara Scifi. Like Francis, she came from a wealthy Assisi family and left home for the convent only after loud scenes. Destined to found the Poor Clares, one of the Church's most heroic orders of Sisters, Clare had a deep friendship for Francis until his death. There is little in contemporary life to help characterize Francis and Clare's bond; we are hot to understand everything about sex between men and women, but there is little concern about friendship. Couples, we think, must end up in bed or they end up in frustration. Yet, Francis and Clare's friendship is truly modern; enjoying a shared consciousness, each liberated the other to do a life's work. It is odd how seldom the women's liberation movement ever calls on powerful women like St. Clare as models of independence.

In 1220, the Franciscan movement growing, Francis found leadership not part of the spirituality he wanted. For one thing, he had to suffer a saint's most bothersome irk: other saints. In addition, few Franciscans shared their founders uncompromised views on poverty. Calling themselves "reformers," the faction opposing Francis insisted that it was proper for the order to use wealth so long as the members did not own it. A fine technicality, Francis said, but he dismissed it as a form of sanctified capitalism that encouraged not the spiritual life but the soft life. "Who are these men," he cried, "who have torn from my hands my own order, the order of my friars?"

Saddened by his brothers' adjustment to society, Francis retreated to his mountains and caves, to live as a hermit. His body—Brother Ass— was soon to give out, among the chills and drafts. For the reformers, this was high luck; soon Francis would be dead, safely canonized, a profitable shrine at his gravesite could be built and all the while the New Franciscans could amass more real estate and ecclesiastical power.

Chesterton saw the irony of Francis's last days. "As it became more and more apparent that his health was failing, he seems to have been carried from place to place like a pageant of sickness or almost a pageant of mortality. . . . He who had become a vagabond for the sake of a vision, he who had denied himself all sense of a place and possession, he whose whole gospel and glory it was to be homeless, received . . . the sting of the sense of home."

Francis died painfully. He tried to keep the doctors outside, but they came in anyway, even cauterizing his head—the miracle antibiotic of the day. The legends differ on Francis's deathbed wish, whether he asked for a salad, a chocolate eclair or a piece of candy. No matter. The symbol is clear: a final pleasure of innocence, after a lifetime of embracing God and owning all goods because he gave them away.

SELECTED BIBLIOGRAPHY OF ST. FRANCIS

Bishop, Morris. *St. Francis of Assisi*. Boston: Little, Brown, 1975.

Chesterton, G.K. *Saint Francis of Assisi*. New York: Doubleday, 1957.

Erikson, Joan M. *St. Francis and His Four Ladies*. New York: Norton, 1970.

Jorgensen, Johannes. *Saint Francis of Assisi*. New York: Doubleday.

Kazantzakis, Nikos. *Saint Francis*. New York: Simon and Schuster, 1962.

Smith, John Holland. *Saint Francis of Assisi*. New York: Scribner's, 1972.

The Interior Life

WHERE DO WE LIVE? *I don't mean a street address, a city or a zip code. I mean the other where, the place to which we take ourselves when we have had enough talk or motion, a place within ourselves where if friends could join us they would see us as strangers and not know us. We live in our interior, not only when life in the exterior world continues to go haywire and forces us to retreat, but also when nothing within us makes much sense either. But at least within ourselves we have some shot, usually long, at sorting out, of re-connecting with some strengths that have been weakened. The signal for finding it is clear. As May Sarton wrote in her poem "The Work of Happiness":*

> *No one has heard thought or listened to a mind,*
> *But where people have lived in inwardness*
> *The air is charged with blessing and does bless . . .*

We need blessings—from each other, from ourselves. Yet we go long stretches—across whole tundras of emotional dryness—without getting them. It is small wonder, then, that we see joylessness in so many city faces. The air is charged with damnings, from the presence of innumerable threats trying to kill or injure us—dangerous automobiles, the hospitals dispensing large amounts of lethal drugs or allowing so much needless surgery, the food companies that inject fake colors and flavors into foods that may be making tens of thousands of children hyperactive, the roadside hazards that kill us if we stray a yard off the highway—to the many politicians who make decisions that are never accountable. From all these messages pounding at us, devaluing and degrading us, how can we not feel worthless?

One's interior life becomes a necessity as much as a luxury. It is the one place where we can discover that we are worth something, despite all the exterior forces or pressures that say the opposite. "The interior life is a real life," wrote James Baldwin, but the difficulty is that many have never taken the risk to explore it. We mistakenly see it as a make-believe world, or something cooked up by Norman Vincent Peale and his Reader's Digest sermons on "How to Achieve Inner Peace," or perhaps it is seen as a phony Carthusian mystique that cloisters out the world's messiness. But a capacity for interiority is no more than a recognition that not all our nourishment comes from without, however much beauty, truth and goodness we may find. Nutrition for the soul is also found in a condition of inwardness, what Emmanuel Mounier called "the pulsation of a secret life which is the ceaseless spring of its productivity."

A measure of courage is needed to risk the interior life. In Eliot's "The Confidential Clerk," a man who is giving up his career as a musician is told by a friend:

> *It's only the outer world that you've lost:*
> *You've still got your inner world—a world that's more real.*
> *That's why you're different from the rest of us:*
> *You have your secret garden; to which you can retire*
> *And lock the gate behind you.*

The garden is the perfect metaphor. Growth is implied. We tend to think, mistakenly, that the person who leads a full life is the one who is ever opening new doors to involvement and enrichment, rushing in, organizing and getting things done. Activity has come to mean fullness, change means growth. Thus, for example, the woman who sends the children off to day care centers and takes a job—even though the husband earns plenty—convinces herself that she is "growing" when all she is doing is moving. She has replaced the work of the family with the work of the company; instead of finding fulfillment, she meets another illusion. Growth occurs only when newness is added, when there is enough interior freedom to allow one to take on responsibilities to love or service that were avoided before, or perhaps not even known.

It is foolish to be concerned about the interior life only because of some expected "results." This is the productivity illusion: press a button at A and, snapo, something happens at B. The first fruitfulness of the interior life has nothing to do with production. All that will "happen" is a feeling of self-acceptance. It is the great Christian teaching to love your neighbor as yourself, but that can be the easiest of acts, while the hardest is learning to love one's own self. We hear of people going off to "find out who I am," but all too often they know fully who they are: they just can't stand it. Self-knowledge is avoided by unrestrained activity.

Inwardness involves the opposite—going into the secret garden, accompanied by no plans, expectations or other baggage, but only with the notion of connecting again with one's self. It means going on a search-and-find party to locate our center, of being discontent with life on the periphery. Fidelity to the interior life often has the ring of mysticism to it, of opening bottles of Zen and breathing in the ether of otherworldliness. To keep us grounded, it may be useful at first to keep a journal. Writing everyday is a fruitful discipline, even if it involves nothing more than jotting a paragraph on how we feel about someone we know or a few sentences on a thought we had. The writing becomes a way of keeping the secret garden tended, of hovering over the seeds we planted and giving them a chance to grow. This may be called the ordeal of self-discovery but however painful, a good will is present, based on the belief that at least a self is present to be accepted. Many refuse to admit even that, preferring to be carried by the emotions of another, or moving in groups and herds, so that nothing distinct about us will have to be noticed. It is not the fear of flying that gets us but the fear of standing—in stillness, in solitude. A moving expression of this fear was made by Florida Scott-Maxwell, one of those in this section. In The Measure of My Days, a book I have been re-reading for years, she shares this thought: "The ordeal of being true to your own inner way must stand high in the list of ordeals. It is like being in the power of someone you cannot reach, or know more, but who never lets you go; who both insists that you accept yourself and who seems to know who you are. It is awful to have to be yourself. If you do reach this stage of life you are to some extent free from your fellows. But the travail of it. Precious beyond valuing as the individual is, his fate is feared and avoided. Many do have to endure a minute degree of uniqueness, just enough to make them slightly immune from the

219

infection of the crowd, but natural people avoid it. They obey for comfort's sake the instinct that warns, 'Say yes, don't differ, it's not safe.' It is not easy to be sure that being yourself is worth the trouble, but we do know it is our sacred duty."

Florida Scott-Maxwell

THOSE WHO FIND IT HARD to die are inevitably those who once found it hard to live; they fear death in old age because they feared life in middle age. No bridges were ever thrown up between the shores of early life and late life, so passing from one to the other becomes a journey of dread. Stragglers are everywhere; you meet people who are lost at age twenty, others still searching for themselves at forty. Part of the trouble is that few who grow old with grace ever tell the rest of us how they do it, what turns they made or what winds they caught on the road we all must travel. Occasionally on slow days, newspapers carry feature stories about peppy old geezers who reached one-hundred "because I never smoked or drank," but that is longevity not aging. In contrast, one of the few who has lived long and told about it well is Florida Scott-Maxwell. Barely known in this country, she is in her nineties now and lives in Exeter, England. At fifty, her children and her flowers raised and on their own, Mrs. Scott-Maxwell went to Zurich and trained in analytical psychology under Jung. With a second career, she began practicing in psychology clinics in Scotland and England.

In 1965, Mrs. Scott-Maxwell began keeping a notebook, sewing together stray thoughts and feelings into a pattern of wholeness. In 1968, these gathered perceptions became *The Measure of My Days* (Knopf), a small book of high beauty and value, faithful in paying homage to the needs of the interior life but free of any sobbing outcries of the self. "Age puzzles me," she wrote. "I thought it was a quiet time. My seventies were interesting, and fairly serene, but my eighties are passionate. I grow more intense as I age. To my own surprise, I burst out with hot convictions. Only a few years ago I enjoyed my tranquility, now I am so disturbed by the outer world

221

and by human quality in general that I want to put things right as though I still owed a debt to life. I must. calm down. I am far too frail to indulge in moral fervor."

She doesn't calm down, of course, and that is one reason Mrs. Scott-Maxwell continues in the strength of her individuality. "My kitchen linoleum is so black and shiny that I waltz while I wait for the kettle to boil. This pleasure is for the old who live alone. The others must vanish into their expected role." And what a role that can be—old people stashed far back on society's shelves like faded relics. Often this final segregation is not a willed evil but results, at least in the United States, from a lack of tradition on how to keep the old in circulation. America—its economy and culture—glorifies products and production, so when a person slows up as a producer, well, pack him off. If they won't go willingly, offer a "retirement plan." Some of the old resist; for example, the government estimated in 1971 that some 105,000 workers were eligible for retirement but weren't going.

Even wise counsel is suspect. A few years ago, a doctor came to Mrs. Scott-Maxwell and suggested she take it easy. "I must rest," she writes. "How I know that word, have known it all my life, so now I lie and rest. I must also 'take exercise.' [But] anyone living alone, even in a small flat, takes constant exercise. Do doctors think you summon meals by magic, hot water bottles, all the things you think you might be more comfortable with if you had, and have to get yourself? No one is more active, relatively, than the sick person who takes care of herself."

Like a planet warmed by a sun, much of Mrs. Scott-Maxwell's thought is nourished by Carl Jung. In places, there is little way of telling the student from the teacher. In the following passages on our no-fault society, which voice is Scott-Maxwell's, which Jung's?

—"A Modern permissiveness makes it difficult to tell good from bad, as though it were simpler to have no differences at all."

—"Our knowledge of good and evil has dwindled with our mounting knowledge and experience, and will dwindle still more in the future, without our being able to escape the demands of ethics."

The first is Scott-Maxwell. Hers is the first of the next two also

—"If I suffer from my lacks, and I do daily, I also feel elation at what I have become. At times, I feel a sort of intoxication because of some small degree of gain; as though the life that is in me has been my charge, the trust birth brought me, and my blunders, sins, the blanks in me as well as the gifts, have in some long painful

222

transmutation made the life that is in me clearer."

—"The serious problems in life are never fully solved. If ever they should appear to be so, it is a sure sign that something has been lost. The meaning and purpose of a problem seem to lie not in its solution but in our working at it incessantly."

Mrs. Scott-Maxwell—who was born in Florida and moved to Scotland when she married—is a lively and spirited letterwriter. In one recent note to me, she recalled her days in a clinic in Edinburgh. An incident she spoke of reveals her style of therapy: if one visit by a patient is enough for the patient, then let it be one visit—why drag it out for years of analysis? "A farmer's wife came and told a tragic story where nothing could be done, but her compassion and strength made it possible to continue. As usual with these cases, I asked if she would care to come again; she looked a little surprised, and said, 'There is no need, I've told you everything.' She had only wanted to confide in someone she respected, in case there was more she could do, and not to be so alone in her hard life. . . . One visit was enough for her." The best of the Jungian analysts stick to this method: a patient's spirit doesn't always need total rebuilding (at $25 or $50 a session), it may only need temporary relief.

Anyone old is always fearful that ideals once worked for will be voted out of office by the younger crowd. In her notebook, Mrs. Scott-Maxwell has exactly the right worries: rich nations inhabited by poverty-stricken personalities. Wealth is hard. "To organize family transportation with only two cars, to find leisure or quiet in a house equipped with every machine a modern house can contain is not easy. To combine chores with responsible jobs, not to mention illness, accidents, and the new poverty of the highly paid, all this demands stamina of the highest order, for the strain of it is great. Now when so many have so much, many work harder than their forebears. So why does having much create strain, dissatisfaction and confusion? Could it be that austerity kept life simple, simple pleasures remaining real pleasures, while plenty makes for complication, and having much leaves us sated?"

The Measure of My Days received few reviews when it came out; the busywork bookstores—crowded with today's smashes—don't carry it, nor do most libraries. More available is an earlier volume, *Women and Sometimes Men,* also by Knopf. Written in 1957, when no tough referees of feminism were on the field telling men what the new rules were, Mrs. Scott-Maxwell found that marriage and freedom are possible. "Poor shivering egos, what else are we after much of the time? We evade each other, we evade all knowledge of ourselves, we pretend and we lie, we do everything to avoid the naked humility of relationship. But marriage does force it on us in spite of all our efforts to avoid it, and gradually we are known. It is being known that makes marriage into relationship, that makes us capitulate and admit we are ourselves, and when a companionship has lasted a long time we each become a witness for the other."

Mrs. Scott-Maxwell is still concerned less about world conditions or causes, but more about the only effort that is truly important anymore: the struggle of the individual to make sense of it all. The testimony of someone who has lived nearly a century, and whose house of memories is not crammed with useless antiques, is crucial. This aging woman, alone in her Exeter cottage, continues to write down her thoughts daily, as though the lights will last forever. That is another similarity with Jung: we are in the hands of what seems immortal.

SELECTED BIBLIOGRAPHY OF FLORIDA SCOTT-MAXWELL

The Measure of My Days. New York: Knopf, 1968.
Women and Sometimes Men. New York: Knopf, 1957.

Miguel de Unamuno

O NE DAY NEAR THE END OF HIS LIFE in 1936, Miguel de Unamuno, one of Spain's major philosophers, took his customary morning walk in a wood near the university town of Santander. A student approached the old man and asked for a word; he had read an article by Unamuno in the Madrid newspaper *Ahora,* and, trembling, said he disagreed with it. Expecting an outburst of argument from the famous teacher, the student was amazed when Unamuno replied, "Well, I don't agree with it either." Then the teacher and student sat under a tree and read poetry together.

Less known in this country than his contemporary in Spanish thought, Ortega y Gasset, Unamuno lived most of his seventy-two years bouncing between the walls of contradictions. Biographers have found an endless supply of reversals and paradoxes in Unamuno's life and writings, Cains and Abels forever having it out with each other. Nothing else makes him stand out more among modern philosophers, traditionally a group intent on explaining the balances that men rest on, not the tipovers. Unamuno insisted that the interior divisions of the personality did not have to be destructive, but believed that the struggle to master them was the one existential necessity. "A man is human, is alive according to what he has in common with other men," he wrote. "The somber man without his joys would not be a man, as neither would the joyful man without his somber moods. The weaknesses of the strong, the decisions of the indecisive, the brave sallies of the cowards, the cowardly moments of the valiant, the commonplaces of the geniuses and the aspirations of the simple, all of this, the intimate contradictions of men, is what makes them brothers."

The pictures of Unamuno usually show an owl-faced man, lost

in a silent hoot of grimness. The adversary within is defeating me, his expression seems to be saying, I can't stand it. Examining the face, though, what comes through is not gloom but intensity. His eyes, in a stare of alertness, appear ready to penetrate any darkness, like the vision of certain animals that can see through a night. His mouth, closed tight, is ready to spring open in denunciation against whatever is cheap. The intensity of his expression is matched by Unamuno's belief that a mind works best when the heart is stormiest. The last line of his masterpiece, *The Tragic Sense of Life*, is addressed to the reader: "May God deny you peace, but give you glory." Peace of mind, a commodity that has never been marketed well in Spain but which is a big seller in America—what would the U.S. pill industry do without ads for peace of mind?—is no longer possible, said Unamuno. Instead, faith and reason are forever at war inside us, and the kind of peace settlement we should seek is permanent dissatisfaction. "The satisfied, the happy," he wrote, "do not love; they fall asleep in habit, near neighbors to annihilation. To fall into a habit is to begin to cease to be; Man is the more man—that is, the more divine—the greater capacity for suffering or rather, for anguish." Elsewhere, he said it even more briefly: "Unless you strive after the impossible, the possible you achieve will be scarcely worth the effort."

Unamuno came from the Pyrenees mountain town, Bilbao. He studied at the University of Madrid, a natural standout with the one failing that he enjoyed reminding people of it. Years later, the springs of his ego were still making record leaps; when awarded a medal by the king of Spain, Unamuno said, "I deserved it." An aide to the king, aghast, took Unamuno aside and said that all others who had ever received the medal traditionally told the king that they were unworthy of such a high honor. "They were right," replied Un- amuno. Even here, Unamuno offered a contradiction; writing to a friend, he once said: "This cursed literary profession fills us with vanity and robs us of our innermost being. Always before the footlights!"

In attacking every imperfection he came on, including his own, Unamuno took special pleasure in going after the two dominant Spanish institutions: the church and the government. "Here in Spain," he said, "we're all Catholics, even the atheists!" His main complaints against the church were hardly new: lackey bishops who sidled too easily with the politicians, too much dogma, too little concern for the poor. But his passion disturbed the hierarchy. For his blasts, Rome put his books on the Index, which conferred on

Unamuno a new title of honor: heretic. As for the government, his hostility to the dictator Primo de Rivera led to an exile in the Canary Islands; a few years after, in 1930, he returned to the homeland only to see Franco moving up. He eventually turned against the latter. Unamuno's opinion of dictators was clear: "There is no culture that can come to life and flourish under a military regime. . . . It's impossible, impossible! Under militarism nothing can prosper; they're just blustering fools."

Although he produced poems and novels—few are available in English—Unamuno's most lasting work was the 1921 *The Tragic Sense of Life*. In a useful biography (*The Lone Heretic*. University of Texas Press, Austin), Margaret T. Rudd writes that "had Unamuno written only this one work, it would have sufficed to mark him as a profound thinker." One possible reason that Unamuno is not well known or much studied in the United States is that America has little or no sense of the tragic. This can be illustrated by a number of events, most recently in Vietnam. Few were ever ready to accept the reality that American involvement there could result in a total loss for us, a full tragedy; many of the politicians—the one group most willing to cover up what voters will see as painful—fed the illusion that we could still have a moral victory in Vietnam, "a happy ending" after all.

It is natural to dislike grief, but it is totally unnatural to avoid grief when its reality crushes in—this is the Unamuno meaning of the tragic sense of life. Because America avoids seeing tragedies as tragedies—Vietnam, Attica, highway fatalities, hunger—and prefers viewing them weakly as "problems," "difficulties" or "issues," it follows that the solutions to them are also weak. Thus, the problems, difficulties or issues continue, despite the political parties which promise every four years to control them. With old-style Spanish emotion, Unamuno believed that instead of avoiding the tragic, "I am convinced that we should solve many things if we all went out into the streets and uncovered our griefs, which perhaps would prove to be but one sole common grief, and be joined together in beweeping them. . . . A miserere sung in common by a multitude tormented by destiny has much value as a philosophy. It is not enough to cure the plague; we must learn to weep for it. . . . Perhaps that is the supreme wisdom."

Reading Unamuno is anything but a free-fall of clarity. He is more like going through a dense fog, to be taken slowly, seeking direction from whatever guideposts appear and not stumbling when they don't. Large passages of *The Tragic Sense* go by with the reader not knowing where he is, and wondering if Unamuno knows either. He does; occasionally, he traps himself in another of his contradictions. Why shouldn't philosophers enjoy that luxury; the rest of us share it all the time.

SELECTED BIBLIOGRAPHY OF MIGUEL DE UNAMUNO

Rudd, Margaret T. *The Lone Heretic.* Austin: University of Texas Press, 1963; reprinted edition, Gordian, 1974.
Perplexities and Paradoxes. New York: Philosophical Library, 1945.
Three Exemplary Novels. New York: Grove, 1956.
The Tragic Sense of Life. New York: Dover, 1921.

Viktor Frankl

W̲HEN VIKTOR FRANKL, or number 119,104 as his Nazi captors branded him, rode into Auschwitz in 1941 in a train crammed with fifteen hundred people, he carried under his coat a manuscript. Frankl, a Jewish psychiatrist captured by the Germans, had written a text containing years of thought and research. After the usual receiving line welcome of Auschwitz, whippings and blows, Frankl tried to hide his manuscript. "I know what you will say," he told an old prisoner, "that I should be grateful to escape with my life, that that should be all I can expect from fate. But I cannot help myself. I must keep this manuscript. It contains my life's work."

The prisoner bellowed a curse at this naive plea of Frankl's. The text did not last long, of course, soon ending up in the ovens, as with nearly everything and everyone else at Auschwitz. Years later, the death camp behind him and practicing psychiatry again, Frankl reflected that having lost his work may have saved his life. "My deep concern to rewrite this manuscript helped me to survive the rigors of the camp. For instance, when I fell ill with typhus fever, I jotted down on little scraps of paper many notes intended to enable me to rewrite the manuscript, should I live to the day of liberation. I am sure that this reconstruction of my work in the dark barracks of a concentration camp assisted me in overcoming the danger of collapse."

Frankl survived the camp partly because the goal of one day publishing his book had *meaning*. Fittingly, no one working today in mental health has written more clearly or thoroughly on the value of meaning in the life of bored, depressed and meaning-starved mid-twentieth century man. No charts or statistics are kept, and no hospital insurance covers it, but meaninglessness is easily one of the most pervasive causes of emotional sickness in America; sometimes this mass neurosis strikes only as a recurring ache, as in the desk people who may get no meaning out of their work, or perhaps a student or soldier unable to shake the hollow feeling. Other times, though, it is severe despair, as with a marriage where the daily payment of sacrifice by a husband or wife no longer provides a kickback of meaning. These are not death camps to be escaped from but they are prisons nevertheless, often much harder to survive because the terror is not the presence of physical pain but its absence; one is lulled into a living sleep so easily by American comfort.

Frankl's book that was burned in Auschwitz became in 1955 *The Doctor and the Soul: An Introduction to Logotherapy.* Together with *Man's Search for Meaning* and *Psychotherapy and Existentialism,* this work is the basis for what Frankl calls *meaning therapy.* Logos is Greek for meaning. "Logotherapy," writes Frankl, "focuses on the future, that is, on the assignments and meanings to be fulfilled by the patient in his future. . . . In logotherapy the patient is actually confronted with and reoriented toward the meaning of his life. This striving to find a meaning in one's life is the primary motivational force in man. That is why I speak of a will to meaning in contrast to the pleasure principle on which Freudian psychoanalysis is centered, as well as in contrast to the will to power stressed by Adlerian psychology."

Theorists debate whether man is more driven by his libido, his id, whether he has an urge to kill one parent in order to marry the other; but to large collections of human beings, these plaything questions are restricted to the games of the rich who can afford a fifty-dollar-an-hour psychiatrist-umpire. Instead, the bored and depressed among the middle and lower classes want answers to the simpler riddle, why don't I enjoy life? In many cases, Frankl would say, because one's life has no meaning, you suffer an *existential vacuum.* "Boredom," he writes, "is now bringing to psychiatrists more problems to solve than distress. And these problems are growing increasingly crucial, for progressive automation will probably lead to an enormous increase in the leisure hours for the average worker. The pity of it is many of these will not know what to do with all their newly acquired free time."

What is often needed as a cure to meaninglessness is not freedom from suffering or tension, however much the drug advertisements preach that happy state. Instead, writes Frankl, "what man actually needs is not a tensionless state but rather the striving and struggling for some goal worthy of him. . . . And one should not think that this holds true for only normal conditions; in neurotic persons, it is even more valid. If architects want to strengthen a decrepit arch, they increase the load which is laid upon it, for thereby the parts are joined more firmly together. So if therapists wish to foster their patients' mental health, they should not be afraid to increase that load through a reorientation toward the meaning of one's life."

A classic case illustrates the emotional importance of meaning—the hallway meeting late at night between the scrub lady and the corporation president. She, though poor, is emotionally healthy; great meaning is in her life because her salary goes for a child's education. The fit and groomed executive, though rich, is emotionally depressed; his striving for money has no meaning to him other than to advance the might of the corporation, and what is that to a man? In chatting in the hall, neither understands the other's psychic state. Why is he gloomy, wonders the scrub woman; why is she peaceful, asks the executive. Frankl would measure their lives not by what each does, but by what they do it for.

Scrubbing floors, surviving prison, joining a cause, getting married or staying married, any action whether pleasant or miserable—Frankl applies to all of them the remark of Nietzsche: "He who has a *why* to live for can bear almost any *how*." In *Man's Search for Meaning*, the clearest introduction to Frankl's thought, he writes that "mental health is based on a certain degree of tension, the tension between what one has already achieved and what one still ought to accomplish. . . . Such a tension is inherent in the human being and therefore is indispensable to mental well-being. We should not, then, be hesitant about challenging man with a potential meaning for him to fulfill.

Frankl, an elderly man, physically short, friendly, is now professor of psychiatry and neurology at the Poliklinik in Vienna. He has taught at Harvard and SMU, and is perhaps best known in America on the campuses where he has often lectured. Although his ideas are generally known as the third school of Viennese psychiatry—after Freud and Jung—many Freudians, perhaps in blind devotion to the Master, dismiss Frankl as simplistic. The criticism is not hard to figure. While a Freudian psychiatrist may spend five years analyzing a patient weekly, a logotherapist may treat the same kind of illness by directing-the patient in a few sessions to a goal or action of *meaning*.

Why shouldn't some illnesses of the mind be that simply treated? Must it always be years and years on a couch? Must one's mother always be the cause for neurosis? If some physical diseases can be eased or cured by one or a few visits to a doctor, why not some mental diseases?

Human beings hunger for meaning, especially Americans whose supply is already dangerously low. A few years ago, catchy experiences like "self-realization" or "self-encounter" were big, until some busy selves saw how little interiorly they had to realize or encounter. Going inside oneself for the answers to life is perhaps the hollowest answer of all, since often only more hollowness is run into. Instead, meaninglessness, according to Frankl, is best cured by going outside, extending the self rather than contracting it, in service to others, in upholding a value, in embracing suffering positively rather than negatively. The decisions of attitude that a person makes are often more crucial to mental health than the conditions he makes them in, whether in Germany 1941 or anywhere in the 1970s.

SELECTED BIBLIOGRAPHY OF VIKTOR FRANKL

The Doctor and the Soul: From Psychotherapy to Logotherapy. New York, Random House: 1973 (paperback).
Man's Search for Meaning. Boston: Beacon Press, 1973; revised edition.

Raissa Maritain

RAISSA MARITAIN TELLS of the beginning feelings that led to a lifetime of love and the pursuit of truth with Jacques Maritain. "Our engagement took place in the simplest way, without any proposal. We were alone in my parents' living room. Jacques was sitting on the rug, close to my chair; it suddenly seemed to me that we had always been near each other, and that we would always be so. Without thinking, I put out my hand and stroked his hair; he looked at me and all was clear to us. The feeling flowed through me that always—for my happiness and salvation—that always my life would be bound up with Jacques's. It was one of those tender and peaceful feelings which are like a gift flowing from a region higher than ourselves, illuminating the future and deepening the present. From that moment our understanding was perfect and unchangeable."

So began the lasting union of a poet and a philosopher. The works of Jacques Martain—intellectual light that revived the brilliance of Christian wisdom—are better known and read than his wife's but the thoughts of Raissa Maritain have special qualities of force and a depth of their own. The West has seen many couples who wrote and collaborated—the Durants, Karl and Gertrud Jaspers—but the women in these unions probably would not have become known if they had never met their husbands. Raissa Maritain would have been different, with the beauty of her mind and persistence of her imagination flowering anywhere with anyone. As it was, her husband was on hand to nurture it. Together they created a romance guaranteed to have tenacity—two people who join not only to be together but to do something together. That is the secret of marriage, and few find it.

They met as students at the Sorbonne at the turn of the

233

century. She was the daughter of Russian Jews whose "mother observed the principal Jewish rites; my father needed a little urging to do so." The family fled Russia to escape the purges, coming to Paris where the father struggled along as a tailor. Raissa was ten but already "all my being was intent on listening and understanding. . . . Everything connected with school was one long holiday for me." This early love of learning came from a sense of obligation to her parents: they "had left Russia, suffered the pain of exile, poverty, separation from those they loved—and all this for my sister and for me, to assure the future of my studies, and the conditions necessary to a free and worthy life, sheltered from anti-Semitic vexation. To allow me to study as I liked, nothing ever seemed too difficult to them or too hard. They had understood, even before I could know it myself, that this would be my life—the happiness of my life."

In 1906, married two years, Raissa and Jacques Maritain became Catholics. As she describes it, it was at once a forced entry into a school of discipline where the mysteries of faith could be absorbed but never understood, but also an opportunity to use the grace of religion to attain the freedoms of spiritual liberty: "The Church in her mystical and saintly life we found infinitely lovable. We were ready to accept her. She promised us Faith by baptism: we were going to put her to the test. But in the apparent mediocrity of the Catholic world, and in the mirage which to our ill-seeing eyes seemed to bind her to the forces of reaction and oppression, she appeared to us strangely hateful. She seemed to us to be the society of the fortunate of this world, the supporter and ally of the powerful, to be bourgeois, pharisaical, remote from the people."

Raissa Maritain believed at first that their conversions would force them to forswear philosophy and the intellectual life. It was to be the opposite. She discovered that Christianity has more to do with rules and dogmas but extends also to working toward what she and her husband called theocentric humanism. This is directed "toward a socio-temporal realization of that evangelical concern for humanity which ought not to exist only in the spiritual order, but to become incarnate, and toward the ideal of a true brotherhood among men."

Until her death in Paris in 1960, Raissa Maritain had produced a large amount of poetry, translations and philosophy. Americans know mostly about Paris of the 1920s, when the city of St. Denis was crowded with expatriates trying to make moveable the feast of truth, but the years of a decade earlier—with the Maritains at the center—had equal intensity. Among their friends were such French writers and artists as Charles Peguy, Leon Bloy ("there is only one sadness, and that is not to be a saint"), Jean Cocteau, Henri Bergson, Georges Rouault and Marc Chagall. These are among the people who walk in and out of the pages of Raissa Maritain's two books of memoirs: *We Had Been Friends Together* and *Adventures in Grace.* Both are published by Image Books, of Doubleday, and can be found mostly in the bookstores that dust their shelves bi-annually. Aside from the exactness of her descriptions and the preservation of the color of this period in French culture, the memoirs reveal a woman of remarkable range who cherished the excitement of friendship because she allowed other people to become her inner companions. Most of us, if we have friends at all—and not mere acquaintances—tinker with them rather than allow them to filter through us, entering our intellectual and spiritual life as much as our social life. Raissa Maritain cherished a line from St. Angela of Foligno: "It is not for fun that I have loved you."

As an ardent uplifter of others, she herself took flight through her poetry. In *The Situation of Poetry,* she wrote that "born in a vital experience, life itself, [poetry] asks to be expressed in life-bearing signs, signs which will conduct the one who receives them back to the ineffability of the original experience. Since in this contact all the sources of our faculties have been touched, the echo of it ought itself to be total."

In 1933, the Maritains came to America. Off and on, they were to spend seventeen years in this country. When France fell in 1940, the couple was lecturing here, traveling from their Princeton, New Jersey, home to talk against anti-Semitism and militarism. Raissa Maritain wrote in 1940: "Life for me draws to a close, ended by the catastrophe that has plunged France into mourning, and with France, the world, or at least all those in France and the world who treasure the human and divine values of free intelligence, wise liberty and universal charity."

Life did not draw to a close for Mrs. Maritain. Again, the opposite happened: it grew. She was able to write: "We know that in the midst of every catastrophe—in the fall of empires, in all persecutions and martyrdoms—good goes on, good is at work, good remains."

SELECTED BIBLIOGRAPHY OF RAISSA MARITAIN

Raissa's Journal. Albany, N.Y.: Magi Books, 1974.

The Situation of Poetry: Four Essays on the Relations Between Poetry, Mysticism, Magic and Knowledge, with Jacques Maritain. Millwood, N.Y.: Kraus Reprint Co., 1968.

We Have Been Friends Together and Adventures in Grace. Garden City, N.Y.: Doubleday, Image Books, 1961.

Kernan, Julie. *Our Friend, Jacques Maritain.* New York: Doubleday, 1975.

Carl Jung

C ARL GUSTAV JUNG is perhaps the best read and even the most understood in the competition among himself, Freud and Adler. Jung paperbacks are everywhere, thanks to book companies who know the sales value of the drugstore rack. Purists might twitch on seeing a copy of *Psychological Reflections* sharing shelf space with *The Love Machine*, but why shouldn't genius compete in the shops against trash?

Far from watering down the mysteries of the unconscious, Jung risked drenching the reader with them, knowing that every person is a test-case for psychic experiences. Stand aside from life for a moment, he says, and trust rather than fear the conscious conflicts within you. "We yield too much," Jung wrote, "to the ridiculous fear that we are at bottom quite impossible beings, that if everyone were to appear as he really is a frightful social catastrophe would ensue."

Although Jung wrote in the earlier part of this century, his thought applies to this morning's front page.

• The arms race. "Let man but accumulate sufficient engines of destruction and the devil himself will soon be unable to resist putting them to their fated use."

• Aged cold-warriors who won't quit. "Man is constantly inclined to forget that what was once good does not remain good eternally. He follows the old ways that once were good long after they had become bad, and only with the greatest sacrifices and untold suffering can he rid himself of this delusion and see that what was once good is now perhaps grown old and is good no longer."

• The masks of tough-guy politicians. "The social 'strong man' is in his private life often a mere child where his own states of feeling are concerned: his discipline in public goes miserably to pieces in private. His 'happiness in his work' assumes a woeful countenance at home . . . and the wives of such men would have a pretty tale to tell. As to his selfless altruism, his children have decided views about that."

• Community. "Most people need someone to confess to, otherwise the basis of experience is not sufficiently real."

Those are usable thoughts, but Jung is valuable for other reasons than his wisdom. More lastingly important is his work in interpreting spontaneous symbols of the unconscious, i.e., analyzing dreams. As a doctor of the psyche who kept crashing into the walls of blank personalities—his patients'—Jung often relied on the sick person's dreams as a source of information about him. "No amount of skepticism and criticism," he wrote "has yet enabled me to regard dreams as negligible occurrences. Often enough they appear senseless but it is obviously we who lack the sense and ingenuity to read the enigmatic message from the nocturnal realm of the psyche. . . . Nobody doubts the importance of conscious experience; why then should we doubt the significance of unconscious happenings."

Dreams are essentially that—the unconscious speaking to the conscious, trying to tell it something, offering new points of view about the stale old routines of trapped lives. The language used is not the symbols of words—the conscious medium—but the symbols of objects (for example, the famous phallic symbol so cherished by Freudians), or events (the Fourth of July symbolizes patriotism) or people (the super-mammary sex symbols of Hollywood). These symbols are now familiar enough to be easily interpreted in a person's waking life. But other symbols are not so easily figured, and when found in one's dreams often seem like paste-ups of confusion. Yet who and what appear in our dreams are usually the symbolic messages of the unconscious rapping at the door of the conscious, saying "let my reality come in, too." In each of us, Jung insisted, "there is another whom we do not know. He speaks to us in dreams and tells us how differently he sees us from the way we see ourselves. When, therefore, we find ourselves in a difficult situation to which there is no solution, he can sometime kindle a light that radically alters our attitude—the very attitude that led us into the difficult situation."

Americans, large numbers of whom prefer to take their doses of truth in pill form, like to think they have a taste for things unconscious. It is common now for otherwise steady people to refer to their "vibes" before making a decision. An avid use of astrology, yoga, tarot cards and other parlor pastimes are popular breezes that supposedly get the vibes moving. A trouble with this busywork is the created illusion that one is "inner-directed," when all that has happened is a case of boredom with the *outer.* It won't work, said Jung. "Together the patient and I address ourselves to the two million-year-old man that is in all of us. In the last analysis, most of our difficulties come from losing contact with our instincts, with the age-old unforgotten wisdom stored up in us. And where do we make contact with this old man in us? In our dreams."

Followers of Jung—whether Jungian analysts, teachers, students or patients—are a passionate bunch, and no outsider should mention the master's name without bracing for a stream of stories and remembrances. A Jung Foundation is active in New York. Many cities have Jungian centers where therapy, teaching and discussion is provided. Aside from Jung's own works, a balanced guide to dream analysis and analytical psychology is *The Symbolic Quest,* by Edward C. Whitmont (Putnam's). Slow going in parts, it explains carefully the theories of Jung on his old favorites: individuation, archetypes, anima and animus, myth, persona. Few who ever read a little of Jung ever fail in time to read a lot.

The importance of Jung's method of the unconscious is that, in his words, "the interpretation of dreams enriches consciousness to such an extent that it relearns the forgotten language of the instincts." Forgotten is right. Where else but in this country at this time is the passion for abstracting and objectifying getting such a workout? The phrase, "everything is so depersonalized," is a comment on the West's often sick dependence on logic, or what Whitmont called the disregarding of "the emotional and intuitive sides of man." Thus, instead of a rich nation like America being moved by *feelings* of empathy, *emotions* of generosity or *instincts* of compassion to go and feed the world's starving, these faculties are suppressed in favor of abstractly and objectively solving "the problem" of hunger. Dying people are treated like math puzzles; it is never starving human beings who need food, but always the hunger "problem" or the welfare "problem." Better to solve a problem than feed a man.

This is dangerous, warns Jung. "The psychological rule says that when an inner situation is not made conscious, it happens outside, as fate. That is to say, when the individual remains undivided and does not become conscious of his inner opposite, the world must act out the conflict and be torn into opposing halves."

The Third World, the peace movement, the communes—the best of these are primordial expressions of the collective unconscious by which a hungry, warring and impersonal world can be led away from its worst self and old instincts long ago buried be dug up. As Jung knew, it is not a bad time in history to be returning to the unconscious for our wisdom. So much is there in waiting.

SELECTED BIBLIOGRAPHY OF CARL JUNG

Basic Writings of C.G. Jung. New York: Modern Library, 1959.
Collected Works of C.G. Jung: Spirit in Man, Art and Literature. Princeton, N.J.: Princeton University Press, 1971.
Man and His Symbols. New York: Dell, 1968.
Memories, Dreams and Reflections. New York: Random House, 1973.
Jacobi, Jolande. *Psychology of C.G. Jung.* Princeton, N.J.: Princeton University Press, 1963.
Whitmont, Edward C. *The Symbolic Quest.* New York: Putnam, 1969.

Sir John Eccles

SCIENTISTS ARE IN THE DISCOVERY business, but often for the layman the real surprises are the discoveries about scientists. From appearances, John Carew Eccles—an Australian, knighted, a Nobel winner in 1963, perhaps the world's most successful investigator of the neuronal machinery of the brain—seems to be only another one of those remote lab people in long white coats. A first look at the record would suggest this; in 1925, he wrote a respected manual on nerve function. *Reflect Activity of the Spinal Cord*: another title was the *Neurophysiological Basis of the Mind*.

Not much there, one would conclude if desiring an evening a little more exciting than reading a stamp book. Yet, probing further into Eccles production—the way a mindful scientist endlessly pokes through the kudzu tangle of doubts—an impressive discovery is waiting to be made. Eccles is emphatically a scientist who has gone beyond the hunt for stray scraps of test-tube truth to make a try for whole wisdom. His writing is not in any daring sense as penetrating or original as microbiologist René Dubos (*So Human an Animal*); Eccles's uniqueness lay in having so complete a scientific mind and yet so profound a respect for the non-scientific.

Much depth and no gassiness is found in Eccles's essays on the soul, freedom and creativity, education, free will, self-awareness and death awareness (all of these collected into one volume, *Facing Reality*, Springer-Verlag, New York). Eccles is a professor of neurobiology at New York State University at Buffalo.

A first hint that Sir John is a special scientist is that he is anything but ga-ga about the space industry, the cheerleading for which now, gratefully, seems to be easing off. "There is absolutely no other place for man to live other than on this earth," Eccles believes. In a tone of rue, he acknowledges that there will likely be plenty of hit-and-run raids on the planets near us, but "we must realize the full negative impact of the new knowledge derived from the study of the moon, Venus and Mars, and of the problems of space travel. . . . We and our fellow men of all countries must realize that we share this wonderful, beautiful, salubrious earth as brothers and that there never will be anywhere else to live."

A fear of Eccles regarding space travel is the backlash that science will suffer. When the trips become a bore—if they have not already, with space dockings with Russian the big event—"science will be discredited." Is that all the scientists can do, the public will ask. This hunger for insta-results and catchy discoveries should be ignored by the scientist, Eccles insists. "The general public and even the most enlightened political leaders fail to appreciate the extraordinary conditions that must prevail if there is to be a free-flowering of science."

Among the seeds of this flowering is an openness to the unexpected. "You do experiments and you can have a very good idea of what to expect from your past experience. . . . Usually, however, there is something else coming in, some worrying phenomenon and for a while, you take no notice of it. You even try to look aside when it appears. But it keeps on reappearing, so you recognize that 'here is something that Nature is trying to tell me.' " Politicians, reformers, the corporate men, even—perhaps especially—journalists, should turn an open ear to this advice.

An example of accepting the unexpected is Eccles's assertion that the brain and mind are not one. Many in the scientific community pass off the mind as a mere "ghost in the machine." If anyone would seem likely to agree with that it would be Eccles, yet after an adult life of studying the physiology of the brain he insists a person's life is more than the physical matter in his skull. He supports the counter-attack to scientists who derive or mock the concept of the mind. "Many of us, despite the philosophic criticisms, have continued to wrestle with the problem of brain and mind, and have come to regard it as the most difficult and fundamental problem concerning man." Eccles told a *Newsweek* reporter: "I can explain my body and brain, but there's something more. I can't explain my own existence. What makes me a unique being?"

It would be a happy day for Aristotelians and Thomists if Eccles went on from here to speak of the soul as "the form of the body," as did those two masters. But he doesn't. Instead, Eccles says this view is no longer tenable. Is there a soul then? Eccles believes so, or at least in the way that "the conscious self may be identified as the soul." Oddly, when expressing these views on the brain and the soul—a few years ago at the Berkeley campus in California—Eccles ended with a cold-war appeal to watch out for "the tragic alternative of a totalitarian aggressor" under whose control "enslaved mankind would (lose) its soul in a long dark night of cultural and intellectual barbarism." True perhaps, but it can happen anywhere, even in the supposedly free countries.

Eccles's daily life is in the labs, where his energy and commitment is intense. As with many geniuses who get the hang of something and can't ease up, life at the lab is often more appealing than life at home. In 1967, UPI in Chicago reported that Eccles sued for a divorce from his wife of thirty-nine years. Aside from charging his wife with not wanting to accompany him from Australia to Chicago for a new post, Eccles's suit also said that his wife refused to permit him to work in the evening, "made loud scenes regarding certain female assistants and openly reprimanded him for dancing with Princess Desiree of Sweden during the Nobel Prize ceremony in Stockholm in 1963."

The divorce granted, Eccles took a new bride in 1968, Helena Taborikova; her profession was, like his, neurophysiology. The pair now work together, and having a wife in the lab seems to suit Eccles fine. He told a Canadian audience at about the time of his second marriage: "That's how Science goes on. We are all the time chattering, gossiping about this or that scientific story or scientist—the incessant gossip of the laboratory. In fact, laboratories should be maintained for this purpose even when there is no experimental program!" Definitely. And the same for other coed workshops—faculty rooms, control rooms, newsrooms.

A humility is present in Eccles's writing, an underground dynamite that blasts through the surface pride crusted to so many other scientists. Repeatedly, he refers to a de Chardin, Pelikan, von Hugel, Fromm. Why not consult philosophers, ethicists, writers? "Arrogance," he wrote in a masterful essay on the understanding of Nature, "is one of the worst diseases of scientists and it gives rise to statements of authority and finality which are expressed usually in fields that are completely beyond the scientific competence of the dogmatist. It is important to realize that dogmatism has now become a disease of scientists rather than of theologians." It is Eccles' honor that seeing the follies of his brothers-in-trade has increased; not embittered, his passion to have science serve in the ascent of man.

SELECTED BIBLIOGRAPHY OF JOHN ECCLES

Facing Reality: Philosophical Adventures by a Brain Scientist (Heildelberg Science Library, Vol. 13). Springer-Verlag, 1970.

Neurophysiological Basis of the Mind. New York: Oxford University Press, 1953.

The Understanding of the Brain. New York: McGraw-Hill, 1973.

Physiology of Nerve Cells. Baltimore: Johns Hopkins University Press, 1968.

Simone Weil

Those who try occasionally to clear their head from the hangover of television, newspapers and movies, and consume instead the purity of obscure literary journals, books by the masters and long afternoons in libraries, these are the ones who keep coming upon the name and ideas of Simone Weil. The winter 1969-70 *Modern Age* quarterly review carried a graceful essay on Israel and Rome as viewed by Simone Weil. W. H. Auden quotes her twelve times in his *A Certain World* (Viking). In June 1969, *America* magazine ran a review of a LaMama Theater Club play on Simone Weil—"one of the most powerful theater pieces in New York this season," said the critic.

Dead at age thirty-four in 1943 from malnutrition and tuberculosis, Simone Weil was a French schoolteacher, philosopher, factory worker and mystic. All this was too consuming for her to bother about publishing a large-scale work and meeting the itchy demands of editors, so the writings, letters and thought-fragments of Simone Weil were gathered posthumously by friends. Several volumes were filled, although most American libraries carry only *The Need for Roots* and *Waiting for God*. Her writing should not be dived into for a quick swim in classy intellectual waters; it would be better, instead, to read a page or paragraph at a time and let the force of it sink in like an anchor. *Waiting for God* is full of rich insight and shading, and reinforces what T. S. Eliot once noted: "Simone Weil was by nature a solitary and an individualist, with a profound horror of what she called the collectivity—the monster created by modern totalitarianism. What she cared about was human souls."

The movement of Simone Weil's own soul began early. The daughter of well-off Jewish parents in Paris, at age five she refused to eat sugar—the soldiers at the front did not have any so neither would she. A few years later, she decided not to wear socks, because the children of workers went without them. As a woman, her conscience long having spilled out beyond the boundaries of convention, this spirit of empathy continued—living in England, she refused to eat more than the meager rations allowed her brothers in occupied France.

This self-mortification—slightly reminiscent of a few senators' wives in Washington in 1969 who lived a week on starvation welfare allowances and found the poor were right, after all, poverty is not pleasant—had a touch of foolishness. But it was the folly of all extra-mile compassion, of wanting to march with the endless line of refugees from suffering who flee from war, hunger, unemployment, whatever.

"The love of our neighbor," she wrote, "in all its fullness simply means being able to say to him: 'What are you going through?' It is a recognition that the sufferer exists, not only as a unit in a collection, or a specimen from the social category labeled 'unfortunate,' but as a man exactly like us who was one day stamped with a special mark of affliction."

As a philosopher concerned about the problem of good and evil, and contemptuous of relativism, Simone Weil almost naturally became absorbed by religion. Perhaps repelled as a girl by the legalism of her Jewish relatives, or for some other complex reason, she was markedly hostile to Judaism as a belief. One explanation is her conviction that the ancient Hebrews' worship of power cut them off from a sense of morality. She wrote to a friend that apart from certain books like Job, the Psalms, Daniel and Tobias, the Song of Songs, "almost all the rest of the Old Testament is a tissue of horrors." Much of the baby is thrown out with that bathwater, and perhaps if she had lived longer, Simone Weil would have overcome her vehemence against Judaism.

Attracted to Christianity, she learned only slowly that religious truth is grasped not by running after it but by waiting to let it catch up. "One of the principal truths of Christianity, a truth that goes almost unrecognized today, is that looking is what saves us." That is the essence for much of the mystical experience—allowing oneself to risk interior freedom so that nothing can block the sight of God. Few ever come close. Unlike the mystical experiences of St. John of the Cross or St. Teresa of Avila, who mostly lived apart from society, the mysticism of Simone Weil is understandable to skeptical modern man because she always remained very much with this world, avoiding the machinery of piety and liturgy lest her soul get enmeshed in it.

She describes an early encounter with God: "In a moment of intense physical suffering, when I was forcing myself to feel love but without desiring to give a name to that love, I felt, without being in any way prepared for it, a presence more personal, more certain, more real than that of a human being, though inaccessible to the senses and the imagination. . . ." Enclosing the body of Simone Weil's mystical writing is a skin of self-examining doubt, as if she was well aware that phony mystical experiences are everywhere—as indeed they are, including every night in drug pads from Malibu to Georgetown. Her essay, "Concerning the Our Father," is a masterpiece of mysticism that is simple, pure and totally unmysterious.

Simone Weil never entered the church, interiorly preferring not to officialize her belief and exteriorly because Catholicism struck her as a type of membership-only club. "So many things are outside (the church), so many things that I love and do not want to give up, so many things that God loves, otherwise they would not be in existence."

Regarding her natural aloofness to institutionalized religion, critic Leslie Fiedler—one of the more unlikely Weil admirers—wrote: "To those who consider themselves on the safe side of belief, [Simone Weil] teaches the uncomfortable truth that the unbelief of many atheists is closer to a true love of God and a true sense of his nature, than the kind of easy faith which, never having experienced God, hangs a label bearing his name on some childish fantasy or projection of the ego."

Simone Weil never married, possibly because she knew—like so many others in the twentieth-century—that uprootedness is the common unavoidable curse. Yet, straining the keel of her heart as though a sea change swelled against it, she placed immense value on friendship, the next closest relationship to marriage. It is also about as difficult, one reason why Simone Weil's essay on friendship is among the most useful pieces of her writing.

An outsider, alone, exiled, Simone Weil died an early, worn-out death. She visited America briefly in 1942, but the country was too secure, too free of the true risks of life. She should be here now, insecurity and riskiness being major commodities on our psychic market. Fittingly, it is likely that many Simone Weils now wander our cities, lost-like on the surface but keeping notebooks, believing in belief if not God, and asking the broke and the broken, "What are you going through?"

SELECTED BIBLIOGRAPHY OF SIMONE WEIL

First and Last Notebooks. New York: Oxford University Press, 1970.
The Need for Roots: Prelude to a Declaration of Duties Toward Mankind. New York: Harper and Row, 1971 (paperback).
On Science, Necessity and the Love of God. New York: Oxford University Press, 1968.
Oppression and Liberty. Amherst, Mass: University of Massachusetts Press, 1973.
Seventy Letters. New York: Oxford University Press, 1965.
Waiting for God. New York: Harper and Row, 1971 (paperback).

Alfred Adler

Those with a nose for salvation schemes cannot fail to enjoy the quick times that are producing so many quick answers. Someone floated the idea of "future shock," only to be dunked by another weighty theory called "Consciousness I, II, III." Unfortunately, modern violence, meaninglessness and absurdity may have roots too deep to be pulled out by catchword gardeners just lately arrived. Many of those who are not yet convinced that the future is shocking or that consciousness, like moonshots, comes in stages, want something more. Some have been turning to the teaching of Alfred Adler to get it.

There is a decided upturn of interest in Adler, from college lecture halls to quiet counseling rooms. Although popularly known for the terms *inferiority complex* and *life style*—concepts long abused by amateur psychiatrists—Adler developed what is called individual psychology. Subtle and delicate in application, this theory holds that one basic force is behind all human acts: "a striving from a felt minus situation toward a plus situation, from a feeling of inferiority toward superiority, perfection, totality." That men constantly strive toward goals and power is inherently healthy, Adler believed; what is sick is the forms this striving can take—violence, crime, aggression. Once the striving has been properly refined, however, beginning in early childhood, the goal of going from "a minus to a plus situation" becomes personally useful and a help to society, which now needs it.

As with many thinkers whose ideas survive the first edition of history, Adler's teaching has perhaps more meaning now than when first devised. The black power movement is a clear example of what Adler called "the masculine protest"—treat me like a man. The

249

women's rebellion today was predicted in a paper called "The Psychology of Power." Nothing but resentment and resistance, he wrote, can come in relationships that force the woman to be inferior and subdued merely because she is female and not male. Finally, nothing in the deep originality of Adler's philosophy equals the importance of what he called "the law of social interest." As the core of his teaching and, Adler believed, the prime cure for either neurosis or delinquency, social interest is the psychological capacity to care about others. This is basically the same ethical notion of many religions—love one's neighbor as one's self—except that Adler went further, believing it was highly practical for living in this world, regardless of life in the next world. How much and how intensely a person cares about others is a measure of his mental health.

One of Adler's biographers, Phyllis Bottome, wrote that the psychiatrist's "whole treatment was based on the fact that though neurotics might have perfectly true grievances and grudges against life, they were capable of giving their contribution to the world even with these handicaps, if they would stop putting all their strength and drive into exploiting their weaknesses rather than in seeking to overcome them by freeing their courage toward cooperative living."

This is obviously a simple theory, yet one that demands an activism of the heart that many refuse to give. Rather than follow through on Adlerian analysis where the soul is freed, many prefer Freudian analysis where the libido is released. There is less trouble with that.

Born in 1870, Adler was the second in a Viennese family of four boys and two girls. He originally became a medical doctor in general practice, a vocation he subconsciously chose at age five when near death with pneumonia. "The doctor" Adler recalled, "told my father that there was no point in going to the trouble of looking after me as there was no hope of my living. At once a frightful terror came over me and a few days later when I was well, I decided to become a doctor so that I should have a better defense against the danger of death and weapons superior to combat it to my doctor's."

In 1902, Adler, now interested in the diseases of the mind as well as the body, defended Sigmund Freud whose ideas on dream analysis were attacked in a newspaper column. Touched, Freud invited Adler into his psychoanalytic society. At first, the two shared their theories, but in time, as with all mergers of genius, the theories began to compete. "The main difference between the two," wrote a colleague of both, "was that Freud wanted knowledge and Adler looked for truth."

During World War I, Adler served as a doctor in the Austrian army. It was during these years of closely observing war neurosis that he devised his theory of social interest. Adler later expressed his views on the draftees, views that are remarkably similar to Yossarian's Catch-22 philosophy that the real enemy is not always on the opposite side of the battlefield. "The draftees in general," wrote Adler, "were immature, had no guidelines and were pushed and driven to slaughter. No one told them the truth; their writers and journalists were under the spell of the military and the government. . . .

"From this unbearable situation, where they were robbed of their dignity and their own will, and staggered in the direction in which they had been ordered, they picked up the call to war from the General Staff and their government; and by the psychological device of self-deception, it suddenly seemed that they themselves had uttered the call to war. From then on they felt easier. Now they were no longer whipped dogs, exposed against their will to the rain of bullets, but heroes, defenders of the fatherland and of their honor. Thus they evaded the realization that they were but the story victims of the power urges of others."

Adler died in 1937. What now is his position in America? While less sung than Freud and perhaps less readable than Jung, Adler's teaching appears to have more practical utility than either of the former. Dr. Rudolph Dreikurs, an early disciple and a director of the Adler Institute in Chicago until his death in 1972, insists that Adlerian therapy concentrates on the goals of human behavior. Analysis uncovers the nature of goals and, if mistaken, seeks to correct them. "We have nothing in common with psychoanalysis," explains Dreikurs. "We do not believe that consciousness is opposed by unconscious processes, as though they were two antagonistic halves of an individual. We have more power over our lives than we think."

In Washington, a spirited group called the Individual Psychology Association (Box 11, Garrett Park, Md.) recently formed and now regularly meets to examine and explain the teaching of Adler, plus the educational writings of Dreikurs.

It is in small groups like this that the ideas of Adler are most likely to be understood. Fittingly, during his life Adler often preferred the active intimate group to the passive written page as a means of teaching. It was taking advantage, he said, of "the spirit of the community." More profoundly, the small group is the first seeding place where *social interest* can grow. If a person cannot care about the few people he sees before him, how can he care about the millions beyond the door?

SELECTED BIBLIOGRAPHY OF ALFRED ADLER

Education of Children. Chicago: Regenery, 1970 (paperback).
Individual Psychology of Alfred Adler: A Systematic Presentation in Selection from His Writings. New York: Basic Books, 1956.
Problems of Neuroses: A Book of Case Histories. New York: Harper and Row, 1964 (paperback).
Social Interest: A Challenge to Mankind. New York: Putnam, 1964 (paperback).
Superiority and Social Interest: A Collection of Later Writings. New York: Viking Press, 1973 (paperback).

Rudolf Dreikurs

IS ANY SURPRISE OF ADULT LIFE greater than this: deciding to marry and having children on the notion that they will fit into your life but then, when they come, discovering the opposite, that we must fit into their lives? The percussion of this large awakening bangs loudly in the consciousness of any parent, and sadly for many the din never lowers. We train our young to fight wars, drive cars and become plumbers, but we send them into adulthood with never a syllable about the huge complexities of raising children. Is it any surprise that American parents have countless ways of either ducking or refusing to learn the enlightened ways of parenthood? Child battering is the extreme form of abuse, but other wounds—from amputated emotions to stifled freedom—are commonly inflicted.

Among those who have tried to bring peace to our persistent parent-child wars is Rudolf Dreikurs. He is not as well-known as Plaget, Erickson, Montessori or others whose social philosophy insists that children have value, but evidence suggests that Dreikurs may be as well, even more, studied. In the past few years, in dozens of cities, parent study groups have been using Dreikurs's theories as guides to understanding their children and the mystery of their own parenthood. (In the Washington area, information about Dreikurs study groups is available from the Individual Psychology Association, Box 11, Garrett Park, Md. 20766. This group has information also about study groups in other cities.) Word is spreading about Dreikurs, not in the fad sense—browse through Eric Berne at the airport book rack for that—but in the strength of an accumulated collection of wisdom that is finally being discovered.

Much of the current enthusiasm for Dreikurs's thought is a result of his own earlier enthusiasm for sharing it. From 1937 to his

253

death in 1972 at age seventy-five, Dreikurs tested his stature in forums that included a succession of teaching posts, lectures, child guidance centers and in the production of eleven books. A Viennese-born psychiatrist, Dreikurs consists of two halves—one his discipleship to Alfred Adler and the other the exposition of his own thoughts that extended Adler. When he came to Chicago in 1937—a Jew, he left Austria when Hitler emerged—Dreikurs found that Freudians had the platform and were keeping off anyone who disputed The Master's theories of sexuality as the basis for human functioning. Dreikurs refused to practice psychiatry in the traditional way if it meant accepting Freudian theories. Instead, he set about creating small child guidance centers where the success of Individual Psychology—the basic Adler method—could be proven not among the officials of the mental health community but among the lower class families of Chicago who needed help.

The basic concept of Adler's thought that Dreikurs brought to Chicago was that the individual must be seen as a whole and cannot be divided into parts, however convenient this division may be in explaining illness or confused behavior. Other types of therapy, he said, "look for causes, emotions, the use of background, heredity, while we realize that the use of emotions, the use of background is only in line with what one wants to do in the given situation. There are two kinds of goals. One is the goal of 'life style,' as Adler calls it, developed in early childhood in transactions with brothers and sisters, where one develops his concept about himself and the way in which he can find a place. But within this same general pattern, there is another kind of goal, a hundred different ways in which one can respond to the given situation, a hundred private logics. For instance, when we describe the private logic of children and their goals of disturbing behavior, neither parent nor teachers know that whatever their child is doing is directed toward them. They look for all kinds of causes: deficiencies of the personality, laziness, whatever might explain his behavior. It doesn't explain behavior; it only describes it. We have to understand what his private logic is . . . what he wants to accomplish with his behavior. It is his way of finding his place in the given situation, and you can't ignore that."

We do ignore it, though, because the effort to raise children intelligently cannot be done with a formula or method. Children, Dreikurs believed, quickly catch on to parents who come at them with theories from the talk-show pediatricians. "Children are very ingenious in frustrating the most forceful schemings of their parents, and gain easy victories while their adversaries (the parents) are bewildered and dumbfounded."

A constant theme of Dreikurs is the foolishness of mothers and fathers. "It is difficult for parents to realize that children are human beings like themselves. Parents not only demand privileges which disrupt social order and destroy the feeling of belonging; but often they permit the child privileges that they would not grant to anyone else. Indulgence is as disastrous as suppression. Only rules which govern the life of the whole family, which includes parents and children, train for the recognition of right and wrong." Long before the more sensible parts of today's women's liberation movement began saying it, Dreikurs held that parenthood is a mutual responsibility between men and women. He scorned men who abstain from helping to educate their children because "they consider it the special task of the mother. This abstinence has various psychological reasons. First, we may say that it is rarely a sincere respect for the mother's ability to perform the task adequately. Although fathers very often have a sense of inadequacy in regard to rearing children, they are also suspicious of the mother's ability. Their abstinence is a device by which they let her make mistakes and reserve for themselves the right to put full blame for any disturbance upon the mother."

Perhaps because he was a psychiatrist who preferred to use his time among parents and nonspecialists, Dreikurs's prose is unadorned with polysyllables and slogans of scholarship. His analytical work, *The Challenge of Marriage* (Hawthorn) is written without the flashy language common to current books on sexuality—always illustrated, as if people forget what they look like—but contains every shade of meaning needed to understand marriage. Dreikurs has a wit, as when he wrote in his book that getting a divorce is often the first cooperative effort between husband and wife. In 1964, *Children; The Challenge* (Hawthorn) appeared; it is the volume used in most of the study groups because it develops the basic sociology of parents living with children, and surviving to tell of it. Dreikurs, free of platitudes, delights in showing the daily absurdities. "Parents' soothing references to changing age—'You will be able to do that, too, when you're older'—are meaningless to the child. In two years he will be able to do what his brother can do today; but by that time the older brother is again two years ahead."

In his personal life, associates report that Dreikurs had a taste for simplicity and humility. Both virtues had their practical side.

"For years," one friend said, "the psychiatric community and the psychological community did not treat him well, and yet he just went about doing his job." What other way is there? Tenacious myths and the decay of the times can be contended with, and possibly removed, only when persistence is fused with wisdom, whether one is loved or hated by the community.

SELECTED BIBLIOGRAPHY OF RUDOLF DREIKURS

The Challenge of Child Training. New York: Hawthorn, 1972.
The Challenge of Marriage. New York: Hawthorn, 1946.
The Challenge of Parenthood. New York: Hawthorn, 1948.
Psychodynamics, Psychotherapy and Counseling: Collected Papers. Chicago: A. Adler Institute, 1956.
Psychology in the Classroom: A Manual for Teachers. New York: Harper and Row, 1968.

Josephine Johnson

IN THE AUTUMN OF 1974, REPORTS had been coming in from the farms that a barren summer had impoverished the land. Little rain had fallen; growth had no source. But the hard weather of such a period is seldom discussed in its victimization of the farmer, what shadows his emotions are led into, what new tensions it adds to his family. Instead, those in the cities are told that because of the rainless summer bread prices will go up in two months, pork will cost more than last year and the futures market will be insecure. It is always the eminence of the dollar, the sign of the times being only the dollar sign. About the farmer—his feelings of ties to the ancient earth, his emotions of sorrow and loneliness in seeing the home of his soul suddenly empty—what are we told?

It is necessary to return to *Now in November,* one of American literature's most personal and intense novels about a family on the land. Few libraries carry all the books of Josephine Johnson—eight—but *Now in November* is usually one of them, forty years old now and sure to live on without pretensions. Simon and Schuster, the original publisher in 1934, recently issued a hardbound reprint. The novel's narrator, who came with her family to a piece of mortgaged Midwest land that was "sanctuary though everything else was gone," forbids us to be tourists traveling through romanticized scenes of farmcult. Following "the long drouth," she summarizes: "I do not see in our lives any great ebb and flow or rhythm of earth. There is nothing majestic in our living. The earth turns in great movements, but we jerk about on its surface like gnats, our days absorbed and overwhelmed by a mass of little things—that confusion which is our living and which prevents us from being really alive. We grow tired, and our days are broken up into a thousand pieces, our years chopped into days and nights, and interrupted. Our hours of life snatched from our years of living. Intervals and things stolen between—between what?—those things which are necessary to make life endurable—fed, washed, and clothed, to enjoy the time which is not washing and cooking and clothings. . . . We have no reason to hope or believe, but do because we must, receiving peace in its sparse moments of surrender, and beauty in all its twisted forms, not pure, unadulterated, but mixed always with sour potato-peelings or an August sun."

The story line of *Now in November* is not intimidating. Instead, one of the powers of Josephine Johnson is in showing the separatism of the family, the divisions between parents and children and the three daughters themselves, all of them unconsciously building crosses for each other to carry. Parts of the mental health community are beginning to realize that the illness of one family member is not isolated from the behavior of the supposedly healthy ones. Therapy is needed for the whole family if wholeness is to return to one member. In *Now in November,* one of the daughters is Kerrin, who "had a strange way of not seeming to notice things or care about them, but years later we'd find the feeling was there, living and fierce, under a thin slab of indifference." She moves slowly to tragedy. Does she carry the heaviest mental weight of all, the subconscious of her parents? The mother "lived in the lives of others as though she hadn't one of her own," and the father soured his own spirit with rage and fear. The novel is a sourcebook for examining the theories of family therapy.

Josephine Johnson lives in Ohio. In 1969, she wrote *The Inland Island,* a month by month account of her feelings and thoughts of a year on a thirty-seven-acre farm, one that had been spared by the stripminers and the industrialism bunch. "This beautiful slice of land is all that's left. It's my lifeblood. The old house is abandoned down in the valley where the mammoth bones were found in the quarry. We are on this side of the ridge from that valley now. The children are gone. The horses gone. The old house gone. What's left? A world of trees, wild birds, wild weeds—a world of singular briary beauty that will last my life. The land—my alderliefest—the most beloved, that which has held the longest possession of the heart."

As with all genuine naturalists, Miss Johnson knows the fragility of the nerves that keep her island in balance. "I can't separate the beauty of this place from the destruction of this place—the sewer water, the soapsuds, the hunters, the trappers, the dogs, the decay of the trees, the planes overhead . . . the target practice of the neighbors, the pollution of the air from sewers and burning garbage, from factories in the valley and even dust from Oklahoma. A world of war and waste." Miss Johnson writes of tanagers, possums and turtles, of her love for the natural world, but balancing it always with a loathing for the unnatural, whether wars or the politicians who start them: "They just go on talking and flailing away and falling down on the young with their tons of dead weight and their power." Such thoughts, as some critics of Johnson have charged, are not polemics. If it is anything, a nature book, as this is, should first be natural—in expressing contempt for those who cheapen or destroy the chances for life.

Josephine Johnson has never marketed herself by becoming one of the publishing world's "hot properties," but appears to have preferred to let a public come find her through her words. She is now in her sixties, widowed—her husband of thirty years was Grant Cannon, who edited the *Farm Quarterly*—and the mother of two daughters and a son. The latter served two years in jail rather than fight for the military. Miss Johnson's literary life suggests that she is the rarest kind of writer—an undeceived one—but in one book, the memoir *Seven Houses,* it is not so much cold truth she is after as its warmer relative, honesty. She describes the houses of her life, the girlhood homes in Missouri and the relocations to Ohio. But she tells also of her husband, portraying in a few lines the essence of a kind of man few women ever marry: "He was always doing things for me. Sparing me. One never knows how much went on inside. What torment he took to himself. Or whether it was really easier for him, as he claimed. I think he had a greater capacity to draw on. A greater love of life which is a physical thing when you come down to it. Man is an ocean inside, they say. Maybe Grant was born with more nutrients, living tides of internal refreshment. We are all different. Some with hearts bigger, livers smaller, kidneys upside down, adrenal glands sidewise. . . ."

The exuberance of Josephine Johnson suggests a woman who hasn't given up: on reason, on caring, on seeing. Many tanks have rolled over our institutions in recent years, flattening them so that our vision at times sees straight to an horizon bare of solace or hope. On that landscape, no writer is more valuable than one of sensibility who confirms that resisting the fake and affirming the real is an effort worth making.

259

SELECTED BIBLIOGRAPHY OF JOSEPHINE JOHNSON

Circle of Seasons. New York: Viking, 1974.
Inland Island. New York: Simon and Schuster, 1969.
Now in November. New York: Simon and Schuster, 1934.
Paulina. New York: Simon and Schuster, 1939.
Seven Houses: A Memoir of Time and Places. New York: Simon and Schuster, 1973.

Tu Fu

THE PRACTICAL CITIZENS OF CHINA have traditionally advised their poets in much the grim manner practical Americans advise theirs. Get a job, we tell them. Conform, earn your keep, learn to write a memo not a poem. This is the standard line, nothing lost in translation. But the attempts to put a corrective lens on the creative eye of the poet, and thus focus it better on the "real" world, has worked no better in China than America. Early in the life of Tu Fu, the Eighth-century Chinese poet honored everywhere as a bright star in the wide sky of China's past culture, the young man had spent a number of years traveling the countryside; he was gathering the raw materials—beautiful scenes and sounds, true visions—by which a poetic imagination is built. During these particular years—around 730, well into the T'ang Dynasty—the building was easy. China had peace, land was lightly taxed and villagers were friendly to strangers. Tu Fu cut short his travel plans, though, and scholars speculate that he had been receiving letters from home saying come back and get a job. Whatever, the pulley of responsibility hauled him back; in the spring of 736, Tu Fu went to Ch'ang-an in central China to take the imperial examinations for an appointment to "officialdom." Tu Fu flunked. This close call with work was unnerving but the young man survived. He lit out again, and until his death in 770, worked at producing verse that was to last until today and earn him the title of China's greatest poet.

Many of Tu Fu's poems depart from the style of soaring images but instead are verse comments on the low events of his day. Eastern poetry, and much of the greatest in the West, has often been topical; in 1972, for example, the touring Russian poet, Yevtushenko, visited the bombed offices of Sol Hurok in New York, and wrote a poem about it. Americans like Robinson Jeffers or Denise Levertov have written beautiful poetry taken from the morning's headlines. In much the same tradition, Tu Fu wrote about war, poverty, even on his son's laying hens. Commenting on war, he wrote "A Restless Night in Camp" (translation by Kenneth Rexroth in *One Hundred Poems from the Chinese*, New Directions):

> *In the penetrating damp*
> *I sleep under the bamboos...*
> *The thick dew turns to fine mist.*
> *One by one the stars go out.*
> *Only the fireflies are left.*
> *Birds cry over the water.*
> *War breeds its consequences.*
> *It is useless to worry,*
> *Wakeful while the long night goes.*

The literary world of the T'ang dynasty held no prospects for publishing poems in the way we know it now; instead, poets would often write a verse for a friend and send it to him. This custom is not so strange. The American greeting card industry is based on it, except that Hallmark and other firms write what the sender is too lazy to write for himself. One Tu Fu greeting card was the nostalgic poem, "To Pi Ssu Yao":

> *We have talent. People call us*
> *The leading poets of our day.*
> *Too bad, our homes are humble,*
> *Our recognition trivial...*
> *Who cares about either of us,*
> *Or our troubles. We are our own*
> *Audience. We appreciate*
> *Each other's literary*
> *Merits. Our Poems will be handed*
> *Down along with great dead poets'.*
> *We can console each other.*
> *At least we shall have descendants.*

Although Tu Fu is known by too few in America, we are lucky that a number of scholars have pursued him. Kenneth Rexroth is one. The deepest digging among the shelves of Oriental libraries was done by Professor William Hung of Harvard. In 1952, when good Americans were supposed to be hating China, he published *Tu Fu, China's Greatest Poet*, an excellent and thorough reconstruction of the poet's life. Translation and analysis of many poems are included. "Next only to the Psalms," Professor Hung wrote, "the poems of Tu Fu have given me the greatest fascination, joy and consolation." The

262

Hung biography is high appreciation, but the professor refuses to legendize Tu Fu. If the poetry of the master could cure malaria, as one legend had it, then "Tu Fu himself would not have been a frequent victim of it."

Tu Fu, with a weakness for early drinking and late hours, was on his way to becoming a public wastrel, but at age forty-one fame arrived when the emperor noticed his verses. Americans may find it hard, even unbelievable, to imagine a nation's leader caring for poetry but this has always been true in the East. With good reviews from high places, Tu Fu received an appointment as Reminder to the emperor. A reminder's job is roughly the equivalent of today's American presidential counselor, reminding the Mighty One of the little dial nobs of ethics and honesty that tend not to be turned in the affairs of state. It is not known how often reminders to U.S. emperors raise ethical questions, but Tu Fu raised them without fear to his employer. On one occasion, the emperor had no ear for it and ordered reminder Tu arrested and tried by the Supreme Censor. At the trial, with his dragline to good luck held steady, Tu Fu was chided but pardoned.

In the later period of his life, China's warlords became weary of peace and the T'ang dynasty suffered from misgovernment in much the way the Roman Empire was falling in the West at the same time. Inspired by the marauding of towns, Tu Fu wrote "By the Winding River;" again, it is a poem of verbal tautness suggesting a telegram's economy of message:

> Every day on the way home from
> My office I pawn another
> Of my spring clothes. Every day
> I come home from the river bank
> Drunk. Everywhere I go, I owe
> Money for wine. History
> Records few men who lived to be
> Seventy . . .
> I cry out to the Spring wind,
> And the light and the passing hours.
> We enjoy life such a little
> While, why should men cross each other?

In his last days, Tu Fu enjoyed the pleasure of his slowboat. He died on it, following a fever. Lines from one of his last poems include (Hung translation): "It is useless for a stumbler to try keeping step with the times; he might as well halt and be grateful that there are those who understand." Today, many do understand Tu Fu, but the number should be greater. Perhaps when American entourages go to China, an enterprising reporter will leave the herd to do some digging and bring back the latest on Tu Fu scholarship. If so, that will be the big news, not what Kissinger said to Mao. Nor will they be remembered as long as Tu. He is already twelve centuries up on them.

SELECTED BIBLIOGRAPHY OF TU FU

One Hundred Poems from the Chinese, translated by Kenneth Rexroth. New York: New Directions, 1956.
Hung, William. *Supplementary Volume of Notes for Tu Fu: China's Greatest Poet.* Cambridge, Mass.: Harvard University Press, 1952.

Henrik Ibsen

NOT LONG AGO, officials of a textile mill in Grafton, Massachusetts, were told by federal lawyers that they were violating the Refuse Act of 1899. Dyes, soapy wastes and other gunks were being poured into the Blackstone River that coursed near the town. The mill's owner protested that he could not comply with the strictness of the law without going bankrupt. Perhaps in sympathy, a state court ordered the twelve thousand citizens to vote on a water treatment facility costing $10 million. Nothing doing, said the town, not voting a penny. Shortly after, with federal lawyers still pressing, the mill owner said he would close down his business and move out of state. A lawyer for the mill, crying foul about the foul water law, was quoted in the *New York Times:* "Ecology is here to stay, but you cannot undo in one day the practices of centuries. Remember these mills came to the advantage of the water power in New England. Now to come in and give these men criminal records is destructive of the business climate in the area." Also quoted was another view, that of the assistant U.S. prosecuting attorney: "All this talk about how complex the problem is is as bad as inaction. We cannot wait for the economic solution to come about—we have to have the courage to do what is necessary. We have to face this as a moral question, not an economic one, and we are drawing the lines of morally acceptable conduct."

The drama in this small New England town, an environmental victory as solid as poured concrete, sounds like a new one. It isn't Barely seven years before the 1899 law was written in this country, Henrik Ibsen wrote a masterful drama filled with many of the same kind of characters who played roles in Grafton. *An Enemy of the People* does not share the shelf of greatness that holds Ibsen's better-known plays—*Hedda Gabler, Peer Gynt, A Doll's House*. But it has a bluntness to it, a type of static that may jar an ear accustomed to only hi-fi tones, but which nevertheless soothes the mind in search of reality. What else counts from a play, except that it tells us what is real? *The Enemy of the People* is more for the 1970s in the United States than the 1880s in Norway.

The tension in *Enemy of the People* is created quickly. The local industry of a small Norwegian town is a health resort where people come to take the waters. The life of the town centers around the baths. Money has come in, rents rise in value and many citizens have jobs. The baths have a medical officer, Dr. Stockman, and he too is proud of the booming industry. By chance, one winter the doctor discovers that the waters have been contaminated from a nearby factory. "Do you know what they really are, these mighty, magnificent, belauded baths? . . . I tell you, the whole place is a poisonous whited sepulchre; noxious in the highest degree. All that filth up there in Mill Dale—the stuff smells so horribly—taints the water in the feed-pipes of the pump room . . . [The water] has become absolutely pernicious to health, whether used internally or externally."

In his innocence, the doctor believes the townspeople will raise him to their shoulders as a hero. He has helped avoid a potential disaster, hasn't he? He has blown the whistle of safety, and who could not thrill to hear its tone of conscience? Soon, though, Ibsen's whistleblower learns that there are other informations—economics and politics—that easily drown out. Think about the money the town will lose, says the burgomaster, if word about the filthy water gets out. Besides, there's really no imminent danger. Act in moderation. A committee will be appointed. Go back to your medicine, doctor.

The room of Stockman's conscience has no rug to sweep his facts under. He prepares a newspaper article about the pollution of the baths, and talks it up around town. The burgomaster, full of civic concern, tells the doctor: "As you have not had the sense to refrain from chattering to outsiders about this delicate business, which should have been kept an official secret, of course it cannot now be hushed up. All sorts of rumors will get abroad, and evil disposed persons will invent all sorts of additions to them. It will therefore be necessary for you publicly to contradict these rumors. . . . We expect that, after further investigation you will come to the conclusion that the affair is not nearly so serious or so pressing as you had at first imagined. . . . The matter in question is not purely a scientific one; it is a complex affair; it has both a technical and an economic side."

Seeing the score now—with himself losing—and being told by the editor of the newspaper that ruination will visit the town if the article runs, the doctor blows even harder on his whistle. A town meeting, the all purpose silencer for neighborhood cranks, is called. The editor says that the doctor seems intent on ruining the town. "Yes," Stockman replies, "so well do I love my native town that I would rather ruin it than see it flourishing upon a lie. . . . You'll end by poisoning the whole country; you'll bring it to such a pass that the whole country will deserve to perish. And if it ever comes to that, I shall say, from the bottom of my heart: Perish the country. Perish all its people." A voice from the mob cries out that the doctor sounds like an enemy of the people. The whole assembly joins in, shouting agreement. The chairman of the meeting seeing a safe position, says: "Dr. Stockman has unmasked himself in a manner I should never have dreamed of. I must reluctantly subscribe to the opinion just expressed by some estimable citizens. . . . I therefore beg to move that this meeting declares the medical officer of the baths, Dr. Thomas Stockman, to be an enemy of the people."

Although Ibsen had other abuses in mind when he wrote his play—for one, the idea that the majority always know best—he loudly condemned the habit of silence as the worst affliction. "I was only following orders" is the standard text of those who clutch a whistle but don't blow it. Large numbers of organizations, government agencies, corporations, armies and hierarchies have potential Dr. Stockmans. But going public with horrors learned in private is a lonely vocation, and the optic nerve easily sights the darkness that may follow—loss of job, libel suits, brush-offs, or having to bear the most lethal of all American insults: "He's not a team man." And, of course, the powers of the board room will stew and pout. In 1971, James Roche of General Motors, hardly aware his opening words paraphrased Ibsen, said: "Some of the enemies of business now encourage an employee to be disloyal to the enterprise. They want to create suspicion and disharmony. However this is labeled—industrial espionage, whistle blowing or professional responsibility—it is another tactic of spreading disunity and creating conflict."

Conflict is exactly right. Ibsen's plays are filled with characters hounded by the essential dilemma of citizenship: how do you keep your integrity while living in a society that accepts the sell-out or cave-in as normal values? "If a man claims to live and to develop in a human way," Ibsen wrote, "It is called Megalomania." Ibsen gave his wife the highest praise by saying she never yielded to the temptation of inertia found in society. With little use for politicians or party leaders—the burgomaster typified the surrendered conscience—Ibsen believed "that the time will soon come when political and social conceptions will cease to exist in their present forms. . . . I believe that poetry, philosophy and religion will be merged in a new category and become a new vital force."

Will they? Or is Ibsen another dreamer, asleep in his idealism while most others are awake before sunrise holding onto their crafty power? A precise answer is not important. It is enough that the restlessness of Ibsen's time is still with us, that whistleblowers keep at their lonely craft and that philosophers and poets, if no one else, hear them.

SELECTED BIBLIOGRAPHY OF HENRICK IBSEN

Eleven Plays of Henrik Ibsen. New York: Modern Library.
Meyer, Michael. *Ibsen: A Biography.* New York: Doubleday, 1971.

INDEX